Y0-DBX-390

$ 14.95

Into The Dragon's Jaws

The Fifth Air Force Over Rabaul, 1943

Into The Dragon's Jaws

Lex McAulay

Champlin Fighter Museum Press
Mesa, Arizona

Barrett Tillman, Publisher

Copyright © 1986 by Lex McAulay

All rights reserved. This book, or parts thereof, must not be reproduced in any form without permission of the publisher.

Printed and bound in the United States of America

Library of Congress Cataloging-in-Publication Data

McAulay, Lex, 1939–
    Into the dragon's jaws.

    Bibliography: p.
    1. World War, 1939–1945—Aerial operations, American. 2. United States. Army Air Forces. Air Force, 5th—History. 3. World War, 1939–1945—Campaigns—Papua New Guinea—Rabaul. 4. Rabaul (Papua New Guinea)—History. I. Title.
D790.M23   1987   940.54'4973   87–695
ISBN 0-912173-13-0

Acknowledgements

This book would not have been possible without the time and assistance given by many people in Australia, the USA, Japan and Papua New Guinea. In Australia, the staff of the Australian War Memorials gave of their best, and among them Bill Fogarty and Barry Saxby must receive a special mention. Nothing was too much trouble, no question too minor and no distant shelf too far to consult. Bill Moran, ex-90BG, and Ted Dorward, ex-Beaufort pilot answered my questions, put up with more and trusted me with their photographs. Steve Birdsall, himself a busy author, assisted whenever he could. Kev Ginnane proved himself to be a master photographer and I take this opportunity to wish him all the best for his own photographic book on the 5th AF in the Southwest Pacific Area (SWPA). In the USA, many people too numerous to mention here but who are included in the text also put up with questions from half way around the world about events forty years ago, wrote long letters, made voice tapes and also, and not least, trusted me with their photos. The MacArthur Archives in Norfolk proved outstanding in their knowledge of their holdings and their quick response to my requests for specific material. In Japan, many veterans of the Rabaul days assisted with their answers to my questions, sent me many books by Japanese authors and did all they could on my behalf. In Papua New Guinea, Bruce Hoy of the Aviation and Maritime Museum gave what help he could despite his own busy schedule and lack of finance.

Introduction

In 1943 Rabaul was the most significant base for the defence of the southern reaches of the Japanese Empire. Possession and development of Rabaul would allow domination of a huge area extending west to Australia and New Guinea, south into the Solomons and east into the Pacific. Rabaul possessed a good, easily-defended harbor, space for airfields and a savage, undeveloped hinterland. If an invader chose to not land in the face of Rabaul's formidable defences, but come ashore elsewhere, he would be forced to fight and advance through a wilderness. Four airfields, scores of fighters and bombers, 360 land-based anti-aircraft guns plus those on ships would make air attack hazardous in the extreme, yet it was with air power that General MacArthur intended to destroy the military effectiveness of Rabaul.

Rabaul had been constantly attacked by US and Australian aircraft since February 1942, but these were small raids, usually at night. It was not until October 1943 that the US 5th Air Force (AF) began large daylight attacks intended to destroy Japanese air power in the region. Later the campaign was continued by US and Royal New Zealand Air Force (RNZAF) units, maintaining pressure until the end of the war. However, it was the 5th AF which began the attacks and it is with their operations in the period 12 October to 11 November 1943 that this book is concerned.

If the Home Islands were the heart of the Japanese Empire, then an aerial attack on Rabaul, with its volcanoes, fighters, anti-aircraft guns and thousands of determined defenders could be seen as a flight into the jaws of the Japanese dragon.

CONTENTS

1

Background

In the irresistible flood of Japanese conquests of 1942, the occupation of Rabaul on 23 January was hardly noticed in the news of battles for Malaya and the Phillippines.

In fact, the Japanese expended little effort taking Rabaul. The pitiful Wirraways, Australian-made version of the AT-6 Texan trainer armed with three .303-inch machineguns, were swept aside by the superior Japanese Naval Air Force, and sole battalion of infantry was flung back into the jungles. Only a handful survived the trip by foot and boat to New Guinea. Japanese losses for the invasion of Rabaul are recorded as 16 killed and 39 wounded in an action of less than a day.

For these small losses the Japanese had purchased a harbor and two airfields of strategic significance. They lost no time in utilizing its facilities, and headquarters of the Southeastern Fleet were quickly established. Rabaul became the base for an area of operations ranging from the Equator in the north, to Nauru in the east, south to a line between Fiji and Samoa and west to the center of New Guinea. Lae, on the north coast of New Guinea, was only 385 miles away and Townsville, the largest northern Australian town with a harbor and airfield, was 1,095 miles distant.

Rabaul is somewhat unusual for such an important base. Six volcanoes are in the immediate area, which is shaken by frequent earth tremors. In May 1937 a devastating volcanic eruption had occurred, almost completely destroying the town and killing about 500 people. Typically for the tropics, seasonal variations are mild and about 90 inches of rain falls annually.

Staging through Rabaul, Japanese 17th Army units moved to New Guinea while naval forces went to the Solomons. Japanese naval forces in the Coral Sea battle had sailed from Rabaul, and were supported by bombers from nearby Vunakanau airfield. During the ferocious Guadalcanal campaign Rabaul was the centerpoint of Japanese operations, with naval sorties, air attacks and troop reinforcements all being launched from its harbor and airfields.

In December 1942, General Imamura's 8th Area Army Headquarters was established in the town. At this time the Japanese were fighting in the Solomons and in New Guinea, where their ground forces were bitterly resisting the Australian advance north from Port Moresby.

In early 1943, the Japanese conducted an operation on each of these flanks. Between 1 and 8 February the survivors of Guadalcanal were successfully evacuated. Then came the disastrous attempt in the first days of March to transport reinforcements from Rabaul to Lae, in New Guinea. The convoy was annihilated by low-level bombing and strafing by USAAF and RAAF aircraft, going into history as the Battle of the Bismarck Sea. Four destroyers and eight transports were sunk, for a loss of five Allied aircraft. The Japanese 18th Army's Medical Report for March 1943 stated that 6,828 persons participated in the Lae convoy, of which 2,978 (44%) were missing in action, excluding ship and gun crews.[1]

The boot was now on the other foot, and the days were gone when Japanese air forces had swept Pacific seas clear of the enemy. At the same time, on the other side of the world, the German *Luftwaffe* and Italian *Regia Aeronautica* were beginning their downward slide into oblivion.

General MacArthur had one main aim for 17 months after assuming command of all Allied forces in Australia in 1942: recapture Rabaul. It was to be a major US fleet base. In August 1943 the Combined Chiefs of Staff met in Quebec and decided to bypass Rabaul, thrusting into the Central Pacific, to the Carolines. MacArthur wished to attack and secure Rabaul, followed by Wewak on the north coast of New Guinea, but the US Joint Chiefs of Staff decided that Pacific forces—that is,

US Navy and Marines—would attack the Gilbert and Marshall Islands first, then western New Britain, in the summer of 1943-44.

However, the formidable Japanese garrison at Rabaul would pose a considerable threat to the Allied forces moving to surround it, and MacArthur decided this threat would be beaten down by air power. He proposed that while his air forces were attacking Rabaul in October and November, the US Navy would conduct its landings, and then in late December and early January his own units would land on West New Britain and North New Guinea.

So, on 22 September 1943, MacArthur issued orders for the occupation of western New Britain and instructed the US 5th AF to begin neutralization operations against Rabaul "on or about 15 October".

Meanwhile, in Tokyo, Japanese Imperial Headquarters was reviewing the situation and looking to the future. In September it also decided on a "New Operational Policy," which was basically to establish a fortified perimeter along the extent of their present conquests and prepare to engage the US Fleet in a decisive action during a counter-offensive in both the Central and South Pacific in the spring of 1944. Rabaul was to become a fortified position to wear down expected Allied offensives in the region.

To put the South West Pacific Area (SWPA) into perspective, it may be worthwhile to look briefly at the war situation around the world, and in particular at the airwar. In February the Russians had destroyed the entire German 6th Army at Stalingrad, and in the Pacific the battles of the Kokoda Trail, Buna and Gona in New Guinea and for Guadalcanal had been hard-won victories for the Australian and US forces. In May the North African campaign ended with total capitulation of all Axis forces on the continent. In July the Allies invaded and occupied Sicily, then made landings on the coast of Italy, leading to the overthrow of Mussolini and collapse of the Fascist regime. At Kursk in Russia the Soviets first held, then counter-attacked the Germans in the greatest tank battle in history. By September the Germans were pushed out of the Ukraine, and in the SWPA successful Allied landings captured Lae, and the nearby Markham Valley was becoming a nest of Allied airfields.

In the skies, 1943 had seen both successes and defeats for the advocates of independent air power. The Axis victories of 1940-42 had been achieved with tactical air forces subordinate to land or sea forces. While the British Royal Air Force (RAF) and German Luftwaffe were services in their own right alongside their armies and navies, most other air arms remained a branch of those services. The struggle for independent air power has been well reported, but it should be remembered that in this middle year of the war the RAF was still threatened by take-over moves, and the USAAF was still a branch of the Army.

Allied bombing had done little damage to Germany, and Japan had been raided only once—the propaganda gesture of the Doolittle Raid. US bombers had not reached German targets until January 1943, at Wilhelmshaven. But in March USAAF and RAAF aircraft destroyed the Rabaul-Lae convoy; in May RAF Lancasters breached the Mohne and Eder dams; in July the first man-made firestorm was raised by RAF bombing of Hamburg and up to 40,000 people died. Then on 1 August US B-24s from Libya lost 54 planes on the Ploesti raid but scarcely affected oil production; on 17 August the US 8th AF from England attacked Regensburg and Schweinfurt, losing 60 four-engined bombers over Europe and the English Channel, abandoning another 30 in Africa. And of those which did return to England, 28 were of use only as parts for other aircraft. That night RAF Bomber Command sent 596 heavy bombers to attack the German missile development base at Peenemunde, aiming at accommodation buildings to kill the scientists and technicians. In August, General Kenney's 5th Air Force executed a series of smashing raids on Japanese Army Air Force bases in the Wewak area, decisively altering the balance of power in the region. 9 September saw the Luftwaffe sink the Italian battleship *Roma* with two hits by radio-controlled bombs.

Winning some battles, losing others, the air arms were learning, adapting and developing. By October 1943 the Luftwaffe was on the defensive everywhere, despite mounting victory claims by the fighter *experten*. In the Pacific, poorly armed and armored Japanese bomber formations were regularly decimated by Allied fighters. Japanese fighters were basically those of the beginning of the war, while the Americans were introducing more advanced aircraft.

The lessons had been learned—never turn with a Zeke—and the strong points of American machines were exploited against the weak ones of the Japanese, to the fury of their pilots, who in 1942 had swept from the skies the collection of unsuitable and obsolete aircraft opposing them over China, Hawaii, the Phillipines, Malaya, Burma, the Netherlands East Indies, Ceylon, Rabaul, Port Moresby and Darwin. Only over China and Burma against Chennault's Flying Tigers, the American Volunteer Group, had any appreciable losses been suffered in the drive from Tokyo to Darwin on the Australian mainland.

But after the Coral Sea, Midway, the Solomons and New Guinea the "old hands" were melting away. The initiative was passing to the Allies, and the review of the situation by Imperial Headquarters had led to a defensive directive.

At lower levels of command the problems facing

the Japanese serviceman were apparent. The ever-increasing material superiority of the Allies was to be countered by Japanese spirit. Men against steel. Their leaders had sown the wind and the individual Japanese serviceman was about to reap the whirlwind, though few could see it coming.

One report distilling the lessons learned from recent air battles apparently was written by the Japanese Army's 248 Fighter *Sentai* (Regiment), on 19 December 1943, by Captain Kozuki and other experienced pilots. It refers to problems flying the Nakajima Ki-43 *Hayabusa* (Oscar). The report repeatedly admits the inferiority of the Oscar, while including all the tried and tested rules of air combat, linked to the admission that "Allied aircraft are hard to destroy at ranges greater than 100 meters". The Oscar had only two 12.7mm machine guns. The recommended counter to the superiority of Allied planes was to rely on manoeuvrability at low level. Significantly, the authors repeatedly emphasize being alert at all times—especially during take-off, adopting formation and landing—watching for attack from above and below, watching the rear, maintaining formation, always leaving some top cover, supporting and protecting each other, never becoming separated, use of clouds, always breaking into an attacker, maintaining height and possession of offensive spirit. Single aircraft returning from battle were to fly fast at low level, not dawdle along at medium height.

To deal with the deadly Lockheed Lightning, it was recommended that "the method of attacking the P-38 is to open fire on its left engine from a position of medium steep dive at an altitude of 500 meters while it is in the middle of a right turn."

Trainees were urged to have an offensive spirit and not "pay attention to pessimistic stories of those returning from front areas".

The report concluded, "if, at the right moment, we attack the enemy vigorously and press the attack boldly we are certain to gain victory. It is also necessary to take countermeasures against the enemy's surprise attacks. The occasions are few when we have the advantages of height, surprise attack and close combat, the three essentials helpful to victory. We must be constantly prepared for combat at low altitude and much depends on the skill of each individual." Interestingly, use of the sun is not included in these vital points compiled by presumably experienced pilots, but all the other golden rules of fighter combat were described. Significantly, emphasis was on manoeuvrability at low level, obviously the primary means of survival against Allied fighters.[2]

The general tone of the report was defensive: what to do and not to do to avoid being shot down. By comparison, a survey of 5th AF fighter leaders made about the same time shows the other side of the coin, emphasizing use of height, speed, firepower and teamwork to destroy the enemy.

So, by September and October 1943 the Allies were growing stronger and more experienced while the Axis powers tried to defend their frontiers, and the Japanese at Rabaul were still confident of final victory.

Notes

1. ATIS Bull 839
2. ATIS EP 202

2

The Japanese at Rabaul

Headquarters for 8th Area Army and Southeastern Fleet were at Rabaul, with six months supply of all materials necessary for all Japanese units in the area of operations. This complex of headquarters, airfields, harbor facilities and supplies was protected by defences which were constantly improved in expectation of Allied assaults following the Solomons Campaign.

As this book is concerned with air attack, the anti-aircraft defences are of interest. It can be seen in the table below how the AA defences increased.

	12.7cm	12cm	8cm	7cm	40mm	25mm	20 & 13mm
Aug 42	—	4	4	—	—	—	—
Dec 42	—	11	16	8	6	—	32
Nov 43	8	15	20	75	?	92	157 (1)

On 1 January 1943, Colonel Nagaaki Kawai assumed command of the 19th Field Anti-Aircraft Command, comprising seven AA battalions, an independent AA company and five field machinecannon companies, plus three field searchlight battalions.[2]

By November 1943, Rabaul was protected by 367 AA guns. Even allowing for 100 inoperable weapons, 260 were still available, and would be supplemented by guns on shipping.

By October 1943, most Army aircraft had gone to the compaign in New Guinea, leaving only a small force of transport, liaison, replacement and reconnaissance aircraft. However the Navy air presence was considerable, exercising its power well to the south and east.

Observation and reconnaissance were provided by the 938 and 958 *Kokkutai (Ku)* with about 56 Mitsubishi F1M2 (Pete) and Aichi E13A1 series (Jake) single-engined floatplanes, while 501 *Ku* operated 20 Yokosuka land-planes.

Fighters came from 201, 204 and 253 *Ku*.

Bombers were provided by 552 *Ku* with 36 Nakajima B5N (Kate) and Aichi D3A2 (Val) single-engined planes, while 751 *Ku* operated Mitsubishi G4M twin-engined bombers (Betty), and included the remnants of 702 *Ku*, which had been annihilated in earlier air operations.

This air force operated from a network of four airfields captured or built by the Japanese. Using natives, Chinese and Indian Army prisoners, the fields of Lakunai and Vunakanau were improved while Rapopo and Tobera were constructed. A fifth, at Keravat, was not really operational due to drainage problems. Around the four airfields a total of 265 fighter and 164 bomber revetments were built.[3]

The harbor at Rabaul, Blanche Bay, is six miles long by two-and-a-half wide, divided into four internal harbors, and provides good anchorage in all seasons and winds. The actual port of Rabaul was Simpson Harbor, where there were seven wharves and an average alongside depth of 21 feet. Simpson Harbor alone could accommodate 300,000 tons of shipping.

Ted Dorward, of RAAF 8 Squadron, flew night torpedo attacks into the harbor, recalling it as a "nasty target", and the distinctive smells of the missions—stink of sulphur from the volcanoes and odor of cordite from Japanese guns.[4]

Sister Berenice Twohill, a teaching nun of the Order of Our Lady of the Sacred Heart, captured in the Japanese advance, recalls the cone of searchlights illuminating the harbor waters at night, and the admiration with which the missionaries watched and prayed for those night intruders.[6]

In daylight, in November 1943, American B-25s and P-38s hurled themselves into that six-by-two basin, through a smoke screen, bomb splashes, AA fire, exploding ships and attacking Zekes, in a raid which aroused the admiration of the Japanese defenders.

The Japanese defensive system included a network of radar, observer posts, telephones and radio which could provide up to 60 minutes warning, but on one occasion there was none at all and on another only a few minutes.

The Japanese forces at Rabaul were products of the military system which had evolved through the industrialization of Japan, victory over the Imperial Russian forces 35 years earlier, combat experience in China, fighting the Soviets in 1939, and not least the military dictatorship which controlled the nation. While tactical and even strategic setbacks were possible, national defeat and surrender were unthinkable. Personal surrender or capture was repugnant in the extreme.

An Army Instruction on the problem of capture gave examples of cases when Japanese soldiers had been captured while unconscious due to wounds—one had a broken leg and elbow wounds—but observed that "actually this is no excuse." Other examples were the unfortunate soldier who could not keep up with his marching unit because of piles and while alone was captured, and the private who saw the enemy approaching his guard position, but took so long trying to think of a way to give the alarm that they hit him on the head and took him.

After listing the ways in which a soldier could be captured, the Instruction deduces that such "regrettable circumstances" may be produced by materialistic or "Christian ideas" and urges greater attention to "national ideas" in training. It goes on to discuss action after capture, resistance to interrogation, escape and return to Japanese forces, when,

"no matter what may come, one must realize his misdeed and show his penitence. Also he must state all the matters and quietly wait for the decision of higher officers. Upon release one should return to duty with the will to wipe out the humiliation and to seek death with the courage of the will to die. However, if an officer of high principle, usually the only course is to commit suicide."

The Instruction ends with the keynote of the prisoner-of-war counter-plan, which is that "when in doubt whether to live or die, death must be selected", and "although there are sympathetic feelings towards people who have fallen into enemy hands due to severe wounds, no matter what the excuse may be it is the greatest disgrace to be captured alive as a Japanese soldier."[5]

When a soldier did escape after four days in the hands of the Chinese, he was sentenced to two years wartime imprisonment for desertion as it was believed he could have escaped sooner.[6]

The Japanese Inspector General of Military Aviation also issued orders in the *Rules of Conduct for Aircrews*, which included "when return to Japanese territory is impossible, the aircraft, documents and crew must not fall into the hands of the enemy," and that "under no circumstances should you cling to life by accepting defeat nor should you forget the dignity of our Imperial forces to the extent of enduring the disgrace of being taken prisoner."[7]

In such an environment, it is no wonder diary entries like the following were made: "During yesterday's raid the Navy shot down three enemy planes, one of which made a forced landing and five crew members were captured. I think the Army would probably spend a long time questioning them while the Navy would execute them immediately."[8]

But like any army, the Japanese had their share of those who breached rules and regulations, and between April and October 1943, 18th Army HQ recorded 13 courtsmartial, for such offences as killing a superior officer, threatening same, avoiding the front by self-inflicting a wound, desertion, destruction of military property, embezzlement, gambling, theft, taking bribes and intimidation.

The Japanese had also reasoned that citizens of Italy and Germany in the newly occupied territories who had not been found interned or imprisoned must be sympathetic to the Allies. These people, if found at liberty, regardless of whether they were missionaries, doctors or business people, were often harshly treated.

Even friendly and neutral citizens were not treated well, as the Kyllerts found. Mrs. Kyllert, born in Hamburg, was married to Peter Kyllert, a Swedish national, living at Stockholm plantation, and they had remained after the Japanese occupation. In June 1943 Mrs. Kyllert went to Rabaul for medical treatment. She was made to stand in the sun for three hours, then taken to the *Kempeitai*—the dreaded military police—and made to stand for another hour before being taken to a room where there were 12 Japanese. She resisted when told to remove her clothes, was beaten and placed in a cell with Japanese and Chinese prisoners, some of whom had been tortured. Next morning she was taken from the cell, beaten again and returned to it until five p.m. She was then told that although she had assaulted a Japanese soldier she would not be punished and could leave. She returned to the plantation. After the Allied landings on New Britain, the Kyllerts and other civilians made their way to the beach-head, were evacuated and interviewed.[9]

However, Mrs. Kyllert was luckier than many others, such as the coolies described in the diary of First Lieutenant Oda, of an airfield construction unit.

"8 Apr 44. I must be calm. If I am nervous in front of the spectators I may fail. When I thought of this it was imperative to remain calm. I sprinkled water on my sword and took a deep breath. The spectators on the road watched. I aimed at the shoulder, neck and chin. I raised my sword and swung. The head fell forward and the body slumped to the ground. Blood was surging from the neck in a jet. I was shaking. The pulse of the artery was visible for a while. There were bloodstains on the blade. No-one said a word. I could see the white flesh, muscles and the bone. I washed my sword and returned to my force. I kept saying, 'Be calm, be calm,' to myself, but from the instant I swung my sword I was not conscious of my movements. I know when I swung but I cannot remember seeing the head fall to the ground. I was trained to leave a skin on the neck when I beheaded a person. I beheaded him completely; I need more practice."

Two references to other officers beheading coolies follow, then the diary goes on:

"I was a person who could not eat when I saw a wound. But now after beheading a person I am nonchalant. I can eat and sleep at night. Maybe I have strengthened spiritually. It is true that I have been indoctrinated in warfare, so this is a natural reaction. I killed a man on 8 April. I will pray for the repose of his soul."[10]

Before the actual arrival of the Japanese, the considerable Chinese community had left Rabaul town and gathered at two missions. The leaders of the Kuomintang were asked to identify themselves, did so, and were immediately executed. The remaining Chinese were then lectured on their need to be loyal to the puppet Emperor of China.

The local people, the Tolai, were mostly hostile to the invaders and reluctant to assist them, but the Japanese established a native police force, the *Li Ming Tai*, from native people from other areas brought to Rabaul to work. This unit oppressed the Chinese with beatings, raping and robbing.

The Japanese themselves were restrained in their treatment of the Chinese. As Sister Berenice Twohill noted, the Japanese commander did not want a further brutal episode added to those credited to the Japanese in China.

Though the Chinese were generally used as laborers, those with skills such as typing, carpentry, driving ability and so on were employed in relevant work. Naturally, when the great expansion of defence works began, Chinese were used for much of the work, especially underground.

Another part of the labor force was composed of units of the British Empire's Indian Army, captured at Singapore or Malaya. At that time they were told they were not prisoners, but would be used as labor forces by the Japanese. Sent to Rabaul early in 1943, they were employed as just that. They performed a great deal of heavy work, unloading ships, digging defence works, caves and tunnels, moving AAA weapons, repairing airfields and so on.

A speech by the commander of a Japanese military police unit on New Britain was given to village chiefs, who were told they could rely on the MPs for support in controlling their people, and,

"As I have mentioned before, the Japanese Army has come to this island to protect and educate you. If among the countless Japanese troops there are a few who enter your villages and loot your goods, your taro, bananas, coconut, etc, notify us immediately. The Japanese Army will never take things without paying. If at any time they steal or rob by scaring you with a bayonet, report it at once."

The chiefs were then exhorted to report any English, Australians, Chinese, Filipinos or Malays who were hiding, any strangers interested in the Japanese, any weapons, letters or clothing belonging to such people. If in future any aircraft were seen to crash, or parachutes appear, to send word at once. After telling the audience that if the English or Australians came back to the island they would kill the natives, the MP commander encouraged the chiefs to get their people to cooperate with the Japanese and grow plenty of food for sale to them.[11]

Censorship was exercised by the Japanese, as well as the Allies. On 13 October 1943, 8th Area Army was informed by the MPs that the censorship situation was satisfactory. Of 124,700 items of mail censored, only 11 contained demoralizing or homesick material, five were of interest from a counter-intelligence view and 94 others were returned to units for such things as unit stamp.[12]

Military organizations around the world have many similarities, not the least of which is concern by senior officers that they are not being shown adequate respect. Like some of his more well-known contemporaries in the Allied camp, General Imamura, commander at Rabaul, believed this to be the case. An order was issued about saluting him, and described the special flag on his car: yellow background, red-white-black roundel surmounted by a red-over-white rectangle.[13]

In general, the Japanese were as hard on their own people as they were on foreigners under their control, though they found it hard to understand the Western concept of mercy and respect for a brave but captive foe.

All organizations, however faceless they may appear to observers, are composed of individuals, and it may be appropriate to introduce some of the Japanese who would witness or take part in the coming air attacks.

In October 1943, Lieutenant Makoto Ikuta was a 21-year-old pilot of a Mitsubishi Ki-46 (Dinah) reconnaissance aircraft, in a detachment of 10 *Sentai* at Lakunai airfield. He arrived at Rabaul in October 1942, and had flown many missions over the Solomons and New Guinea. Most of 10 *Sentai* had gone there, leaving a detachment of five or six aircraft under the operational command of General Imamura.[14]

Further south along the bay, at Kokopo, 33-year-old Doctor Tetsuo Aso was medical officer to the 60th AAA Battalion. A Christian, Dr. Aso had seen service in China and on Guadalcanal, and on arrival at Rabaul was "perfectly ignorant of the area." His immediate concern was with diseases in the area—malaria, dengue and scrub typhus (called *Tsutsugamushi*). While on Guadalcanal, Dr. Aso began to suspect that the frontline situation was worse than IHQ admitted. At Rabaul he became sure of it.

Aso's experiences at Rabaul have been the subject of books and magazine articles in Japan. Malaria was a great problem, and after Rabaul was isolated, he designed an ingenious machine made of gas cylinders from 20mm Oerlikon cannon, motorcar springs and other items, to produce 200,000 quinine pills for the battalion. The quinine itself was extracted from a shipment of damaged tablets, which arrived as a mixture of shattered glass and broken powdered tablets. Like his Allied counterparts, Dr. Aso struggled against disease until the last day of the war and beyond.

But unlike his Allied counterparts, he took an active role in the warlike activities of the unit, standing watch in the gunpits, salvaging 20mm cannon from wrecked planes on the airfield and preparing them to give extra firepower to the positions.[14]

Commander Takeo Shibata led his Zekes of 204 *Ku* first to Buin airfield on Bougainville, then on 4 October 1943 to Lakunai at Rabaul, where they would fly in the coming air attacks.[14]

Takashi Makino, soldier in the 53rd Regiment, arrived at the end of September, and with the rest of the men was put to work constructing air raid shelters.[15]

751 *Ku*, with its Betty bombers, had also arrived in September, absorbing the planes and men of its destroyed predecessor. Hiroshi Suda had been at Vunakanau since May, had managed to go to Rabaul town two or three times, seen other aircraft and realized other units were in the area, but did not know where they were. To this extent he knew more and had travelled more than many others.[16] Hideo Hatani was also in 751, and was restricted by the order that men were not to go beyond 1,000 meters from their quarters and working place. Guards and patrols enforced the regulation.[17]

Another member of 751 was Leading Airman Noboyoshi Asakura, who had flown night bombing missions to New Guinea and the Solomons. He had not been far enough away from his unit at Vunakanau to know of the Army Ki-61 *Hien* (Tonys) based at the far side of the field.[18] Chief Petty Officer Kunishige Kuwaori, a 751 pilot, had seen the Tonys, but was not allowed to look at them close-up and did not know who flew them.[19]

Nobuko Tsujimura was head nurse of the 8th Naval Hospital, arriving in May 1943, and like most of the

men, knew nothing of the place before she did.[20]

Some of the Japanese were not military people, but civilians like Koichi Owada, an employee with 8th Naval Munitions Depot, on Mango Avenue.[21] Others had very little training, such as Satoshi Ota, conscripted on 10 January 42, when the train trip to Sasebo Naval Base was the longest journey he had undertaken—and paid for the ticket himself. He had been trained to clean sparkplugs, and after a long plane flight had arrived at 751 *Ku*.[22]

"Moto" was an unknown diarist in a shipping engineer unit, arriving at Rabaul on 27 August 1943. On the 29th, he wrote: "Disembarked at Rabaul. I was surprised to see that there were many more papayas, coconuts, etc than I had expected. When I think this is where my unit will be based, a feeling of gladness arises in me."[23]

For most of the Japanese there was scanty leave, and most did not leave their unit locations. Some knew there was a harbor nearby only because they flew over it on the way in. Radios were few, usually held by an officers' mess. Information came from superior ranks, garrison newspapers or letters from home. In this sixth year of war—for the Japanese it began in 1937—home was increasingly drab, with queues and shortages, reduced beer supplies and shorter opening hours for geishas and other places of entertainment. One letter informed the reader that "it is difficult to live in Tokyo, too, especially for women whose husbands are absent. A person who wishes to buy vegetables would have to wait for two hours, and when she obtains them she finds she has to pay for extra unwanted things. I really feel like crying. It is easy to spend three or four yen a day and one usually spends at least one yen a day. Even if I wanted to buy clothing for the children I cannot very well pay 15 or 20 yen. I am hoping you would send me lots of things from there. I cannot send you anything for there is nothing to send. We are not afraid of air raids so do not worry about us."[24]

Masao Takashiro, 5th Company, 54th Regiment, believed that by 1943 the conditions in Japan were at 80% of the pre-war standards, but the population endured the situation in order to win the war and would fight for 100 years if necessary.[25]

An Australian civilian prisoner who later left a record of his time in captivity was Gordon Thomas, editor of the local newspaper. He and three other men were to be the only survivors of the Europeans who had been taken by the unstoppable Japanese. Selected to work at the freezing plant, they remained when all the others were sent to Japan aboard the *Montevideo Maru*, and were lost when it was sunk by a US submarine. Thomas worked at the plant until it was destroyed by bombing, then survived until the arrival of Australian forces after the surrender. Thomas described himself as "a rather cranky man in his middle fifties. Having lived in the islands over 30 years I had developed that natural Island intolerance for any interloper who had arrived later than 20 years before, and having been the editor of the local paper for so many years naturally possessed that dogmatic, self-satisfied attitude which editors invariably cultivate all over the world."[26]

Another Australian was Sister Berenice Twohill, who observed of the Japanese that "the Air Force fellows were fit, tall and seemed to be educated but were very arrogant. We never had anything to do with them, they just came to look us over."[27]

Sister Catherine O'Sullivan was a nursing nun who was working among Australian sick and wounded when the Japanese landed on the beach near Vunapope. Staff and patients were lined up on the verandah of the hospital, covered by machineguns manned by Japanese soldiers who "appeared as apprehensive as we were." Later the scene became more relaxed, with discussions in broken English taking place, until the "arrogant and ruthless" officers arrived. The missionaries were sorted out and the Germans separated and strictly guarded.

At first the missionaries were allowed to go for walks and swims. "Apart from an arrogant attitude, we could not complain of their treatment. The CO in Rabaul was enforcing discipline on the troops on account of the bad name they had won for themselves in their sweep through Asia, and Japanese soldiers were executed for interfering with native women in any way. Their general attitude to us religious sisters was one of respect and we were protected by the officers of the Kempeitai from the advances of soldiers, which was not common."

Up to the time of the Coral Sea battle in May 1942, Sister Catherine describes the Japanese attitude as "happy and glorious", but after the military setbacks, particularly at Guadalcanal, hostility grew and deepened. The missionaries were thought to be communicating with the Allied forces, and "marked disapproval was shown on 3 October 1942, when we were ordered out of our mission homes into the workshops. A barbed wire fence was built around us and we were officially prisoners or internees."[28]

One of the Japanese officers who moved into the church buildings was Lieutenant Kiyoshi Yagita, pilot of a Mitsubishi Betty in 702 *Ku* at Vunakanau. He stayed there until mid-October 1943, in "the church building that had a view of the inside of the harbor."

So, in October 1943, Rabaul was still the largest Japanese base in the region, garrisoned by units which gave real meaning to the phrases "no surrender" and "fought to the last man". Despite recent setbacks, the 50,000 Japanese there were determined to fight and die for the Emperor.

Control of information to the junior ranks naturally assisted the intentions of Imperial HQ. At Rabaul, as on the other fronts, the average Japanese serviceman was far away from home, many days by ship and hours by air, across new expanses of the Empire. Great victories had been won, and news of those events were shown to be true. Further claims would not be doubted, even if untrue.

Restricted in movement out of their unit areas, given little news, part of a military system demanding instant and total obedience to all superiors, indoctrinated unceasingly to die for the Emperor, the Japanese awaited their orders and flew, sailed or marched to their enemies.

The local people tried to accommodate these occupiers as they had the Germans and Australians, unaware that fire was about to fall upon them from the skies, as impersonal and deadly as from the volcanoes. The enslaved local Chinese, the Indian Army and Allied air force prisoners and the missionaries lived day by day, clinging to what hope remained after up to 20 months of captivity.

Against the 50,000 Japanese defenders, fewer than 2,000 Allied airmen were preparing to attack, across merciless seas and jungles, through dangerous flying weather, knowing prisoners rarely survived.

Notes

1. CICSPF Item 1182
2. CICSPF Item 749
3. USSBS
4. audiotape to author 1983
5. ATIS Bull 1478
6. ATIS Bull 1370 and 1578
7. AAF Int Memo 31 and 32
8. ATIS Bull 1453
9. AWM file 779-3-93
10. ATIS Bull 1379
11. ATIS Bull 580
12. ATIS Bull 741
13. ATIS Bull 688
14. letters to author 1982
15. AWM file 779-3-29
16. AWM file 779-3-62
17. AWM file 779-3-100
18. AWM file 779-3-36/17
19. AWM file 779-3-36/17 and PW Intg 187
20. letter via Henry Sakaida 1984
21 letter to author 1982
22. AWM file 779-3-62
23. CICSPF Item 938
24. ATIS Bull 1541
25. AWM file 423-6-36
26. ANU Menzies Library Pacific Manuscripts microfilm 36
27. audiotape to author 1983
28. letters to author 1983
29. letters to author 1983

3

Kenney's Buccaneers

By September 1943, General George Kenney led a 5th Air Force which was a far cry from the struggling organization he had taken over 13 months previously. Now the Allied air forces totalled 102 squadrons—59 USAAF and 43 RAAF. While employing some units on other tasks in the theater, Kenney was able to provide a considerable force for the attacks on Rabaul. Four-engined B-24s would come from the 43rd "Ken's Men" and 90th "Jolly Roger" Bomb Groups. Twin-engined B-25s, for low-level bombing and strafing, came from the 3rd, 38th and 345th Bomb Groups. Fighter escort would be provided by six squadrons of P-38 Lightnings. They came from the 80th "Headhunters" Squadron of the 8th Fighter Group; 39th Squadron, 35th Group; 9th Squadron, 49th Group; and the three squadrons of the 475th "Satan's Angels" Fighter Group. The 475th was the first complete P-38 group in the Southwest Pacific Area (SWPA). The other groups were equipped with the inferior P-39/P-400 and P-40, and it had been decided to convert one squadron from each as P-38s became available.

RAAF aircraft for the Rabaul raids were the Beaufighter, a strafer and attack aircraft, and the Beaufort, used on night raids against shipping and airfield targets. RAAF 6, 8 and 100 Squadrons flew day and night anti-shipping missions in the New Britain area, and as the Japanese had resorted to using naval vessels on supply runs rather than merchant ships, it was believed the missions had some success.

The American aircraft have all been well described in books dedicated to the subject and it is not intended to do so here. It should be remembered that all-metal aircraft flying easily at 200-300 mph were relatively new in 1943. The last few years of the 1930s had seen the beginning of the explosion in aviation technology which has continued to this day, but flying then had only recently moved from fixed undercarriages, bracing wires, open cockpits and the proverbial white scarf around the neck of the dashing pilot. As one former B-24 crewmember put it, "we were still learning to fly those things and our friends were being killed in them."

The Consolidated B-24, like the B-17, had been designed to provide long-range reconnaissance from the US coast, to detect hostile fleets. It was not intended to be the heavy bomb-carrier evolving in the European airwar.

The North American B-25 had recently been field-modified in Australia, and tested by the legendary Paul "Pappy" Gunn, to become a flying gunship, nose bristling with eight .50 caliber machineguns which poured a devastating hail of fire onto a target.

The Lockheed P-38 had been a case of "love at first sight" in the Pacific, where the Japanese Zeke had proved superior to all other Allied fighters. Fast, twin-engined, with superior high-altitude performance and with firepower of four .50 caliber machineguns and a 20mm cannon concentrated in the nose, the Lightning climbed to fame in the SWPA.

It will be seen that the 5th AF provided fighter escort whenever possible for the Rabaul raids, with all available P-38s. At this time in Europe the 8th AF was losing B-17s and B-24s by the dozen, in attempts to prove heavy bomber formations could protect themselves beyond fighter cover.

The US aircraft were serviced and flown by men from all across the United States, representing all walks of life in the 1930s. Before beginning training, some had no more knowledge of machinery than Satoshi Ota, who had gone from the farm to Sasebo and been taught to clean sparkplugs.

At Chanute Field, Cy Stafford of Arkansas raised a laugh when he placed his hand on a strange object in the classroom foyer and asked what it was. It was an aircraft engine, and Cy vowed then that before the laughers left the training base they would be asking him questions in an attempt to improve their knowledge. In New Guinea,

Cy served with the 8th Service Group's 482nd Squadron, a unit commanded from inception in 1942 until his departure in mid-44 by Major J.J. Summers. The 482nd provided such good support that flying units did not want to release it, requesting its services.

Another member of the 8th Service Group was John Brogan, a line chief. Being young and adventurous, John had gone to Spain to fight in the Civil War, but found he cared for neither the Communists nor the Fascists. He tried to join the Foreign Legion, but was told it could only offer North Africa, with roadbuilding and marching in the sun. He returned to the USA, joined the Army and found himself in Panama, building swimmingpools and marching in the rain.

In the early days of the war against Japan, after the fall of all territory north of New Guinea, there were few aircraft available in the Allied Air Forces (AAF). Those that were came in many different types, with few spare parts and tools sometimes had to be made by the men who would use them. Improvisation and making-do were the only ways to keep aircraft operational. After the fall of Java in 1942, Cy Stafford was working on a collection of aircraft at an Australian airfield, of which no two were the same, there were no instruction books or tool kits, no torch batteries for night work or seeing into the dark recesses of the aircraft, in all, "a shambles".

For aircrews there were also shortages of basic requirements. Charles King, 39th Squadron, was one of a formation flying P-39s from Mount Gambier in Australia's south to Williamtown, 160 miles north of Sydney in mid-1942. Most of the wingmen had no maps, and the flight leaders had Shell roadmaps.[4]

Larry Tanberg later commanded the 38th Bomb Group, and retired as a major general. His opinion of the maintenance crews: "As for the maintenance of the aircraft, not enough praise could possibly do justice to the work of these men. Parts shortages were an everyday fact of life. Only through the ingenuity and perseverance of our maintenance personnel were they able to keep the aircraft going. The Wright engine on the B-25s was our major problem with a fairly high internal failure rate. This was gradually corrected over a period of time through trial and error, but continued to plague us throughout.

"Perhaps the hardest work fell on the shoulders of the armorers, who had to keep the .50 caliber guns working and loaded, and loading and fusing of bombs. Most frustrating was the frequent necessity to change bomb load configuration to meet a change in mission from higher headquarters. Often this resulted in two, and infrequently three, different bomb loads before the mission departed. The fewer number of aircraft in the theater then caused headquarters to have to do this, but to us at the lower end of the line, it was most unpleasant.

The armament sections carried a tremendous load and responsibility. Fuse settings were critical to the low-level mission at hand and the performance of the guns was vital. Today they are still vital to any Air Force mission and I believe too infrequently get justice given their mission."[5]

The 5th AF Statistic Book for 1943 shows that it required 89 men to maintain and fly one aircraft. Manpower strength was composed of about 5% flying crews, 21.3% maintenance men, 14.9% clerks, 11.1% vehicle operators and maintenance, 3.1% cooks; the remainder being medics and officers for the above categories.

Allied units began moving in strength to New Guinea when the decision was made to resist and hold them there rather than in Australia. On 30 July 1942, Cy Stafford arrived at Port Moresby aboard a ship which ran aground in the middle of an air raid warning. About 10:30 p.m. it was decided to off-load the passengers in the hope that the ship would be lightened enough to float free. After a dangerous descent through the blackness into a small boat, Cy and the rest were taken ashore and told to "bed down, there is nothing that can hurt you", but in the next raid Cy found himself momentarily sharing his trench with what he later realized was a wallaby as frightened as himself, and "skinned my legs climbing and jumping out of there."

The Americans were puzzled by the trees in their camp site. All had been chewed off about 18 inches above the ground. Then they found the place was called Death Valley: Japanese daisy-cutter bombs had levelled the area. The air raids ceased to be a spectator sport after the first personal experience of one. Raids were so frequent that the common signal to take cover was a series of three loud noises, such as blasts on a car horn, shots, or similar. Cy recalls one night when "some of the boys were sitting on the latrine and by accident three of them got up at the same time and the lids closed with a bang 1-2-3, the guys were jumpy and some that were half asleep thought it was the red alert, rushed out and jumped into their foxholes."

Clint Solomon, 3rd Group, flew both A-20s and B-25s, preferring the A-20. He landed in Sydney in September 1942, and made the long boring train trip to Townsville with no dining cars, getting off the train to eat. He recalls that there were more crews than aircraft, and "if you damaged a plane you were in trouble." A year later John Stanifer, 19-year old P-38 pilot, made the same boring journey, getting out to walk alongside the train as it slowly climbed hills and shooting his .45 pistol at wildlife, though he inflicted no injuries or deaths. An adequate comment on a boring and frustrating means of getting to the war.

In the 43rd Bomb Group's 64th Squadron, Harry Young was a B-24 pilot. In the well-known fashion of military organizations the world over, he had trained on B-17s and was sent to a B-24 unit. The quota for B-17s being filled in December 1942, the last 34 names on the list were simply passed to B-24s. Harry's conversion from flying a tail-wheeled, Wright-engined, electrically-powered B-17 to a nose-wheeled, Pratt & Whitney-engined, hydraulically-powered B-24 was brief. A single flight, consisting of a dual take-off, 100-mile flight, solo landing rolling into take-off, return 100-mile flight, land, take-off, return to base. "The captain said, 'Young, that checks you out day and night. Go and meet your crew and take it up for four hours.' " Harry collected his crew and found the co-pilot just came from single-engined advanced training. After a further three months training, they collected their B-24 at Topeka and on 1 June 1943 set out for the war via San Francisco, Hawaii, Canton Island, Fiji, New Caledonia, Brisbane, Townsville and Charters Towers, then on to Port Moresby. To find the 43rd flew B-17s. The group was converting to B-24s, but kept a B-17 hidden away for hack runs to Australia and the fleshpots. Before his Rabaul daylight raids, Harry had flown 18 missions.

Among the fighter pilots was Cornelius "Corky" Smith, in the 80th "Headhunters". Graduating as a pilot in September 1942, he joined the squadron at Milne Bay in November, flying P-39s and P-400s. Moved from Milne Bay because of rampant malaria, the squadron re-equipped with P-38s at Mareeba, in northern Australia. Returning to New Guinea in April, by the time of the first large daylight raid on Rabaul, "Corky" Smith had flown 68 missions and had four Zekes credited.

Another fighter pilot was Marion Kirby, who flew with both the 80th and 431st Squadrons. His class graduated on 12 December 1941 and were all immediately posted to combat units, receiving no gunnery training. Their first shooting was in combat, and Marion believes this had much to do with their initial reluctance to engage the enemy. When the 80th brought its P-39s to New Guinea, the only maps available were National Geographic productions showing "the outline of the coast and a few, very few, peaks inland." When returning to base from Buna they would fly on 180 degrees until reaching the southern coastline. If reefs were seen, they turned right; is no reefs, they turned left. "That was it, the summation of our navigation," Marion recalls.

His description of the P-400: "It had to be the worst aircraft a major power has ever asked one of its citizens to fly to defend the nation as well as himself. Our maximum altitude was 23,000 feet, after a long and grueling climb. At that altitude it was so unstable that if you rolled your eyeballs from side to side a wing would dip and you'd lose a couple of hundred feet. When the Japs would raid Moresby we scrambled 50 miles down the coast. There we would watch the Japs fly over in perfect formation, Zeros in trail, having the durndest ratraces you ever saw. They were having a ball!"

Of course, to people on the ground in the target area it was not good to see the fighters fleeing, as Cy Stafford recalls, "take off like a swarm of bees and go out over the ocean until the Japs had bombed us and gone, then they would come back and land." Some called the exodus "the Kingfishers," others "the Fishing Fleet" and less polite terms.

The 80th's alert shack in 1942 was a grass hut at the end of 12-Mile Strip. (The Port Morseby airdromes were named for their distance from town.) A telephone switch was at one end, a card table in the center and cups along the side. Headquarters was worried about Japanese infiltrators, so the line was checked every 15 minutes to see if it was intact. "The corporal on the switch answered every call the same way, with no indication the call was routine or perhaps one that would send the waiting pilots into combat." Pilots reacted with nervous urinating, so much that when the 80th left not a tree was alive within 25 paces of the shack!

However, when the P-38 became available, in Marion Kirby's words, "the handwriting became more legible on the wall." His first combat in the P-38 came in May 43, near Wau, New Guinea. "The first rule of combat was push everything forward, firewall it! With all this added thrust the nose came up and I began climbing. I had so much I could not push the nose down, so just climbed out of the combat. Once clear I turned and dove back . . . as soon as I reached the center of the melee I poured the coal to it . . . and here I went again right up out of the fracas! Sure, I could have used the trim-tab, but who wanted to have a silly thought like that in the middle of your first combat?" Climbing, he noticed the airspeed indicator showing well over 200 mph at 22,000 feet, climbing at an unknown rate, but equal to well over 400 mph true groundspeed. "It was love at first sight!"

At the time of Pearl Harbor, Bill Martin was a 20-year old sophomore at San Jose and joined the USAAF. During training he survived a mid-air collision in BT-13s, getting out at 700 feet, parachute opening at 200, putting a shaken cadet on the ground a few yards from the burning wreck with the instructor still in it. With 200 hours in his log-book, he went to B-24s and 8.5 hours later was a first pilot. Collecting a crew and a B-24, he had further training and set off across the Pacific with 280 hours flying time.

Only a few years previously, the first pilots to cross the huge expanses of oceans and continents were feted as heroes, yet in 1942 and 1943 inexperienced crews were taking their aircraft, often not long out of the experimental stage, over those oceans as a mere first step to combat.

When he arrived in the 90th Group's 321st Squadron, only three B-24s were flyable, the rest used for parts. By July, the number had risen from 16 to 18, and by October, the time of the Rabaul raids, the squadron could launch 20 planes on a mission.

Charles King spent three years, from January 1941 to December 1943, with the 39th Squadron, commanding it for the last four months after Tommy Lynch returned to the USA. King began his combat flying in May 1942, in P-39s and P-400s, flying 25 missions before converting to the P-38, and flying another 176, gaining five confirmed victories. In King's opinion the poor performance of the US fighter units in mid-1942 resulted from a combination of poor mechanical expertise, poor pilot training and poor leadership in some units, plus confronting the superior Japanese aircraft. The 39th had the benefit of proper training for pilots and groundcrews, plus good leadership, but the opposing planes were better. Then came the Lightning.

Danny Roberts, from New Mexico, had intended to become a minister of religion but left his studies to take pilot training, graduating shortly before Pearl Harbor. He did not drink, smoke or swear. Roberts flew his early missions in P-39s and P-400s, then came the P-38. When a cadre of experienced pilots was provided for the newly-formed 475th Group, Roberts went to the 433rd Squadron, taking command on 4 October 1943.

In the opinion of Charles King, the greatest fighter leader in the area at the time was Tommy Lynch. Lynch took the formation to the target, into combat and back home, bringing back convincing camera-gun evidence of his personal combats. While other pilots such as Bong and Sparks were renowned for individual kills, Lynch was as good and a leader, with only Gerald Johnson as his equal.

John Shemelynce, a photographer with the 3rd Bomb Group, arrived in Melbourne, Australia, in March 1942, after a 21-day voyage from San Francisco. He arrived at Charters Towers when the 3rd was equipped with A-24s, most of which were soon lost in action against Japanese landings on the north coast of New Guinea. A-20s and B-25s arrived to replace the lost aircraft. At Charters Towers, the group was "spoiled on the plentiful steaks. The mess hall would even serve you a steak for breakfast. In addition we would have a whole beef given to us from a local cattle station (ranch), which we would barbeque on a Sunday. The town of Charters Towers looked like a Western movie set, with places to tie your horses in front of the pub. In fact some of the Yanks purchased horses to ride into town."

Tom Fetter, bombardier, had been with the 90th since July 1942, and had flown the group's first combat mission. By the time of the Rabaul raids he was an experienced aircrew member, having been through the "bad news" Wewak missions of the earlier months and in particular one reconnaissance mission with Major Thornhill in December 1942, when the lone B-24 was set upon by ten Japanese fighters.

Bill Martin's first mission had been a shipping recce to Kavieng, New Ireland. As the B-24 neared the port, a lovely target in form of a ship was seen. Martin's experienced co-pilot, along to show the new guys the ropes, was horrified as they prepared to run in and bomb, saying it was live and let live up in this area. Then the front gunner said he could see Zeros taking off so Bill wheeled away into some cloud, thinking it was no way to win a war.

A final word on the 5th AF, about its commander, from Larry Tanberg: "Much has been written and said about the late General Kenney. It was he who gave us young 'punks' the opportunity to command and lead. He felt we had been there from the early days and deserved the chance to move ahead. More so, we knew how he wanted to operate. This was a great morale factor in a theater which was low on the priority totem pole. That, plus the high loss rate of some of our leaders gave some of us 'lucky' ones the chance to command at a very early age. This all was a classic example of learning from the school of hard knocks at its best. Everything, or perhaps I should say almost everything, was learned the hard way. No one could tell us much about what to do, but I think perhaps the smallness of the overall operation worked to advantage. We used to meet with those who were flying fighter cover or on the same mission next day and it became a very personal operation. It wasn't just a P-38 up there, it was a P-38 with Dick Bong, or Charlie MacDonald or some other known friend flying it.

"I have felt for some time that perhaps the late General Ennis Whitehead did not receive the credit due him for that war. Kenney recognized a brilliant tactician in Whitehead and I don't know anyone who worked harder to beat the enemy than General Whitehead. He was always scheming, planning and working for better ways to meet the foe. He was extremely hard on his staff, but for those of us flying combat for him, we could do no wrong. Perhaps his only fault was that he tried to do too much—even to the extent of determining and deciding bombloads, take-off times, etc. He was a stern taskmaster and there were those after the war who remarked in admiration that 'Whitehead was as tough as LeMay thinks he is!' "

Notes

All information this chapter from letters and tapes to author 1982-83, or books quoted in text.

4

Service Squadron Scene I

A recurring problem for the maintenance and repair units was "souveniring" of the high-quality clocks in damaged aircraft. The instrument shop then had difficulty in replacing the "lost" items. Cy Stafford carried a screwdriver blade fitted to a pocketknife so he was always ready . . . just in case.

One day he saw an A-20 taxi into a ditch, collapsing the left main landing gear. He decided there was one clock which was not going to be stolen. As the pilot climbed out, Cy walked up the wing, leaned in, removed the two screws, pocketed the clock and climbed down. Two officers appeared on the other side of the plane, and one said, "Let's get the clock." They scrambled up, looked in, and were amazed. "Someone done got the clock! How did they do that so quick no one saw them?" A grinning Cy walked away to arrange collection of the A-20.

While in the Port Moresby area, the 482nd Service Squadron had wanted a small boat for fishing and pleasure sailing, but of course there was nothing like that for sale and no suitable wood to build one. One day, Cy noticed two of the men driving a 30-foot flatbed trailer into the area; about 20 or 30 men climbed aboard and off it went. He realized something wanted by the 482nd had been seen. About an hour later the posse returned with a sailing boat, which was speedily unloaded, upturned on wooden horses and attacked by three men from the paint shop, spraying the gray hull a distinct red. Later, MPs were in the area, looking for a stolen gray boat. Of course, no one had seen such a thing. A sort of justice was done. Soon after the 482nd had to pack and move, leaving the boat sitting there, unused. Cy often wondered who got it, what happened to it . . .

The 482nd sometimes used a fast method of timing P-38 magnetos. One man sat in the cockpit to operate the throttles, while the other lay flat on the wing, reaching into the engine bay at rear of the V-bank of cylinders on the Allison engine. The latter made adjustments to

the points with the screwdriver, then walked out to the wingtip and waited while the other man ran up the engine to check timing and mag drop. He signaled the man on the wing to advance or retard ignition and in that way the job could be done in ten to 15 minutes. "Of course," Cy recalls, "you could expect the fire to flash all around the screwdriver and sometimes you got a good electrical shock."

Sometimes P-38 squadrons were unable to fix an engine problem, so they sent the plane to the 8th Service Group with a supposed sheet metal problem, knowing the engines had to be run and checked before the plane was returned. One such came in for a minor repair, was found to have an engine running hot and it could not be fixed. The problem was found in a cooling line. A cork had been placed in it at the factory, reducing coolant flow by about one-third.

When the P-38 turbosuperchargers got out of synchronization, "they were one mean devil to get synchronized," according to Cy, "so the 482nd carpenters made a special set of chocks. Fourteen inches high, with steel spikes six inches long, to be dug into the ground. Then metal posts were pounded in and the landing gear was chained to them. When the engines were opened up to 76 inches of manifold pressure the P-38 would climb the chocks, bucking and twisting, trying to get free. Everyone gave them plenty of room when that check was being made."

Flying There

Nature was regarded by many in the Allied Air Forces as more dangerous than the Japanese enemy. Before, during and since the war, aircraft and crews have been consumed by the flying conditions in this region. Certainly in the bombing campaign against Rabaul the weather intervened more often than not to give the Japanese respite from sustained attack. Better than a general description of the hazards of flying there are personal descriptions and comments from men who experienced them.

Bill Martin, 321st Squadron, 90th Bomb Group: "I've never seen such horrible weather in my life! The darn Owen-Stanley mountains were an absolute weather factory. Every afternoon, gigantic thunderstorms towering out . . . at night, tremendous thunderstorms . . . what a frightening experience! Here I am with 200 hours as a cadet, 80 or 90 more by the time we went overseas, and we did get a little weather crossing the Pacific, but nothing could mentally prepare a pilot such as myself for what we went through flying over the Owen-Stanleys and Bismark Sea.

"What I did learn from experience on the night raids was to get down to about 6,000 feet over the water and there seems about the best level for taking what a thunderstorm wants to give. It wasn't uncommon for my co-pilot and myself to be holding the wheel all the way forward, watching the altimeter climb two or three thousand feet a minute, sometimes higher, up to about eight or ten thousand, hit the top, a tremendous crash, the wing would almost break off and down you'd start. It took the strength of two of us to keep the thing level. The auto-pilot couldn't hold it, they weren't good enough in those days. So it was a tremendously trying psychological experience. And we lost people due to weather. They finally lost control and spun in, that was all there was to it.

"As I got a hundred hours or so experience I began to get a little cocky and try to use the things I'd learned, like fly between the flashes of lightning, things of that nature. I'm sure my crew must have been horrified to sit in the back and be thrown around, praying the pilot knew what he was doing, because there just wasn't any rescue if we went down. There was no air-sea rescue at all, even in daylight. Accidents and weather got more American crews than the Japs ever did."

John Stanifer, 80th Fighter Squadron, 8th Fighter Group: "I always regarded weather as the greatest enemy, that and the lack of navigational aids. We relied strictly on pilotage, hoping the weather did not close in as you returned from the target. You read wind direction and velocity from the whitecaps and hoped it was the same at the altitude you were flying."

Larry Tanberg, 38th Bomb Group: "While there are many good and bad memories of those days, I'm afraid the bad ones have the edge, and leading that list was the necessity of having to fly across the Owen-Stanley range to most of our targets. With no oxygen and a very limited amount of fuel in those first aircraft, coupled with the fact that we had no navigational aids, made that flight over the mountains pretty much a night-

mare. As I am sure it still does today, the cloud cover began building about 10:00 a.m. each day. On returning from missions in the Buna or Lae area, generally with low fuel, we'd climb to 11-12,000 feet, plough into the clouds and hope to hit the saddle of the range. Frequently we would break out of the clouds over the sea. It was then standard procedure to turn north towards land. Our navigational aid then was the coastline and whether or not there was a reef. As I recall, if we were west of Moresby there was no reef and if we were east there was a reef."

"Corky" Smith, 80th Fighter Squadron: "The weather from Kiriwina to Rabaul was always a factor to be carefully considered. The Bismark Sea is noted for its towering cumulus clouds, the severe squalls beneath and the numerous waterspouts along a weather front. Weather curtailed several missions. The height of clouds precluded overflight and the squalls and waterspouts beneath made low-level on the deck penetration a very hazardous undertaking. We flew needle-ball-airspeed in those days, and that type of instrument flying in turbulent weather and in formation was not a welcome challenge to any of us. Although the P-38 had an artificial horizon instrument, we had little confidence in its merits as it was prone to tumble in turbulence. Hence, missions were aborted both by individuals and groups of planes because of the instrument flight conditions that were encountered."

Harry Young, 64th Squadron, 43rd Bomb Group: "I was on standby reconnaissance to Rabaul, for weather. We sent two aircraft, one to Wewak and one to Rabaul. It was terrible, and they sent the first plane to Wewak. It did not report and they sent the standby and it didn't report. The Rabaul plane did not report. It was really stinking weather. Then they made me go. Our usual route over the Owen-Stanleys was to take off and fly south to 10,000 feet, then head back, climbing to 20,000 feet over the Kokoda Pass. I knew that once I was airborne I was in command, so I decided to fly around New Guinea over the sea towards Milne Bay. About 50 miles from Port Moresby the weather broke and we made a leisurely flight, climbing to about 25,000 feet 20 miles from Rabaul, reported the weather, which was OK, then had the pleasure of hearing the raid on the radio. Incidentally, we lost the three weather recces that night. I was the only survivor."

Charles King, 39th Squadron, 35th Fighter Group: "First of all, we tried to avoid it. It is probably difficult for today's fliers to realize how little we had to work with in 1942-45. In the P-38 and P-39 it was not unusual to have a magnetic compass 30 or more degrees in error. Gyro horizons easily tumbled with the kind of flying that we did and they were more often than not out of technical order limits.

"Another factor was that weather in the tropics was seldom in horizontal layers but vertical formations and had the associated turbulence. We discovered the tops of the clouds went far higher than predicted. More than one of us found as we struggled to gain altitude to top the afternoon thunderstorms that clouds were building up faster than the plane could climb. Perhaps the primary factor was that the success of the mission we flew depended on the formations of fighters and bombers getting to the target together. Since the poor weather we often encountered precluded us staying together, such missions were often scrubbed before we took off or caused us to turn back when we encountered it on the way to the target."

For all the unlucky ones who disappeared for years, decades or forever, there were the more fortunate people. On 31 December 1942, Clint Solomon, 3rd Bomb Group, was in Port Moresby and decided to fly to Charters Towers, Australia, for the New Year. Despite being clipped on the head by a prop blade, he took off, flying through bad weather with no radio aids from New Guinea to Australia, by dead reckoning. At the right time they gently let down through the clouds, coming out 200 feet over the water, right smack between the mountains forming the mouth of Cairns Harbor. For miles on either side jungle hills sloped into the sea.

Flying fully loaded heavy bombers in such conditions was hard on the crews, especially the pilots. Harry Young briefly describes a bomber pilot's task. "I would like to emphasize the necessity for a pilot flying a wing ship in formation to glue his eyes only on his leader. Now we are ready to explore the problems of a combat pilot if he is not leading the flight. Number one, he does not know where he is, only that he is looking at another airplane and maintaining his position. Two, he is either on inter-phone or command radio jack. Three, he has a turret with two .50 caliber machineguns directly over his head. I remember once we approached Rabaul and asked my navigator the ETA. He gave it to me and I glanced at the clock. About 15 minutes before the ETA I reached down and put on my steel helmet and really started to fly a tight formation. My co-pilot asked me what I was doing and I pointed to the clock. He told me to loosen up and pointed down . . . we were still circling Kiriwina as the Rabaul weather was bad.

"Now we approach the target and the machineguns start making a lot of noise. If the pilot is on command radio he hears fighters calling where the enemy are hitting the bombers. If he switches to inter-phone he hears his co-pilot calling out targets for the gunners and all the while he doesn't know what the hell is really happening."

Bill Martin, 90th Group: "Hell, being the pilot of a crew of ten at age 20, that was an ego satisfaction sort of thing. There's no question about it. But as a pilot, until I got to be a flight leader and later squadron operations officer, I was flying formation. A B-24 was no easy thing to fly in formation . . . that's an ungainly cow. Especially at altitude, when the turbosupercharger was the only thing you had your hand on as the throttles were already fully forward. You'd have four sticking up, none in the same position, one'd be an inch ahead, another half an inch back, and so on, and it drove you mad trying to get your fingers to hold 'em all equal. I didn't see much of anything. I saw the other airplane, and occasionally I'd see a Zero going by, and I'd hear the crew talking, but I'd have loved to have sat back and watched what was going on, instead of concentrating on that B-24. Later, when I became a flight leader, I sat out there on autopilot and let the guys on my wings worry about formation."

The jungles and seas were merciless to those who fell into them unprepared for survival. Most crews were philosophical about it—they returned or they did not. Bill Moran, 90th Group, cannot recall any survivors of downed aircraft returning to the unit. "Corky" Smith, 80th "Headhunters", did not worry about it, though he and other pilots strafed huge sharks seen below them. Catalina flying-boats were sometimes able to pick up survivors on the water, and coastwatchers sometimes had aircrew survivors brought to them by friendly natives. But the crews were generally young and confident, particularly in the fighter units, and did not worry, or admit to worry, about what to do if they did not make it back to base.

The quality of equipment had much to do with an individual's frame of mind. While flying the P-39, Marion Kirby did worry about being shot down, but once in the P-38, "did not think of it again." Some items of equipment were an annoyance and sometimes more than that. The rubber dinghy supplied was so designed and positioned under pilots that the valve was "right in your A-hole." The discomfort caused on the trips around New Guinea was bad enough, but the later seven- and eight-hour missions to Borneo were uncomfortable in the extreme. After the Rabaul missions it was decided to test a dinghy. "The cord was pulled . . . nothing happened. Another one tried . . . again nothing. The entire batch was tried . . . nothing. All the time they had thought they were sitting on a life-saver," says Marion, "but all they were getting was a pain in the you-know-what."

Bill Martin: "We knew if we crashed in the jungle the chances of survival were practically zero. I traded my .45 for a carbine. It never dawned on me till later that if I pulled the ripcord with that thing across my chest the opening shock of the parachute would probably have fractured my jaw. We had no jungle training. We had a little jungle kit in the back of our parachutes, and this little card with crossed Aussie flags, half in pidgin and half in English. We were supposed to read this if we met a native."

This very basic amount of equipment was the least that could be provided. The supposition or hope that natives would be friendly was an optimism badly misplaced in some instances. Many survivors were taken to the Japanese, though many others were led to safety. Much depended on the attitude of the local chiefs and headmen. In some areas the first visits by Europeans were only a few years before the war. Some tribes bore blood grudges against whites, and in fact were hostile to all visitors. At least one case of cannibalism is known, when a 90th Group crew was killed and eaten by locals after surviving the combat and parachute jump.

John Shemelynce, 3rd Bomb Group: "The jungle also offered diseases—malaria, fungus growth in the ears and a variety of skin rashes. I only know of one person who died of malaria in our unit, and he was one of the medics. I was unfortunate, as I had it. I had never been so sick before. I lost 30 pounds, and turned totally yellow from atabrine tablets."

Larry Tanberg: "Rescues were few and far between. We seldom recovered anyone from a jungle location. I believe most aircrews secretly said to themselves that a bailout was a last resort, while you might survive and be found if you crash landed the aircraft."

"Corky" Smith: "I knew that if I went down at sea, was able to get into my life raft and was known to be in a certain area, then a PBY would be there shortly. I witnessed several such pick-ups and was content. My greatest concern about going down in the water was the shark threat. Some of those creatures were longer than 20 feet, and it appeared there were hundreds of them in given areas. They were more to be feared than the Japs! As for going down inland, I was not confident at all about being rescued. We had a few chaps—damn few— return, and their stories weren't at all encouraging. All you had to help were your feet. The injured pilot in the jungle had utterly no chance of rescue. If shot up, our instructions were to head for the sea."

On 16 June 1942, the great Tommy Lynch found the limits of the P-39 against the Zeke, ending up in the water off Port Moresby, close enough for natives to paddle out and collect him in a dug-out canoe. There were no pilot's life rafts or dinghys, but the 39th Squadron had received its first Mae West-type life jackets. Back at the unit, he was asked how it worked. Charles King recalls his reply as 'typical of a thinking man': "With the things I've heard about sharks I didn't want my swimming slowed down by a bag of air!"

Many natives assisted crews, performing great feats of carrying and giving the very best care they could to injured survivors. Charles King again: "We always gave them some rewards, small things to us, but big to them. Certainly we knew they were not enough to show the enormous gratitude we all felt in having friends in a most unfriendly environment where the Japs, the jungle and sea were our enemies. One of our pilots survived because they carried him back in a continuous march of 24 hours. He had a leg wound and internal injuries, and the doctor said the natives' quick evaluation and action probably saved his life."

The 'best' 39th Squadron survival story is the events that befell Charlie Sullivan (now O'Sullivan). Both engines of his P-38 gave up on a return from Wewak, forcing him to land in the Ramu Valley, cutting his head on the gunsight in the process. Later, he contacted natives, but was wary of them, realizing Japanese had been there recently. When they tried to grab him he shot two and escaped. For nearly three weeks, barefoot, he walked towards the Allied lines. One day he walked right into the camp area of a company of Australian Commandos, who were so scruffy and bush-worn that they thought Sullivan was one of them until he spoke and they heard the American accent. A light plane answered signals, landed and picked up Sullivan, who dozed off in the cabin. A short while later, it had engine trouble, landed and turned over onto its back, waking him. His luck held—he was still uninjured, and another plane came by, landed, collected him and delivered him safely to Marilinan, from where he returned to Moresby and the USA.

In 1943, at the start of the bombing campaign against the greatest Japanese base in the region, pilots and crews of the 5th—and all the other air forces in the Pacific—were operating with few radio and navigational aids over primitive areas, through frequently bad and dangerous weather, with little chance of survival if they did not return to base. The Japanese were only one of the dangers facing them.

In 1944, the 5th organized a rescue system, but before that many trained and experienced crews were lost to weather, sea and jungle.

Notes

All personal quotes are from letters or tapes to author, 1982-83, including the Sullivan story, which came from Charles King.

5

Early Attacks on Rabaul

The obvious importance of Rabaul had resulted in attacks by the Allies as soon as strength could be gathered. The first was by B-17s of the 19th Bomb Group on 23 February. From then until the opening of the major bombing campaign, small formations, mostly at night, attacked the harbor and airfields. By October 1943, 619 sorties had been flown. The Japanese admitted the loss of some 40 aircraft destroyed in the air or on the ground, and shipping lost included *Komaki Maru* on 17 April 42, *Italia Maru* on 27 December 42, and *Tomiura Maru* on 30 December 42.[1]

Sister Berenice Twohill and the other imprisoned missionaries watched these attacks, praying for the men dodging searchlights and AA in the night sky. In harsher, military imprisonment were a small number of Allied air crews captured in New Guinea, the Solomons or on New Britain itself. Listening to these raiders were Jose Holquin, navigator and sole survivor of a 43rd Group B-17, and Jim McMurria, B-24 pilot of the 90th, undergoing the long months and years until the end of the war and liberation.

At 2:00 a.m. one morning in November 1942, John Brogan had to go onto the catwalk of a 19th Group B-17, with a screwdriver, to release hung-up bombs, while searchlights and AA lit up the interior of the plane like daylight.[2]

Carl Hustad, 43rd Group, flew a somewhat different first mission, a night raid to Rabaul. An experienced pilot would be in command for the flight. As the B-17s prepared to take off, Japanese bombers arrived and the air raid siren sounded. Carl's pilot decided to press on, so the remaining engines were started and a cold take off commenced through the bombing. Climbing on course for Rabaul, the usual checks were made, and it was discovered that the gunners in the rear were missing and the fuselage door was open. It was decided to go on to the target, so Carl manned the top turret while the engineer 'tripled-up' on the waist and tail. Naturally enough, it

was their B-17 engaged by a Japanese nightfighter. Carl and the engineer fired lots of tracer at him, the pilot slipped them into a cloud and the fighter was seen no more.

Back at Moresby, they taxied to the revetment to find a sheepish collection of gunners who had waited for the plane to return, not daring to tell anyone that their plane had gone on a mission while they took cover during a Japanese raid. (Author: Some things will never get into official histories!)[3]

Gordon Thomas, prisoner at the freezing plant: "At night there would be what we called 'the naggers', one or two planes just circling round and round all night long, making it necessary to go to earth, where the troops had to sit until the *Kaijo* (All Clear) sounded. To me, that word *Kaijo* was the sweetest in the language

sitting cramped in a deep dugout for five to six hours, catching only a few winks of sleep. It meant that one more death-dealing raid was over, that life could still be lived—possibly—until the next raid. It always seemed to me that as soon as the *Kunchu* (Warning) sounded something inside me was wound like a giant spring, and it stayed wound up until the *Kaijo* was sounded, when it was released."[4]

Sister Berenice: "In January 1943 Allied planes began to liven up our tropical skies. We would watch the little silver planes in the searchlight beams. They seemed utterly unafraid. We could not recall seeing any shot down over the harbor, though we watched every night. We did not think of going to the trenches, but would unroll a large bolt of white material which we had hidden, to make a 'V' sign, but never heard if anyone ever saw it."[5]

Rabaul AA and fighters claimed a high-ranking member of Kenney's staff on 5 January 1943. Six B-17s and six B-24s attacked at noon, led by Brigadier General Kenneth Walker, Commander V Bomber Command. Both the timing—noon—and Walker's presence had been against Kenney's direct orders. Two B-17s were lost, and a large search was commenced when it was realized a man with Walker's knowledge of Allied affairs was in Japanese territory. The other crew was found, but not his. Hit and slowed by AA, attacked by fighters, Walker and his crew were not seen again.

Later, during a visit to Washington, Kenney was present when Walker's son received the Medal of Honor posthumously awarded his father, from President Roosevelt.

In the context of the times, and particularly the airwar, it is easy to find explanations for Walker's action in flying on the mission. The 8th AF had yet to hit Germany. On the first US heavy bomber mission in Europe, General Ira Eaker had led the formation to Rouen. A general officer flying the 5th's first daylight bombardment mission to the largest Japanese base in the region would be an expression of airman's leadership.

(Author: At least one crew member, a gunner, was captured and interrogated by the Japanese. I have been unable to ascertain his identity and fate.)

Initiative, ingenuity and a desire to try something new were strong points of the Allied air forces, and the 5th was no exception. B-17 skip-bombing, converting B-25s into heavily-armed strafers and use of parafrags on airfield attacks are obvious examples. It did not take much imagination to link the volcanoes at Rabaul with the presence of Japanese bases. Rabaul had been destroyed by volcanic eruption in 1937, and perhaps another could be induced. Carl Hustad, 43rd Bomb Group, flew the mission, "one of those End The War Quick schemes that didn't work. The mission was planned in conjunction with an attack on Lakunai fighter airdrome the night of 22 May 1943. My plane was loaded with two 2,000-pound bombs. Fuses were set for 45-second delay to allow deep penetration of the volcano. I was not to make my run until the other bombers had cleared the area for at least 15 minutes, to avoid any losses due to the expected 'conflagration'. We had 45 seconds to go from bombing altitude to a dive over the crater, to get something between us and the explosion. It was quite dramatic for a crew of non-geologists.

"I found out later we would have been more effective if we had dropped soapsuds and plugged it up with foam rather than relieving the pressure with explosives. The mission went off quite smoothly. We ran into a fair amount of AA fire, dropped our bombs, scooted over the rim of the crater and headed home in a low sweep over the water north of Rabaul, waiting for the 'shock wave' that didn't come. It sure sounded like a good idea at the time."[6]

Other people tried the same idea, and after the war, Bill Moran, 90th Group, was disgusted to find their bombs had only been piling dirt inside the craters, opposite to the desired effect.[7]

On the wider scene, it was realized early in General MacArthur's planning that bombers would require fighter escort on the Rabaul missions. On 30 June Australian and American forces occupied Woodlark and Kiriwina Islands, nearly halfway to Rabaul from New Guinea. By early August 5,000-feet strips were operational, with negligible Japanese reaction.

Here fighters could refuel and all types of damaged aircraft find haven in the coming missions.

Notes

1. USSBS
2. letter, 1982
3. letter, 1982
4. ANU PMB microfilm 36
5. letter, 1983
6. letter, 1983
7. letter, 1982

6

Intelligence on Rabaul— 11 October 43

Much has been made in recent years of the alleged advantage Allied commanders received from interception and reading of enemy radio traffic. Other books have examined this in some detail and it is not intended to do so here, except show that in this bombing campaign "Ultra" information in itself was of little use to MacArthur, and always needed confirmation, usually by photographs. Copies of the "Ultra" information issued in Special Intelligence Bulletins (SIBs) by the Military Intelligence Section, General Staff, GHQ SWPA are part of the holdings of the MacArthur Archives. All SIBs referred to are from this source in all following chapters.

SIB 160, in its Air Section, reports:

2. North-eastern Sector: (24 hours ending 1800I/11):

a) Navy: Activity declined, a minimum of 33 aircraft being observed (Author: on radio). These appeared to be based as follows: Rabaul area 12, Kavieng 8, Vunakanau 7, Faisi 3 and unidentified 3. 14 aircraft of 958 Naval Air Group were aloft, the majority being from Matupi (Rabaul). Three floatplanes of 938 *Kokkutai* (Group) were active from Faisi, probably on reconnaissance over the Central Solomons and the surrounding areas. Seven divebombers of 582 *Kokkutai* (Group) were active from Kavieng.

b) Army: Activity slightly increased, a minimum of 5 bases and 13 aircraft being noted. There were no significant flights. (Paragraph 3 dealt with the North-Western Sector—West New Guinea and Indonesia.)

4. Adjacent areas:

a) 12 October is the beginning date of "E" Operation, in which shore-based aircraft in the Bismarck-Solomon-New Guinea area are involved. The operation is estimated as a series of shore-based air attacks against Allied positions and surface units in the area.

Comment. The high concentration at Rabaul of 294 aircraft, as revealed in photographs taken yesterday, is doubtless related to this operation.

The final paragraph of the report, in the Navy Section, is:

6. It is believed that two heavy cruisers, probably *Myoko* and *Haguro*, accompanied by an unknown number of destroyers (probably anti-submarine escorts) are enroute from Rabaul to Truk.

The General Staff's Daily Summary had wider distribution than the SIB.

Summary 568, 11-12 Oct 43. "The mounting air strength at Rabaul, to which attention previously has been called, reached culmination yesterday. Photographs taken at 0915L showed a count of 294 planes, or as large a concentration as ever photographed at that base. The day before, 10 October, photographs with incomplete coverage revealed 143 planes. The sharp rise undoubtedly is in fighters. Photographs 10 October showed 37 fighters; photographs yesterday showed 145 fighters. *Estimated* air strength for 10 October was 83 fighters and 146 bombers, a total of 229 planes. Not since 13 August has so much air strength been shown at Rabaul; then, 287 planes were counted." The report details other dates and numbers, then goes on:

"There are, of course, several possibilities for this increase, but the answer may rest in the facts that the sharp rise is in fighters and that good weather will now permit Allied raids on Rabaul. The photographed total of 128 bombers represents no marked change and this bomber strength has not been utilized for months. Hence, it is more probable that the enemy has brought in the fighters as a defensive precaution. His aerial combat defeats, even when his striking force was heavily protected by fighter cover, possibly have been too calamitous for him to risk further diminution of his air strength."

The report goes on to describe the Japanese air effort in New Guinea, Kiriwina and nearby locations.

Shipping also had increased each day on the 9th, 10th and 11th, photographs showing an estimated 120,000 tons in the harbor. Thus, on the day preceding the beginning of the daylight bombing offensive against Rabaul, photographic intelligence had informed Allied commanders and staffs of an increase in Japanese fighter strength, while in SIB 160, it was reported for 11 October that flying "Activity declined."

Rabaul's reputation, ranking with London and Berlin in AA defence was "of interest" to the crews, but despite being called the "Japanese Gibraltar" and so on, they did not particularly worry about it. The 5th had recently executed several highly successful strikes and morale was high. Wewak had been hit hard—Clint Solomon burned out the guns in his strafer, never having seen so many Japanese planes—and the enemy air force was receiving visible punishment. Corky Smith: "Little was really known about Rabaul and its defences to the fighter pilots, who were not concerned with details."

The Japanese, to the Allied crews, were a faceless mass. Little or no interest was shown in unit identifications or identities of opposing pilots. The Navy was known to defend Rabaul and the Army to defend Wewak. The only Japanese unit recalled by any 5th veterans, in reply to a question, was "The Cherry-blossom Squadron." Several men mentioned this unit, which was said to be an elite sent to the defence of important places in the Japanese Empire. Its aircraft were reported to be black, with small pink cherry blossoms painted over the surfaces. However, no record of it can be found in any Japanese document, nor do surviving Japanese veterans remember it.

Tom Fetter, bombardier, 90th Group: "We all rather admired the enemy pilots for their courage and skill. The feeling among the men at the time about the Japanese was bitter. We knew of the death march from Bataan and the execution of some of the Doolittle Raiders. None of us wanted to be taken prisoner and as history has revealed we were right. Most of our people died in enemy hands. However, we didn't blame the Japanese fighter pilots for this."[1]

Rabaul's AA defences were reported to be strong, but before experiencing it, most crews' opinions of it were similar to "Corky" Smith's: "We did not really grasp the situation until we were confronted with the stuff. Then we flew around the areas of heaviest concentration, as did the Zeros . . . we had never experienced any really good AA until Rabaul, we did not know what good AA was! Further, our AA at Port Moresby was most ineffective in my view so I did not worry about it until I saw theirs!"[2]

However, for the bomber crews, Rabaul loomed somewhat larger, probably because they had been there at night. Larry Tanberg: "Just hearing the word Rabaul in those days was a scary proposition and sent shivers through us. We knew it was a stronghold of the Japanese and knew it would be an awfully rough go when the time came for the strafers to hit it."[3]

Bill Martin: "Rabaul was a terror point in our fear and anxiety. Rabaul at night was bad enough, but the thought of going to Rabaul in daylight was absolutely horrifying. The psychological thing was Rabaul. At Wewak we ran into more fighters, but Rabaul was worst. On the 12 October briefing, they said, 'The target today is . . .' and they said, 'Rabaul', and you should have heard the groan. But there were so damn many pilots and crews in the briefing we knew we could whip 'em by that time."[4]

Notes

1. letter 1983
2. letter 1982
3. letter 1983
4. audiotape 1983

7

Service Squadron Scene II

A little game enjoyed by men of the 482nd Squadron, was "Hoss." It was often played with pilots of aircraft which had a minor problem, but which the pilot believed to be greater than it really was. Three members of the 482nd would take part. On hearing the pilot's version of the problem, one of the mechanics would kick the ground, and say thoughtfully, "It looks bad", then to one of the others, "What you think, Hoss?" The second man would agree, and ask the third, "Yeah, what about you, Hoss?" In turn, he would pass it back to the first man, and around the circle with puzzled fliers trying to identify Hoss. Then one man would say, "Remember Hoss, on that same problem you took a hammer, hit it, and that fixed it?" One of them would turn to the pilot, "You can go on off now, we know how to fix it as soon as we get the hammer."

A colonel suddenly appeared at the 482nd, de-manding a P-40 which had been left by an outfit which moved out. A backlog of 15 planes needing repair were ahead of the P-40 in question, but Cy Stafford told the colonel to come back in two hours. A change of spark-plugs had the P-40 running sweetly. When the colonel returned, Cy told him the job was done and mentioned that the mechanics were now waiting on the colonel to remove the P-40 from the area. "He got in a huff and piled into the cockpit. I always checked the pilot to see the straps were put on correctly. As he didn't even hook up the crash harness, I said, 'Sir, are you not going to buckle in?' He said in a gruff voice, 'No'. I said, 'Sir, it don't make any difference to me. I have pulled some dead ones out that didn't buckle up, I can pull a colonel out as easy as anyone.' The wind went out of his sails in a flash. 'Maybe I better button up', he said."

8

'The Japanese Pearl Harbor' 12 October 1943

TO: GHQ SWPA (FOR MACARTHUR)
FROM: WASHINGTON
NR: 9166 14TH OCT 43

ACCEPT PLEASE MY HEARTIEST CONGRATULA-TIONS ON YOUR VERY SUCCESSFUL ATTACK ON RABAUL. WOULD APPRECIATE YOUR EXTEND-ING MY COMMENDATION TO KENNEY AND HIS AMERICAN AND AUSTRALIAN UNITS WITH THE STATEMENT THAT THE ATTACK SERVES TO STIMULATE PERSONNEL IN THE TRAINING AND PROCUREMENT ESTABLISHMENTS WHO ARE BEHIND HIM HERE IN THE STATES. THIS SMALL PEARL HARBOR IN REVERSE IS ALSO A BOOST TO THE MORALE OF THE WHOLE COUNTRY. WE BELIEVE YOU ARE NOW GETTING STARTED IN A BIG WAY.

ARNOLD (1)
14 OCTOBER 1943

TO: GHQ SWPA (FOR MACARTHUR)
FROM: WASHINGTON
NR: 9142 FOURTEENTH

PLEASE GIVE KENNEY AND HIS AIRMEN THE CONGRATULATIONS OF THE ENTIRE STAFF HERE FOR THEIR GREAT ATTACK ON RABAUL.
MARSHALL (2)

Finally, on 12 October, everything was ready for Rabaul to receive the full weight of the air power collected to hit it as hard and as often as possible. Selected targets were to be attacked with a solid blow, a one-two punch from 349 aircraft. One: B-25 and Beaufighter strafers were to go in first and create havoc on the airfields among the 290 Japanese planes there. Two: B-24s would bomb shipping in the harbor. P-38s would escort the force.

Rapopo and its fighters would be attacked by Colonel D.P. Hall's 3rd Bomb Group; Vunakanau's bombers by Clinton True's 345th and Larry Tanberg's 38th. Squadron Leader Boulton's 30 Squadron RAAF Beaufighters would strafe both Tobera and Rapopo. All flights and squadrons of 43rd and 90th Bomb Groups had been assigned targets in the mass of shipping. Nothing was allocated to strike Takeo Shibata's Zekes at Lakunai.

The available aircraft had been allocated as best the commanders and staffs could arrange. Now the flight crews would execute the plans.

At Rapopo, Doctor Tetsuo Aso was feeling a little feverish and unwell. On Rabaul Harbor—Simpson Harbor—was Masasui Adachi, civilian employee on a fishing boat. He hardly noticed the large amount of shipping, it was a common sight. Sister Berenice Twohill and the other internees and prisoners began yet another day of captivity. At Vunakanau were the twin-engined Bettys, tails numbered in 300-series marking of 751 *Ku*. Leading Petty Officer Hiroshi Suzuki began work on them. Engines were to be checked, practice flights were on the program, like the other days since he arrived in September.[3]

Dobodura, New Guinea, 7:30 a.m.: Lieutenant-Colonel Clinton True, leading the 345th, began his take-off. Over 100 other B-25s were ready and followed, lifting over the New Guinea jungle, forming up for the flight to New Britain. The resulting dust haze forced the RAAF Beaufighters to postpone take-off, so they missed the rendezvous and set off alone for the targets at Rapopo and Tobera.

The P-38s refuelled at Kiriwina and the RAAF ground-crews slaved to get the big American fighters airborne again, while overhead droned the four-engined heavy bombers, still climbing en route to the target. The B-24 crews had been up early, but waited 45 minutes after the B-25s were gone. Climbing steadily, they were at about 18,000 feet when they reached the coast of New Britain and continued gaining height.

At 1,000 feet the B-25s went on to Kiriwina, then slanted down to minimum altitude for the flight up St George's Channel. The formation thundered past Peter Figgis, Australian coastwatcher near Cape Orford, who noted in his subsequent report: "The first really heavy daylight strike on Rabaul was made and as nearly all the planes taking part flew over Cape Orford the effect on native morale was great." And no doubt on the morale of the coastwatchers themselves.[4]

At the mouth of the Warangoi River the B-25s swung left and set course for their targets: 67 with Clinton True for Vunakanau, the remainder banking right for Rapopo; 100 strafers, each with eight nose-mounted .50 caliber machineguns and bomb-bays full of fragmentation bombs.

Behind, and much higher in the 90th Group's 321st Squadron, was Bill Moran, on his third mission. A photographer-gunner, his job was to photograph targets during strikes, record hits and anything else catching his attention. "This was not the easiest of jobs, particularly with flak and fighter interception. From a photographer's point of view, it was an understatement. At 21,000 feet, hovering over an open hatch, wind blowing in your eyes, sometimes tears running down your face, trying to balance a 24-inch cone camera, encumbered with heavy flying suits. . . ."[5]

Bill Martin: "Until June or July, I wasn't convinced we were going to win the war. The Japs outnumbered us, they were jumping all over us with fighters and we only went to places like Lae and Salamaua because we didn't dare go any further. We'd bomb Wewak and other places at night, but as for the biggies, no way. We took that Rabaul raid and I saw the sky full of B-24s, P-38s all around us, and I said, 'Now I know we're gonna win the war.'"[6]

Undetected, the largest Allied air attack so far launched in the Pacific was about to hit the Japanese at Rabaul, bringing to them a demonstration of airpower experienced and regretted by their units on New Guinea.

Rapopo

60th AAA Battalion, on the bluff at the end of the runway overlooking the water, had just been putting gun-crews through training exercises. Now the guns were lowered under their canvas covers, and the men gathered outside the gunpits climbing into trucks to take them back to the living area. Doctor Tetsuo Aso, battalion surgeon, had a temperature and was in his bed, "when I heard the strangest explosion from our airfield. I thought one of our aircraft had an engine failure and crashed. Then I heard the cry of a guard and hit the floor . . . 'Enemy attack!' It was not only a surprise attack but a low-level attack. I rushed out of the tent, through the clinic, to the bomb shelter which was at the bottom of the cliff. Running along, I saw enemy aircraft, one after another, violently machinegunning. The patients in the clinic rushed for the shelter, too. On my way I saw Driver Wada crouched beneath a tree, looking up at the enemy aircraft. Shouting at him that the shelter was this way, I managed to throw myself into it. Private Sato followed me, and after my initial feeling of relief, I noticed that his leg was dangling limp, hit by machinegun fire. There was continuous gunfire spattering into the wall near the entrance and at one stage I dug out from the wall a warm 12mm bullet. The thickness had just prevented the large bullet from going through.

"It seemed the first wave of air raids was over. People were shouting, 'Doctor, doctor!' as I ran to the clinic. There seemed to be many dead and injured. But parachute bombs were dropping quietly . . . sliding onto the sides of tents like raindrops on the eaves . . . then exploded. Petty Officer Ohira and a few others on the floor died instantly. Sergeant Matsui was carried on a stretcher to the clinic with a big hole in his chest and his lungs hanging out, looking like balloons. As we were treating him on the floor, each time another wave of enemy approached we had to leave him. There was nothing we could do for him despite his cries of pain, and he passed away shortly afterwards.

"First Battery had just finished gun practice and they came under attack so suddenly there was no time to organize and prepare the guns. The battery commander, Lieutenant Shiramizu, did not have a helmet on. He was hit on the forehead and went into a coma."[7]

The wave of strafers doing such damage was the 8th Bomb Squadron, its B-25s beginning the attack at 10:30 with a long sweep from south to north over the target, at first firing the formidable nose armament of massed .50 calibers, then releasing their parafrags. Nine Mitchells roared up the eastern side of the airfield, claiming six of 16 parked bombers.

Five Sallys had taken off for Alexishafen and a sixth was beginning its roll when the Mitchells struck. The B-25s shot the right wing off the Sally flown by Captain Tero Kurano, commander of 2 *Chutai*. All the crew were killed. Four other Mitsubishis escaped but the sixth, flown by Lieutenant Yasuda, abandoned its takeoff and was damaged.

The 8th Bomb Squadron started fires in the fuel dump, and .50 caliber rounds hailed into the AA positions and trucks nearby, mowing down or scattering the gunners. The other six B-25s strafed along the western perimeter, hitting personnel, a radio station, aircraft in revetments and small ships offshore. Crews saw a Japanese shot down over the mouth of the Warangoi River as they sped along.[8]

A short distance away, Sister Berenice Twohill and the other captives were startled, then interested spectators of the sudden attack. From their building they watched the waves of speeding machinegunning strafers, explosions, black smoke clouds rising, Japanese planes trying to get airborne:

"There was a roaring of engines and we watched the Japanese planes trying to make it, hurrying, scurrying, but not one did. Dense black clouds soared into the sky."[9]

Another 13 Mitchells of the 13th Squadron followed—one had turned back with engine trouble—claiming a Betty and a Nell destroyed, other Nells damaged, and fire started in a fuel or ammo dump, while counting about 50 bombers and unidentified aircraft in the area. Only one B-25 received damage, two small holes which may have come from a parafrag.[10]

The "Headhunter" Squadron arrived overhead with 17 P-38s, four others having failed to make the entire flight. Captain Wilson shot down one Hamp from the only four Japanese fighters engaged, for the squadron's sole victory.[11]

Also close by was Captain Sen, of the Indian 5/2 Punjab Regiment, who had been looking after some of the sick men in his unit. Sen was sitting in the open, looking at the crater of the Mother volcano, when suddenly there was the noise of many aircraft and "we looked around and saw a lot of planes coming in one behind the other just about two feet off the water. That was a raid of about 100 planes. Then we heard a lot of machinegunning on top of us . . . from Jap AA guns. The only cover was the stumps of coconut trees. The Japs were not expecting the raid. It was the first time I had seen a Lightning in the air. It was all on its own and two Zeros tried to fight with it. Then we realized our Allies were trying to do something in this war. We were beginning to doubt we would ever get out."[12]

The 90th Squadron put 12 B-25s and an A-20 into the attack, thundering along the sides of the runway, over personnel accommodation and dump areas. Smoke and dust from preceding waves prevented accurate observation of results, but one of a formation of 'white-tailed' Sallys was shot down and seen to crash and they hurtled past the canvas-covered guns of the 60th AAA.[13]

Sister Catherine O'Sullivan: "12 October 1943 remains vividly in my mind as we were, at the time, very dejected as very few planes had been over and we thought we were forgotten. This was the fatal attack on Rapopo and Tobera. We watched the Japanese planes try to take off, but because we of the surprise element in the attack they were caught on the ground and we believed this was the turning point in their victorious thrust towards Port Moresby . . . We did not see the planes which came in on the 12th, but we did see one American fighter shoot down one Japanese plane right over us. The Japanese guards raced up, covered the red ball on the plane and assured us it was American. But we had seen the American plane leave safely."[14]

Vunakanau

Practising take-offs and landings was part of normal routine of flying units around the world, and 751 *Kokkutai* was no different. Neat, three-point landings were a matter of pride with Navy pilots, whether they flew fighters or bombers, and the Bettys of 751 *Ku* were active around the field, all unaware of the 67 Mitchell strafers speeding toward them.

The 498th Squadron, attacking 12 abreast, fell upon the peaceful scene, and the roar of the Mitsubishis' engines drowned the noise of the attacking Americans, until, with absolutely no warning a rain of .50 caliber bullets struck along the airfield.

Hideo Tani, mechanic, was working on an engine, deafened by the sound of Bettys taking off, when the assault enveloped him in a roar. Shigeru Hoki, a fellow groundcrew member, was astounded by the speed and violence of this, his first experience of strafing.[15]

The 498th reported it was obvious the target was taken by surprise: men were running in all directions and AA guns were pointing the wrong way; three Bettys in the traffic pattern were hit by the strafers; a taxying Zeke was hit by bombs, swung to the side of the strip and stopped, and crews passing later saw it burning. Aircraft, refuelling trucks and AA positions were shot up by the passing Mitchells, only one B-25 being hit six times by light AA. Crews claimed 30 planes destroyed, plus two airborne Bettys, and as they swung away from the target counted 40 or more fighters parked on the south end of Rapopo.[16]

The 71st Squadron was unable to observe damage as they crossed the target, but counted up to 15 fires burning behind them. Japanese fighters made "half-hearted" passes, breaking away when attacked by P-38s, who shot down the fourth member of the Japanese flight when he pressed his attack alone, as the single victory of the 433rd Squadron. Leaving the target, crews noted large columns of smoke rising from Simpson Harbor, Rapopo and Tobera.[17]

At the south side of the airfield, 15 bombers in their revetments were thoroughly strafed by 12 Mitchells of the 405th, flying through the heavy pall of dust and smoke thrown up by leading flights. Nine Zekes attacked over the target, six concentrating on and bringing down one B-25, flown by Lieutenant Sidney Crews, while three Japanese were claimed in turn, as they chased the withdrawing B-25s as far as the southern side of the Warangoi River. Though themselves under attack, 405th crews noticed an unidentified aircraft pursued by two fighters south of Rapopo, and saw it burst into flames. This may have been the Beaufighter from 30 Squadron RAAF, flown by Stone. Behind them the 405th Squadron counted twelve fires, believed ten of them to be aircraft burning and claimed ten destroyed.[18]

36,000 rounds and 750 parafrags were expended by the 500th Squadron's 12 strafers, who claimed six Bettys and a Helen destroyed on the ground, along with three fighters in the air and two as probably destroyed from a formation of 12 Zekes which pursued them, making passes as far to the south as Wide Bay.[19]

Behind the 501st Squadron eleven fires were counted burning, and crews noted 40 bombers and 20 fighters in revetments as they machinegunned their way across the airfield. Passing Tobera they saw a radar and encountered light inaccurate machinegun fire, but counted 20 to 30 black-colored Zekes and Hamps parked on the southwest end of the strip 'wingtip to wingtip', as well as observing heavy black smoke at Rapopo.[20]

The B-25s passed in a storm of engine noise, machinegunning, tracer, explosions, smoke and dust. For the Japanese below them the effect was devastating. Hiroshi Suzuki knew of "at least 50 people killed and 80 wounded. Hardly any of 751 *Ku*'s bombers were undamaged;   20 were destroyed by fire, 5 were able to be salvaged." However, "of about 1500 parafrags, 600 were duds due to landing at a slight angle off the vertical."[21]

Shigeru Hoki, under stafing for the first time, believed the attack went on for a long time, as it took him "thirty minutes to crawl from the plane to the trench, with parafrags falling between flights". He estimated that "200 planes took part in the attack and 120 flew over him." Six planes were destroyed close by him.[22]

In the relative silence after the attack, among the burning bombers, dead and wounded, and everywhere the unexploded parafrags, the Japanese began to determine the damage and get the airfield operational again. Many casualties had been caused when men came out of shelter after the strafers passed and thought the parafrags were paratroops—until they exploded around the watchers. Sueyoshi Oyama saw 20 killed and 50 wounded from his unit, plus another 30 killed from the nearby construction battalion. Morio Yamanaka believed 80 casualties were suffered and 30 planes were damaged or destroyed. To Hideo Tsutani the parafrags were an effective weapon.[23]

They were hanging everywhere—from trees, from revetments, on vehicles, dangling from aircraft tails and wings, laying on the ground and sitting in the grass, all fused to explode on contact. Several men were killed trying to remove them, so it was decided to detonate the remainder with machinegun fire. Hiroshi Suzuki estimated that about half the parafrags failed to operate as intended, and hindered activity, but "the field was clear by evening and 100 men worked for seven or eight hours to repair the runway."[24]

A pilot of 702 *Ku*, Kiyoshi Yagita, thought the "time of dropping was bad. In the jungle belt on the south side of the airfield there were quite a few parafrags dropping from the disturbed trees, and occasionally as the wind blew they crashed to the ground and exploded." This was the only parafrag attack he saw in the Rabaul area and he wondered if it had been intended as a one-time-only surprise, or abandoned due to heavy US losses.[25]

Tobera

30 Squadron RAAF, with 12 Beaufighters, was to strafe Tobera, but took off late due to the dust haze caused by over 100 B-25s ahead of them. Consequently, the Beaufighters, led by Squadron Leader Boulton, set course for the target alone. As Boulton reported, "When approximately 10 minutes from Tobera Strip, the Beaufighters, who were flying at sea level, met head-on two squadrons of B-25 and fighter cover of P-38s who were leaving the target area. The leading B-25 squadron was at a height of approximately 80 feet and the second approximately 150 feet. The P-38 cover was at approximately 1000 feet. On sighting the Beaufighters the lower squadron opened out formation and fired on the Beaufighters without scoring any hits. The P-38 top cover went into position for an attack, but were stopped by the Beaufighter leader calling up and identifying themselves as friendly planes. The leaders of the B-25 squadrons both stated subsequently that they mistook the Beaufighters for Sallys."[26]

Going on to the target, the Beaufighters received "the attention of most of the enemy fighters which were able to take off on the approach of the B-25s. There were nil sightings of planes on Tobera Strip."[26] The 30 Zekes seen by the 501st were up and hunting.

The Beaufighters, under a cloud of Japanese, tried to carry out their attack, but their attention was necessarily given to the fighters around them. Some of the pilots' reports give an impression of the action.

Flying Officer McRobbie: "When over Rapopo Strip at a height of 300 feet, a large number of Zekes and one Nate were sighted. The majority of Zekes were in threes and appeared to be all around our formation. I was forced off Rapopo Strip by 3 Zekes attacking from 11 o'clock. Fired a burst at Nate from 6 o'clock but observed no results. I then pulled up and fired a burst at a Zeke, stall-turning onto leader. He fell off in opposite direction—observer in leading aircraft says he was smoking. Was attacked from 3 o'clock by a Zeke. Turned into him and made for home. Later attacked again from 3 o'clock. Took same evasive action. Two Zekes chased off our tail by rear gun. Flew down coast underneath 3 Zekes who did not see me. Proceeded home low on trees. Method of breaking off engagement—turning into attacks, using full power low on water and getting over trees for use of camouflage. One Zeke is claimed as possibly destroyed—last seen diving towards ground smoking."[26]

Squadron Leader Boulton: "On approaching the target, one Nate was dead ahead going across from left to right at same height (200 ft). One burst from approximately 300 yards was delivered as enemy aircraft turned in towards and under us. A few hits observed on port wing. On disengaging, a Zeke was seen dead ahead flying straight ahead. Zeke started gentle turn and short burst delivered from 300 yards. Few hits observed on port wing. One Zeke observed 500 yards ahead attempting to intercept two Beaufighters at 3 o'clock 200 yds ahead. Full deflection shot delivered from 400 yds, no hits observed. Zeke pulled up and over to deliver attack from dead above. Chased from Tobera to Cape Archway at full power. Was able to pull away from Zekes. Attacks delivered from rear. Method of breaking away: applied full power and took gentle evasive action. Sight settings: range: 250 yards. Span 40. Deflection as required. Length of burst: all approximately one second."[26]

Flying Officers Stone and Hadwell, in Beaufighter A19-97, did not return. They were last seen climbing to fire on a Zeke. Japanese claims for B-26s destroyed in this action may have been in mistake for Beaufighters, as both have a cylindrical fuselage with single fin and rudder, twin engines, and were fast at low level. Stone's was the only RAAF aircraft lost.

Flying Officer A.G. Claire, in A19-139, had been at Rabaul in February 1942, and was shot down by Zeros. This was his first return visit. Later, he told war correspondent H.J. Summers of the *Sydney Morning Herald*: "It was then 100 to 5 in the Japanese favor. This time it is good to know we are taking the offensive."[27]

The Harbor

Colonel Art Rogers, CO of the 90th Group, was leader of the B-24 force. He had been up late the night before, checking every detail with his staff, then went out to the aircraft in their dispersal positions before going to bed for a few hours rest and the alarm waking him at 3:30. Seven squadrons climbed behind him in the 400th, meeting the P-38 escort over Kiriwina. Twenty miles out of Rabaul, Rogers waggled his wings, signalling the squadrons to break into six-plane bombing formations. But this made the B-24s spread out so much that the Lightnings could not cover them properly—only 28 had made it to Rabaul, another 19 had turned back with mechanical problems and 25 Liberators had also dropped out. Four of these were from the 400th, with whom Rogers was flying.

It had been hoped the chaos caused by strafing the airfields would have disrupted the fighter defence, but as Lakunai had not been hit and Tobera only slightly the realities must have been apparent to those who thought about them.

As Colonel Rogers led the remaining 16 B-24s of the 400th over the harbor, and the lead bombardier, "Ace" Dunmore, began his bombing run, the sky rapidly became peppered with flak bursts, and looking down, crews could see plainly the muzzle flash of warships below. Some people mistook the flash for bomb hits.

Bill Martin: "The ack-ack was pretty good at Rabaul, but we'd learned how to fox these guys. The minute we saw the firing I'd take off the autopilot, slowly turn about three or four degrees to the left or right, then when the shells burst I'd immediately turn back in the direction I'd come from originally. Then the next ones would be on my right, then on my left, and I could zigzag my way, take my formation through all this ack-ack until my bombardier took over and you had to fly straight and level. Then you just pulled your steel helmet down over your head, sunk down in your seat, looked through your instruments and did not worry about outside."[28]

"Once I began my run," Rogers remembers, "I kept my eyes on the instruments, preventing me seeing the many large bursts in and around our formation. I could tell by the indication of my instruments that my bombardier, 'Ace' Dunmore, was making a good run. As the little light flickered on the instrument panel telling me the bombs were away, I glanced out to see which way to turn to avoid the flak so that my entire formation would not be blown out of the air. I was amazed and flabbergasted to see just ahead the biggest swarm of enemy fighters I had ever seen in the air at one time. About this time, Ace's words came clear over the interphone, 'We hit the target, sir.' I had no time to congratulate him or anyone else as the Zeros prepared to attack. They had spotted us and apparently another of my elements that was off to the left of us. As we left the target, by actual count made from the window by General Kenney's aide, Major Kip Chase, who was riding as observer, there were 87 individual attacks made by the Jap fighters. There were equally as many made on the other side, not counting attacks made from underneath and above. The Japs would fly by us in formations of 25 to 30 airplanes on each side of our formation just out of reach of our guns until they were out ahead of us about five miles. Then they would simultaneously turn in from right and left to make their passes."[29]

As Colonel Rogers led the B-24 procession over the harbor, away below them Masasui Adachi, civilian employee on a fishing boat, wondered what all the excitement was about. Flares were shooting into the sky, sirens wailed and shrieked. He presumed it to be some Navy affair. Then he looked up and overhead was an endless stream of four-engined bombers, showering bombs all over the anchorage. The waters seethed around the shipping, and Adachi saw one transport and 'many' smaller vessels sunk. It was his first and last view of an air raid—he never ignored flares and sirens again after that experience and was very rapidly into a shelter at the first warning.[30]

Charles Ray, flight engineer and top turret gunner in the 320th Squadron, was looking ahead of his formation at the solid cloud of AA bursts, thinking of "the poor devils who have to fly through that", then realized his flight was next to go in.[31]

At 1207, through dense but inaccurate flak, the 320th bombed an oil tanker and other vessels, claiming three bombs within 50 feet of the tanker, leaving it listing and smoking. As the squadron passed Lakunai, over Cape Gazelle and down St George's Channel, 20 dark-green Zekes and Hamps attacked, making passes from ahead and below in the 9 to 12 o'clock sector. Maintaining formation, the B-24s turned into the attacks and flew on. Crews reported two ships on fire in the harbor and smoke over Vunakanau. Only 10 planes had bombed, and two others which had problems on the bomb-run salvoed into the sea. Five others had turned back on the approach flight from Moresby.[32]

First Class Stoker Noboru Sakurai observed the heavy AA barrage and thought it strange that no planes seemed to be brought down, and also that it was ironical that large numbers of casualties were caused by falling shrapnel hitting "indifferent" soldiers standing around watching the raid.[33]

Charles Ray was looking back from his turret, down through the open bomb bay, at "a beautiful sight from the air—it looked like half the Japanese Navy was steaming out of the harbor, and a beautiful small plane passed under us, with a big red ball on each wing—it was a Zero."[34]

The leading flight of the 319th Squadron, at

20,000 feet, bombed on a 6,000-tonner, claiming for its 24 bombs two or three direct hits and seven or eight near misses, leaving it burning and sinking. Some bombs hit short, causing a fire on shore. At 21,000 feet, the second and third flights aimed at a 5,000-tonner, claiming their 30 bombs exploded all around it and it was last seen smoking badly. Two large and a number of smaller ships were seen on fire, and 'many small fires' at Vunakanau were noted.[35]

Bill Moran, photographer with the 319th: "The run over the target is not so bad, then the pilot starts his evasive action . . . and now starts the fun . . . get the camera up, lift it out of its ring-rack, and close the hatch, all the while rocking from side to side. Lay the camera so it will not be in the way and get to your gun station. All the earlier fears, anticipations, emotions—all gone."[36]

"Moto", diarist in the Shipping Engineer Unit who had been pleasantly surprised at the quantities of fruit at Rabaul, wrote: "Embarked on the *Bunzan Maru* at 0730. The ship left harbor at 0930. Just as the *Bunzan Maru* left Raluana Point a formation of eleven enemy planes came over and bombed Rabaul harbor and the vicinity of Rabaul mountain. It seems as if two or three of the ships were bombed. Quite a bit of smoke arose. I could see some of the ships which had caught on fire. Six enemy planes circled over the *Bunzan Maru* and one of them dropped bombs but none made a hit. We arrived at Kokopo safely. Our planes went up and engaged in battle but they withdrew calmly. (Author: 90th BG please note!) From the land and from the ships AA guns were fired fiercely, but not one found its mark. I don't know what happened but the naval ships left harbor in formation. *Bunzan Maru* departed for Lorengau. Even now smoke is still rising from the harbor and vicinity of Rabaul's airfield. Tonight I will sleep on the ship."[37]

Five minutes after bombing, over St George's Channel, the 319th Squadron was engaged by three Tonys and three Zekes, also making low frontal passes, from 11 to 4 o'clock. For Dennis Petersen, it had been an eventful birthday. His leather jacket was pierced but he was untouched. Don McNeff, lost from the 400th Squadron, had been a friend at flying school. (After the war, Dennis was flying B-29s out of Okinawa and one day got into conversation with a Japanese taxi driver. This man had been a Zeke pilot, and was shot down over Rabaul on 12th October 1943, by B-24s. He managed to bring the Zeke in for landing but broke both legs and was evacuated, surviving the war. Dennis wondered if he was one of those claimed by his crew. Unfortunately, the Japanese has not been able to be traced.)[38]

Meanwhile, the Lobio dock, warehouses and a 5,500-ton ship moored there were targets of 18 bombs released from 22,000 feet by Flight A of the 321st

Squadron, which reported a small ship sunk and the area burning as they left. Flight B, from 21,000 feet, claimed a direct hit and several near-misses with their 12 bombs aimed at a 5,500-ton freighter, while at 21,500 feet, Flight C claimed several direct hits on a merchant vessel. Again, after the bomb run, fighters attacked. About 20 Zekes, Hamps, Oscars and a Tony made 30 frontal attacks in a 40-minute period. Vunakanau was seen covered with smoke, and four or five ships were noted leaving harbor. One twin-engined and four Zeke fighters were seen to crash.[39]

Another diarist, "Takagi," from the South Seas Administrative Section, recorded for this date: "Lecture by Okawara. Experienced my first enemy air attack, composed of about 100 planes. Antiaircraft fire seems unable to shoot any down."[40]

Lieutenant Hampton Rich, in *Pistol Packin' Mama*, was hit by fighters, losing an engine. Normally, undamaged aircraft would carefully slide out and back into formation behind the damaged plane, making it formation leader and providing protective fire but Captain R.O. Brown, Rich's flight leader, was on intercom, talking inside his plane, and could not hear calls from other aircraft telling him of Rich's plight. Rich was falling further behind and still Brown did not acknowledge calls until a wingman pulled up alongside and rocked his wings, getting the message across that something was wrong. By then *Pistol Packin' Mama* was being savaged by a horde of Zekes. Brown took his flight back in a circling manoeuvre around the cripple, but the Zekes just attacked when Brown was on the far side of his circle . . . and then, on only two engines, Rich was too slow, and beyond help.[41]

Colonel Arthur Rogers, "Jolly Rogers" CO: "I was on the radio calling for help from our fighters, but from their own conversations I decided they were having a problem looking after themselves. As a result, I never saw one of our fighters after I commenced my bomb run. I knew now that something had gone wrong with the plans and wondered if the Mitchells had been able to reach their target. I could not imagine how it would be possible for the Japs to throw this many fighters at us if they had a previous engagement.

"I could see the Zeros flying to pieces in front of us as our good old nose turrets rotated. My plane had received a 20mm shell in the left wing tank and the hole had been so large that the self-sealing material of the tank was allowing the gasoline to seep out. With the exhaust flame not too far from the escaping gasoline our plane became a fire hazard. I had to slow down as one of my wingmens' engines had been struck and was belching smoke. From radio conversations the other flight commanders were all having their difficulties and I began to wonder if any of us would get back. The Japs had

followed us out 75 miles and were still attacking us fiercely as if the fight had just begun."[42]

Charles Ray, 320th Squadron: "We had a very nervous waist gunner from Chicago on our plane, and as we left the target and started for home a group of P-38s (believe they were from Major Bong's group) came in to fly top cover for us. The waist gunner started firing at them and luckily he did not hit any—but that was the last of our cover . . ."[43]

Over the harbor, as the 43rd Group began its bomb runs, the sky was beginning to be covered with smoke, haze and flak bursts, but the fighters had been drawn off by the 90th.

Thirteen B-24s of the 403rd Squadron claimed a hit on a 5,500-tonner, and a 'probable hit, plus damage, to two other ships moored 200 feet apart, where 13 bombs exploded in the space between them.' Twenty bombs were aimed at a 10,000-ton ship, with 'two or three' hits on its deck and 'one just under the stern'. Crews also reported intense inaccurate AA from all around the harbor, and one large and many small columns of smoke at Vunakanau. Only two fighters were seen, well below at 5,000 feet over the harbor.[44]

"Okabe", a civilian cook, thought about 250 planes attacked and counted four US planes, smoking, flying towards Kokopo. He saw two ships of about 5,000 tons each sunk, and two others also sink, as well as three fires in supply dumps and a fuel dump burning the next day.[45]

Thirteen of the 17 B-24s despatched by the 65th Squadron arrived over the harbor, passing at 23,000 feet over the Burns Philp and Customs wharves. Eighteen 1,000-pounders were aimed at a ship at Burns Philp, with another six at the Customs wharf, bursting in a collection of luggers and small ships east of the target. Intense flak was bursting behind and below the formation, and two direct hits were seen on large ships in the center of the harbor, another was on fire, and bubbles, possibly from a sunken ship, were seen in the water. Only two fighters were seen, at 22,500 feet, being chased by P-38s. The 65th had dropped 54 thousand-pounders, but two aircraft had been unable to bomb, so on the return trip they attacked targets at Cape Gloucester and Gasmata.[46]

Near Lakunai was Miyachi Tanaka of 141 Regiment, a veteran of the Bataan campaign, in Rabaul since December 1942. He thought about 100 "Boeings, Consolidateds and North Americans" attacked. The bombing was so fierce he thought he was sure to be killed. There were many casualties in his area, and numerous fires around the harbor; one destroyer and many smaller ships were hit. Tanaka thought there were few fighters and little AA.[47]

Ten Liberators of the 64th Squadron arrived—three

others turned back—and bombed, claiming a hit on an unidentified vessel off Lakunai, possible hits on a destroyer and unidentified merchant vessel near the Beehives (rock formations in the harbor), which was seen burning by other crews, four small vessels in the north of the harbor, a 50-foot miss off the stern of an unidentified merchant vessel north of Malaguna. As well, crews reported seeing one vessel hit by about 20 bombs, just north of Vulcan Crater, and believed it to be sunk, another was seen burning, one more in the north western corner of the harbor was hit, and one off Sulphur Creek exploded.[48]

"Kasato" was a crew member on the ship *No.100 Koeki Maru* who kept a diary. He had served on several ships at Rabaul, and this day noted that the harbor was attacked by "130 fighters and 30 bombers". He wrote that the ship was damaged, but gave no details, and next day was spent "repairing the ship."[49]

Meanwhile, the 90th Group was still under fighter attacks. Charles Ray was shooting at a Zero and "stopped just in time as I realized that I was shooting just below the waist gunner in the plane flying in formation next to us."[50]

Colonel Rogers: "I saw one of my elements off to my left with one of his wingmen losing height rapidly. Apparently all but one engine had been shot out and he called his flight commander and said he would have to make a forced landing in the ocean."[51]

This was Rich, in *Pistol Packin' Mama*, hounded by Zeros.

Rogers: "This he did and it was well done, as the airplane did not break up on landing. He had no sooner come to rest when at least 20 Zeros dove on him, opening their guns on the defenceless plane and crew, 75 miles from land. Before the last of the Zeros passed in attack the plane burst into flames and we were positive there were no survivors of this crash as the men had not launched their lifeboats or were probably killed in the attempt. Another wingman in my element reported an engine out and the air was full of troubles for every flight commander. I kept wondering if these damn pests would ever run out of gas or ammunition since it looked like this would be the only cause for them to leave us alone. They were flying so close you could actually see the Jap pilots as they passed below or above on the completion of their pass.

"With all our airplanes in trouble I sent out a call to all flight commanders and airplane commanders notifying them to head for the Trobriand Islands, which was our nearest base. Other airplanes which thought they could make it as far as Buna were to proceed there and land. I didn't want too many planes landing in the Trobriands because of a crackup on the runway, which almost inevitable, might prevent the other planes from

coming in.

"The Japs continued to dog us until we were 175 miles out. All the planes in my flight had holes in them, but after conferring with the airplane commanders I decided that none of my six planes was damaged to the extent that we could not make it to Buna. My navigator was working furiously as I had used many evasive maneuvers in the running fight across the Bismark Sea. He gave me a new course that would bring me into Buna and after following it for thirty minutes my engineer informed me that our gas loss from the damaged wing tank was greater than expected. It was a question then of could I get to Buna or should I go back to the Trobriand Islands? I decided to try to make it to Buna and we arrived there all right. A nice landing was made but as the plane slowed down to five or ten miles an hour the nosewheel strut gave way and we stopped just off the edge of the runway on our nose."[52]

The target for the 400th on this eventful mission was a destroyer tender, the aiming point for 30 bombs dropped from 24,000 feet. Two direct hits were claimed, plus two or three hits or near misses on the destroyers around the tender, and a hit and several near misses on a 6,000-tonner. During the interception, one fighter was seen going down in flames and three seen to hit the water. The B-24 flown by Don McNeff was also lost, and closer to Kiriwina Lieutenant McMullen had to ditch his B-24, the crew being rescued by PT boat.[53]

The Japanese fighters had concentrated on the leading squadrons, not unlike the Luftwaffe tactic, but the Japanese had been unable to achieve the more spectacular results of the heavily-armed Focke-Wulfs and Messerschmitts over France and Germany.

Back at Rapopo, Doctor Aso was pondering this first day of direct attack on the airfield. "Corporal Wada, who had a bullet wound, had jumped on a truck by himself to have medical attention, so I was surprised to learn Wada died from loss of blood soon after he got to hospital. It seems there is a big difference between 7.7mm bullets in the 'China Incident' and the Yankees' 12mm bullets." He added in his diary: "At last, the day which will close my life will soon be here."[54]

The Chicago *Tribune* was represented by Robert Cromie, who flew in *Satan's Sister*, piloted by Lieutenant John E. Bond. As the B-24 taxied and took off, Cromie stood in the bomb-bay, between the rows of 1,000-pounders. As the Liberators climbed to bombing altitude he described the scenic flying conditions. "Dead ahead of us were nine planes flying in beautiful V formations, and others far to our left were still jockeying into position. The whole sky—well, almost the whole sky—seemed to be filled with Allied planes. It was a lovely sight.

"Someone spoke over the interphone. 'Are we supposed to join fighters somewhere?' he asked, cheerfully, 'because this damn course is taking us right for Rabaul.'

"A little while later we were joined by fighters, and I felt much happier.

"The pilot and bombardier were discussing how to make the bomb run, and concluded their conversation with, 'Then go right over Rabaul Harbor.'

"We passed swiftly over water whose coral reefs were amazing shades of blue and green and then over land with checkered jungle and open spaces and an occasional muddy river. From an extreme height, New Guinea looks like one of those funny-paper lands where the sun always shines, everyone is happy, and no one ever dies.

"A few miles ahead I saw what looked like smoke hanging low along the water's edge. It was Rabaul. By leaning a little way out into the slipstream, I could see a couple of Jap ships beginning to circle frantically in the outer harbor. From the other window I saw dozens of Jap ships, most of them motionless, and a number of bombs bursting among them, throwing water high into the air and leaving black smoke hanging where the bomb had split the water.

"As Powell (SSgt Ralph W Powell) and I watched we could see one ship disappear momentarily as some sharpshooting bombardier scored a direct hit. Then, as we came over the harbor, I lay down and peered thru the bottom turret to see our brown beauties of bombs drop into space and begin the long trip down.

"Someone's bombs—either ours or those of the plane ahead—landed very close to two large ships which still were side by side, perhaps caught as they were refuelling. The bombs made a brisk pattern of near misses, but perhaps even then they did grave damage to the ships.

"The sky became discolored with bursting anti-aircraft fire, which came from a few ships and also from some ground guns near an extinct volcano. Then we turned over the harbor and began to leave the target area.

"Behind I could see the town of Rabaul—which from a height of many thousands of feet looks like a delightful vacation spot—the harbor, where at least two and perhaps more ships were burning with a pleasant persistence, and a couple of airfields, one of which was almost completely wreathed with smoke.

"The ack-ack guns were still firing at our last six bombers. Two Jap planes, apparently bombers, and the only Jap planes I saw all day, were flying far below along the shore line as if their only desire was to get away from there.

"Then we moved far enough from Rabaul so that the only indication that our raid was a success was a

heavy irregular line of dark smoke in startling contrast to the pure white clouds.

"The Allies' two attacks were less than an hour apart. The first caught the Japs thoroughly napping and did a viciously efficient job of knocking out many Jap planes on the ground, and silencing much ack-ack. The second smash was directed against the harbor and shipping as well as waterfront installations."

It was the 29th mission for *Satan's Sister*, since the crew had brought her from Topeka the previous May.[55]

As usual in any large engagement, some units had seen little or no heavy combat, while others struggled all the way in and out under enemy pressure. The 39th Squadron P-38s saw so little that they went all the way back to Port Moresby, a three hour flight, not needing to refuel. Charles King: "Later missions were to be far different."[56]

The *Sydney Morning Herald* reported the attack alongside victories on the Russian and Italian Fronts. The *Herald*'s war correspondent, H.J. Summers, wrote: "General MacArthur spent Tuesday in the operations room of the air force in New Guinea with his air chief, Lieutenant-General George C. Kenney, and the officer commanding the US 5th Air Force, Major-General Ennis C.W. Whitehead. Two days before, at an interview with war correspondents, he had told of the long-range preparations that had gone into the making of this attack on the enemy's key base—how the moves to the Trobriands and Woodlark on June 30 had been a means to this end, and how even planes in the near-pensioned class had been overhauled and patched and brought in to supplement our air strength for the job. 'We intend to smash Rabaul,' General MacArthur said.

Throughout Tuesday he watched the progress of the operation as revealed in radio flashes from the crews, and at the end expressed his satisfaction. 'It was a crushing and decisive defeat for the enemy at a most vital point,' General MacArthur said. 'Once more surprise was predominant. Rabaul has been the focus and very hub of the enemy's main advanced air effort. I think we have broken its back. Almighty God again blessed our arms.' " The remainder of the article described the roles of the B-24s, Mitchells and Lightnings, and quoted Squadron Leader Boulton of the RAAF 30 Squadron.

Another *Herald* war correspondent, H. Mishael, "with MacArthur's Headquarters", wrote: "The Allies have raided Rabaul 122 times since General MacArthur established his South West Pacific Command. Up to the end of July the Allies had dropped approximately 1,000 tons of bombs on Rabaul this year. The heaviest tonnages reported in all raids were 60 tons on October 10 last year and 54 tons on March 24 this year, when 250 planes were hit on the ground. The longest string of consecutive attacks on Rabaul was a six-day attack that ended on February 6 this year. The latest attack against Rabaul, however, exceeds all previous ones in the number of planes engaged, tonnage of bombs dropped and rounds of ammunition fired."[57]

The attacking force was back at base, where the ground crews were working under the tremendous pressure of having the planes prepared for the next mission, to follow on 13 October. Men of the 479th Air Service Group were at full capacity to repair and prepare the mass of airplanes. As well as the three B-24s lost, many of the 90th's aircraft were damaged by flak and fighters; engines hit, fuel tanks holed, hydraulic lines punctured, controls damaged and crewmen wounded.

Over 300 tons of bombs and more than a quarter of a million rounds of machinegun ammunition had been expended. The B-25 Squadrons alone averaged over 20,000 rounds of .50 caliber ammunition fired on strafing runs.

At Rabaul, reports were going to the various Japanese Headquarters, claiming successes or listing damage. 204 *Ku*, led by Sub-Lieutenant Fukuda from Lakunai claimed 10 victories for the day: P-38s and 'new-type B-26s', plus one each P-38, Liberator and 'new B-26' damaged. The 'new B-26s' may have been the RAAF Beaufighters, which they may not have met before. No unit losses were recorded.[58]

4 Air Army received a multitude of reports over the next few days from the sectors which had been attacked, giving damage suffered. An analysis of these reports gives the following list:

Army aircraft destroyed	: six Sallys
damaged	: eight Sallys
Navy aircraft destroyed	: nine Bettys
damaged	: three
Army ships destroyed	: two
damaged	: 25
Navy ships destroyed	: one
damaged	: four
Personnel killed and wounded	: about 200

Five "factories", the main motor transport depot and 1 Field Shipping Depot were burned.

These total 15 aircraft destroyed, eleven damaged, three ships sunk or burned and 29 damaged and about 200 killed or wounded.[59]

When personal accounts of damage given in diaries and in interrogations are considered, the official reports above may well be inaccurate. The Japanese were notoriously bad record-keepers, and pressure of operations may not have allowed efficient staff work. Immediately at the end of the war, all records at Rabaul were burned under supervision. What remains are those captured

elsewhere, and are incomplete. Appendix 1 shows the detail in captured documents and post-war surveys.

Shipping losses for the Bismark Sea Battle in March 1943 were the subject of controversy for some time. Shipping losses at Rabaul claimed by the 5th AF have been disputed by other forces operating in the area. Post-war research into shipping losses resulted in studies producing conflicting tallies of damaged and sunk shipping, and the author has not been able to locate any information to clarify the 5th's shipping claims.

Differences between post-war studies, damage listed in the 4 Air Army reports, diary entries and interrogations done soon after the events indicate a large amount of confusion after the attack, and it is not unreasonable to assume considerable destruction and damage from the bombing. What did not help was that the army and navy each had a large shipping organization, with reports going through separate systems.

If the mission did not achieve total destruction, it did inflict considerable damage, and ominously showed the Japanese again the striking power and flexibility of Allied air formations operating under unified command.

Such a massive blow required an appropriate response from official sources for consumption by the armed forces and by the public. In their Resume of Daily Operations, Allied Air Force HQ reported the attack as:

"The most powerful air raid in SWPA was made against Rabaul in daylight. A preliminary report from Advanced Echelon, Fifth Air Force, summarises: 87 B-24s, 114 B-25s, 12 Beauforts and 12 Beaufighters with 125 P-38s, were loaded with 350 tons of bombs. A hundred and fifty thousand rounds of ammunition were expended by medium bombers strafing Vunakanau, Tobera and Rapopo aerodromes, destroying 100 and causing great damage to 51 more enemy airplanes on the ground. Also 28 of 40 enemy airplanes that managed to take off were shot down by our bombers and fighters. Eight large fires were started around Vunakanau runway. Aerodrome installations, ammunition dumps and fuel tanks were destroyed. The shipping and waterfront were heavily hit by heavy bombers using 1,000-lb bombs, sinking or destroying three merchant vessels of 5,800 or 7,000 tons each, 3 destroyers, 43 merchant vessels of 100 to 500 tons and 70 harbor craft. Also one submarine, one submarine tender of 7,000 tons, and one cargo vessel of 7,000 tons and one destroyer tender of 6,800 tons were damaged. A direct hit set afire Toboi wharf, and another wharf and a warehouse were badly hit. Five of our airplanes were lost.' "[60]

For the Allied forces' internal distribution, HQ's Intelligence Summary 570, dated 13/14 October, described the situation as: "Perhaps the main result of the raid on Rabaul is that the enemy's planned capabilities for both offense and defense in the air are reduced, if not nullified. He is not, of course, devoid of air strength in the N.E. Sector, but he has been pushed back to the levels of early July when he had suffered the crushing loss of 101 planes in one day in the Solomons; he has probably less planes here now than were operative following upon the mid-August raids. In the face of continuing losses, the enemy since August gradually nurtured his growing air strength into a potential force sufficiently strong to counter-engage any attack we planned. Photographs revealed probably more than 300 planes at Rabaul 12/13 October—as large a force as ever assembled in this theater. His carefully prepared plans based on this strength are now obviously defeated.

"Several courses of action are open to the enemy, including the following considerations:

1.   He is scarcely in condition to fight immediately in force, no matter what force confronts him—his operational aircraft, including both fighters and bombers, at Rabaul, are probably not in excess of 50-60 combat planes, nor more than 70 combat planes within the Solomons and New Guinea, assuming 30% serviceability. As a maximum, his estimated total strength in the N.E. Sector would be less than 500 planes, including 75-80 reconnaissance aircraft."

The Summary went on to report small-scale Japanese raids against Finschafen, Morobe and Santa Ysabel (in the Solomons), that photographs showed the strips at Madang, Alexishafen and Nubia were serviceable but few planes were seen, and aircraft at Wewak increased from 48 to 63.

Use of the word 'nullified' was anticipating events by some four months. Much heavy fighting was ahead before the Japanese were pounded back to that state. However, their capabilities had been somewhat reduced. What the correct use of airpower now required was immediate and heavy continuation of the attacks.

The Propaganda Salvos

Both sides launched their versions of the day's events. Allied GHQ issued Public Relations Office (PRO) Communique 551 on 14 October 1943:

"The enemy has sustained a disastrous defeat from air attack at Rabaul. With complete secrecy, the mass of our air force was concentrated and launched against his air and naval forces there using fields made possible by our occupation late in June of the island groups north of New Guinea. Recently we crushed the right wing of his air command at Wewak, this time our objective was his left wing at Rabaul. The division of his air forces into two great groups based upon Wewak and Rabaul has

made it possible to use our main mass first against one flank and then the other, thus acquiring in each case superiority of force at the point of combat and destroying his force in detail. The surprise at Rabaul was as complete as at Wewak. Mustering every appropriate plane available, we struck at midday. The enemy was caught completely unawares with his planes, both bombers and fighters, on the ground. While our medium bombers raked the airdromes, our heavy echelons swept shipping in the harbor. Both were covered by our fighters. A total of 350 tons of bombs was dropped and 250,000 rounds of ammunition was fired. Our low-flying medium bombers striking at Vunakanau, Rapopo and Tobera airdromes, destroyed 100 enemy aircraft on the ground and severely damaged 51 others. So complete was the surprise the enemy could put but forty fighters in the air to defend. Twenty-six of these were shot down in combat. In all, 177 airplanes or approximately 60 percent of the enemy's accumulated air strength at this base, were lost to him in this attack. Operations buildings, radio installations and many fuel and ammunition dumps were demolished or heavily damaged, anti-aircraft positions were silenced and a motor transport pool was wrecked. Fires raged throughout the areas. In the assault on enemy shipping our heavy bombers with 1,000-lb bombs sank or destroyed three destroyers, two merchant ships of 5,800 tons each, and one of 7,000 tons, forty-three seagoing cargo vessels ranging from 100 to 500 tons and 70 harbor craft. In addition they hit and severely damaged a submarine and its 5,000 ton tender, a 6,800 ton destroyer tender, and a 7,000 ton cargo ship. On shore two wharves and a warehouse were destroyed, waterfront installations were wrecked and many fires started. Five of our planes are missing and others were damaged. This operation, including the first phase at Wewak, gives us definite mastery of the air over the Solomons Sea and adjacent waters and thereby threatens the enemy's whole perimeter of defence."[61]

In Canberra, the Australian capital, Members of Parliament cheered after Prime Minister Curtin read aloud the communique and information about damage done to the Japanese base.

On the other side, Tokyo Radio announced in its Home Service at 7:00 pm on 15 October that "IHQ communique announced at 1530 hours on the 15th that when 200 enemy planes attacked Rabaul, New Britain Island, in the morning of the 12th, Japanese Naval units and AA fire scored the following results: Enemy planes shot down in aerial combat, 8; damaged, 4; Enemy planes shot down by AA fire, 5. The Japanese losses were given as 15 planes self-blasted or set on fire; one ship was sunk."[62]

Another Japanese broadcast was included in Allied

Air Force Intelligence Summary 147, on 16 October: "Seven enemy planes were shot down on Tuesday forenoon when enemy air forces raided Rabaul on New Britain Island. The raid was preceded by a reconnaissance flight carried out by 30 Lockheeds which was followed later by a larger unit comprising 100 bombers and fighters. The enemy bombing was concentrated on the airfields and shipping sighted in the harbor. The Japanese land and naval forces offered fierce resistance and brought down four enemy planes by ground fire and three others in aerial combat. About ten others were also downed, but their loss could not be ascertained. The ground defences kept the Japanese losses down to a minimum." A comment was added by AAF: "The heretofore omnipresent Japanese assertion that 'our fighters drove the enemy away; damage was negligible' is decidedly absent."

At about the same time, other Japanese radio items reported services at Yasukuni Shrine, where relatives of war dead were permitted to enter the Imperial Palace grounds, and paid homage later at the Shrine. Other groups were entertained at the Kabukiza and Yurakiza theaters. General Doihara visited the Tokio Theater and met relatives of war dead from Toiyama and Niigata Prefectures.

The Japanese losses were circulated among their forces and references to the 15 planes and one ship lost were found in many captured diaries and letters. However, again differences occurred, probably as witnesses spoke of the events and these figures were relayed from one man to another.

Whatever the exact results of the raid, it was important enough to be spoken and written about by many Japanese in the region, and recalled as the first of the large attacks.

At 8:00 a.m. on 13 October, 70 Liberators of the 43rd and 90th Groups, plus 12 from the 380th which usually operated to the west out of Darwin, set out to continue the attack on Rabaul.

Service units on Kiriwina had performed magnificently, preparing over 100 Lightnings for the mission.

But the malignant weather worsened and about 150 miles from Rabaul a turbulent front to 30,000 feet was met. First the P-38s, then the bombers turned back.

Three fighters and a bomber were lost on the return flight, possibly due to collision.

General MacArthur was aware of the heavy work load borne by key members of the Staff and the groundcrews. He sent the following message to Washington:

"AGWAR   14 October 1943

Although details of Rabaul strikes are amply covered in communiques and operations reports (Personal

for General Marshall from Ritchie), believe the following personal observation to be of interest to you and General Arnold. Was with ADVON Fifth Air Force in Guinea during all final planning and preparations. Outstanding impression to me was the apparently effortless manner and rapidity with which the very limited staffs of the advanced air echelons were able to orient and control such a maximum concentration of their total striking force. Unquestionably the primary reason for the extraordinary effectiveness of the air force is the surprising flexibility. After the general plan is approved by Generals MacArthur and Kenney complete decentralization of detailed planning and execution follows. Final coordination of timing and assembly is accomplished at one short personal conference between the two air task force commanders and ADVON (C-6676) except for the teletype circuit from Moresby to First Air Task Force at Dobodura, there was no increase in the normal levels of communications anywhere in the area.

"The Jap had watched the development of Kiriwina, and with customary consideration had been concentrating his air at Rabaul for two days before the strike, thus assuring us of a good bag of aircraft in addition to the shipping against which the first strike was primarily aimed. Immediate systematic follow up is being made as long as weather will allow. The simultaneous strike at Buin-Faisi was purely coincidental as the Rabaul strike was not co-ordinated with SOPAC for excellent reasons."

"Sincerely hope the final results of this show will merit special approval from the War Department as such word is of outstanding value here as a tonic to the war-weary ground crew and air crews, many of whom have been operating in Guinea for 18 months. As an example of their work, 118 B-25s went out on Rabaul strike and three hours after their return 108 were ready for another mission. The key officers of the airstaffs are few and the experience level drops off sharply below them. This results in their carrying the load continuously. I am concerned over the fitness to which some of them are drawn. Should any of them crack there are no understudies to replace them and the present excellent teamwork would be jeopardized. Will have more detail for this for General Arnold when I return. Generals MacArthur and Kenney returned today from a trip to Moresby especially for the Rabaul show.

MACARTHUR"[63]

One example of the experience level of the staff is that of Clint Solomon, 3rd Bomb Group. He was shot down on 20 July 1943, picked up and made assistant operations officer at Group HQ. The following day, the operations officer himself went home and Solomon was thus his successor. This is not intended to be a slight on

Colonel Solomon's ability, but it is hardly the way to ensure correct functioning of the important functions of the staff. It is eternally to the credit of the men concerned, as General MacArthur realized and stated in his message, that they performed their duties so well in such trying conditions.[64]

In the days following the strike, the 'Ultra Secret' radio intercepts in GHQ SWPA's Special Intelligence Bulletins contained small items of information which needed to be correlated with information from other sources. 'Ultra' was rarely the dramatic revelation of enemy strengths, locations and intentions as has been reported from the European Theater.

SIB 161 reported air activity around Rabaul increased, but no effect of the raid was noted. Naval surface movements included a *Comment*: "All of these ships are proceeding to Shanghai in connection with the three convoys, each composed of four or five transports, leaving Shanghai on 8, 20 and 21 October. These convoys are expected to arrive at Rabaul on 21-31 October and 1 November respectively."

SIB 162, to 1800 hrs 13 October, reported that aerial activity decreased and light cruisers *Tama* and *Kiso*, carrying 1,100 troops, left Shanghai for Rabaul.

In SIB 163, for 14 October, aerial activity at Rabaul was mainly floatplanes possibly due to disorganization and bad weather, and *Tama* and *Kiso* were due at Rabaul at "0730 hrs 25 October via a route eastward of New Ireland".

SIB 164 continued tracking *Tama* and *Kiso*, reporting their expected arrival at Rabaul to be 0730 on 21 October, when they would unload and depart at 1830 hours. Aerial activity was once again mostly floatplanes, but flights increased.

Photo-reconnaissance on the 15th showed more shipping present than on the days preceding the attack: two heavy and one light cruiser, nine destroyers and a destroyer tender, seven submarines and a tender, one minesweeper and 24 merchantmen. Weather barred air attacks.

Meanwhile, in the European air war, American faith in unescorted heavy bomber formations was shaken again. On 14 October, 291 heavies set out to attack the ball-bearing factories at Schweinfurt. Sixty failed to return, 17 crashed or were written off back in England and 121 others needed repairs. Six hundred trained aircrew were lost at a blow. And this was in addition to another 88 heavies lost in the previous week of operations.

Yet on that same day 93 new American crews arrived in the United Kingdom, and for October as a whole the 8th Air Force was expecting between 250 and 300 bombers and crews. But at last it was accepted as essential that fighter escort was needed in the face of coordinated, determined and experienced fighter de-

fences operating over their own ground. On 3 November, 500 bombers set out for Wilhelmshaven—escorted by P-38s.

Another result was that General Kenney, always agitating for more planes, was given a lower priority again. After the Schweinfurt losses, General Arnold, on 16 October, promised the 8th Air Force the majority of P-51 production and one-third of the P-38s. On 30 October this was amended to all P-51s and all long-range P-38s. Other theaters made do with the remainder.

Notes

1. MacArthur Archives
2. MacArthur Archives
3. letters 1983 and AWM file 779-3-29
4. Figgis Report, 1944
5. letter, 1982
6. tape, 1983
7. diary, 1943 to author 1982
8. mission report
9. tape, 1983
10. mission report
11. Squadron History
12. Post-war interview, Lancaster Report
13. mission report
14. letter 1983
15. AWM 779-3-29
16. mission report
17. mission report
18. mission report
19. mission report
20. mission report
21. AWM 779-3-29
22. AWM 779-3-29
23. AWM 779-3-29
24. AWM 779-3-29
25. letter, 1983
26. mission reports, 30 Sqn
27. SMH Oct 43
28. audiotape 1983
29. Birdsall 'Flying Buccaneers' p116
30. AWM 779-3-29
31. letter, 1983
32. mission report
33. ATIS Intg 306
34. letter, 1983
35. mission report
36. letter, 1982
37. CICSPF Item 938
38. letter, 1982
39. mission report
40. ATIS Bull 880
41. letter, Martin, 1983
42. Birdsall p116
43. letter 1983
44. mission report
45. ATIS Intg 344
46. mission report
47. ATIS Intg 318
48. mission report

49. ATIS Bull 917
50. letter, 1983
51. Birdsall p116
52. Birdsall p116-117
53. mission report
54. letter, 1982
55. Chicago "Tribune" Oct 43
56. letter, 1983

57. SMH Oct 43
58. Takeo Shibata, 1983
59. ATIS EP 270
60. AAF Intsum
61. RAAF Historical Office (HO) C45
62. AWM radio transcript file
63. MacArthur Archives RG-4
64. tape, 1982

9

B-25s Over Rapopo and Tobera 18 October 1943

'The Press-on Spirit'

19 OCTOBER 1943

LIEUT GENERAL KENNEY
CG, AAF

PLEASE EXPRESS TO THE MEDIUM BOMBER COMMAND MY ADMIRATION FOR THE STRIKE AT RABAUL YESTERDAY PD IT REALISED THE HIGHEST STANDARDS OF A GALLANT SERVICE

MACARTHUR (1)

Weather continued to interfere with the intention of 5th AF to keep the pressure on the Rabaul targets, and it was not possible to launch another mission until 18 October. Needless to say, crews and aircraft were kept busy on other objectives. Alexishafen, Cape Gloucester, the Ramu Valley, Sio, Madang, Wewak, were all attacked and the fighters reaped a good harvest of divebombers and their escort when the Japanese attacked Allied bases and shipping on the coast of New Guinea.

On 15 October, Marion Kirby of the 431st Squadron got his first victory. Seeing a Val at 7,000 feet below him, he dived in, firing all the way, speeding in so close he could see the expression on the gunner's face as the Japanese watched the huge P-38 come right in on him, four .50 caliber machineguns and a 20mm cannon firing, overwhelming his puny 7.7mm gun. Kirby overshot and was pulling around for another pass when the Val began to burn and fell into the sea. He banked away, looking for another target . . . heard a clunking sound as though he was taking hits, reefed the P-38 into a turn in each direction . . . no one there. He saw a lone P-38 chasing two Japanese fighters, and slid in behind the other American to protect his tail, then as that Lightning broke out of its pass, Kirby moved in, assuming the other P-38 would cover his tail in turn. But the other pilot left him, and as he began his own pass, Kirby started firing all the way in, until his guns stopped "at about the place where I should have started firing in the first place." He broke off and returned to base, landed, and told the crew chief he had run out of ammunition. The cowl flaps were lifted, and ammunition was still in the bins. The crewchief grabbed one of the guns to check it, and it fell out in his hand! Marion's prolonged firing had burned out every barrel, and the clunking noise he had heard was shells "cooking-off."

At debriefing, the wingmen confirmed the Val for him, as he was not sure he could claim it. His gun camera showed no other planes at all, but "the most beautiful panoramic view of the whole north coast of Papua you would ever want to see. Any travel magazine would give their eyeteeth for such good photography."[2]

The Japanese claimed eight fighters shot down, four transports sunk and one on fire. Lieutenant Ikeda led the Vals of 582 *Ku* and Warrant Officer Aoki the escorting Zekes from 204 *Ku*. Both were decorated for their work, but Aoki was killed.

At 7:30 p.m., Radio Tokyo's German language broadcast to Europe informed their friends how well the Pacific War was progressing.

"Thailand-Japan Co-operation. The Thai Minister for Foreign Affairs, Vichitr (sic), who is going to Japan as ambassador, gave a farewell dinner at his residence in Bangkok on 16 October in the presence of representatives of friendly nations. The Japanese Ambassador, replying to his address, said that the victory of Thailand was due to Mr. Vichitr and the active collaboration with Japan.

"Weekly Military Review. Formerly the Anglo-Saxon powers tried to extend the war, believing that time was working for them. Today, however, realizing the reconstruction of Greater East Asia, they have found out that Japan is profiting by time and consequently they are working frantically to shorten the war by all means. The counter-attacks by enemies in the southern parts of Japanese-occupied countries, which again and again have been repulsed, are a sure sign of growing enemy nervousness. On 10th October, 100 enemy bombers and fighters attacked Bougainville Island. This attack was repulsed after costing the enemy 10 B-38 (sic) planes. There were no Japanese losses. During the same period our air forces attacked Finschhafen, Morobe and Oro Bay, during which we succeeded in sinking or damaging 14 war vessels and causing heavy damage to military installations. During an enemy surprise attack at Rabaul by 200 planes we destroyed 15, losing 15 and suffering damage to one light transport. All the efforts of the enemy make it clear that his intention is to overcome his difficulties by sheer numbers. Senator Chandler, just returned to Washington from a tour of the battlefields, reports that all Japan needs for victory is time. If one bears in mind that the enemy, since the outbreak of the Asia war, has lost 24 battleships, 15 aircraft carriers, 105 cruisers, 114 destroyers and over 6,000 planes we can easily understand the enemy's despair. Japan's air force appeared over both Ceylon and Madras, achieving destruction of military installations as well as harbour installations and one heavy transport. All our planes returned safely. In North China the Japanese Army continued its campaign of destruction, destroying or capturing 13,000 Chinese soldiers.'' The broadcast continued in similar vein.[3]

SIB 165, to midnight on the 16th, reported Navy flying activity "sharply decreased", with 20 of the 35 flights detected being floatplanes on regular patrols over the Bismark Sea. Army activity also decreased, though one aircraft "aloft from Wewak belonged to *Hikosentai* (Regiment) 208. *Comment*: *Hikosentai* 208 contains light bombers, and reportedly moved from Rabaul to Wewak some months ago."

SIB 166 reported Navy flying again decreased, 20 of the 25 flights being the regular floatplanes, two others divebombers of 582 Air Group and the two remaining being "Transport aircraft of 782 Air Group . . . in the Rabaul area." Army activity increased, 6 of the 11 flights being in the Madang area. In "Adjacent areas", it was noted that 17 divebombers of 501 Air Group were en route Iwo Jima-Truk-Rabaul, probably reinforcements after the recent losses over Oro Bay, and that 20 fighters from Rabaul were to stage through Tuluvu, east of Cape Gloucester, to attack Finschhafen at 0330L on 18 October. The Navy Section included information on torpedo boats in the Solomons, the movement of a

cruiser and 4 destroyers Kure-Truk, a possible tactical reorganization of the Japanese fleet, a submarine supply run Rabaul-Gasmata 17 October which complemented a report from Cape Orford (Author: Peter Figgis, the Coastwatcher), the unexplained operations of two cruisers from Rabaul and the torpedoing of the auxiliary aircraft carrier *Chuyo* on 16 October.

The Mission, 18 October

The 5th AF hoped for a repetition of the 12 October raid, but again weather made it impossible. Eight squadrons of B-24s—from the 43rd, 90th and the "poor cousins" 380th from Darwin—along with B-25s from the 38th and 345th Groups, met the three-squadron escort of P-38s over Kiriwina and set off for Rabaul. A weather front caused the Lightnings to turn back, and the Liberators began to search along the coast of New Britain for a break in the weather. They could not find one, and either attacked "targets of opportunity" or salvoed their bombs and returned home.

Bill Martin, of the 90th Group's 321st Squadron, determined that he was not going to waste his bombs, and signalled his wingmen to follow. Easing away from the formation, he led them across New Britain to the Japanese airfield reported at Cape Gloucester. En route, his navigator mentioned that some Japanese destroyers had been worked over by the B-25s near the cape, and perhaps the destroyer guns were mounted at the airfield. When the AA did open up on the three B-24s, it was the most intense and accurate Martin experienced in his SWPA tour, with bursts between the planes in the flight, and shells from one gun repeatedly bursting just in front of the nose of Bill's B-24 . . . and his bombs would not release. Sending his wingmen on, Bill turned for another run through that accurate flak . . . still the bombs refused to go. Enough was enough, and the reluctant four 1,000-pounders finally were forced to drop by screwdriver over the sea.[4]

Lieutenant Colonel Clinton True of the 345th was the B-25 leader, and he went down within 20 feet of the water while taking both Mitchell groups under and through the weather. In the Group Evaluation, it was stated that when Colonel True discovered the fighter escort had turned back "it was too late to turn the strafers back and probably more dangerous, for the entire Rabaul fighter force would have been intact to overtake and probably destroy several of the unescorted B-25s." Therefore it was decided to go on to the target and use the confusion of the attack to cover withdrawal of the strafers.

But at 12:21, a radio message from a Japanese

spotter post was intercepted, warning of American bombers heading for Rabaul. The B-25s were still 37 minutes from target.

South of Cape Gazelle, the 345th turned port, across the coast, heading south of Rapopo and the shipping at Vunapopo, while the 38th flew on to Tobera, base of the Zekes of 253 *Kokkutai*.

The 71st and 405th Squadrons (38th Group) roared along the airfield, strafing and bombing. The 71st reported bombing a cluster of fighters gathered in the open, as well as aircraft in revetments, the control tower and other buildings. Two Zekes attacked immediately after the bombing run, but pulled up into clouds and were not seen again.

Most AA fire burst 500 feet above the formation but one aircraft of the 405th had an elevator shot off as they dropped bombs among 12 fighters gathered at the eastern end of the runway, six with engines running. Two fighters followed the Mitchells to Wide Bay, but made no attacks. The 38th claimed 16 aircraft destroyed. Fourth Air Army records give naval aircraft losses for the day as five, including two "missing", plus three damaged, but a later document gives losses as two destroyed and three damaged.[5]

The main action of the day was taking place with the 345th Group, who had turned starboard and moved into attack formation for their pass over Rapopo and shipping at adjacent Vunapope. The imprisoned missionaries were held there.

Colonel True, in B-25D *Red Wrath*, led the 498th Squadron along the length of the airfield, the nine Mitchells firing 33,000 rounds and dropping 108 parafrags and 72 wire-wrapped bombs over parked fighters, bombers and transports, the control tower, revetments and supply dumps, as well as a corvette off Gredner Island, unfortunate enough to be in their path as they came off the target. Swinging right, they raced for home under 40 Zekes, who apparently waited for the nonexistant escort. In a running 25-minute fight, the Mitchells flying close together for defensive crossfire, low over the water, lost none but claimed 10 in addition to 17 on the ground.[6]

On True's wings were Lieutenants Robinette and McCall; behind were Captain Kilgore with Lieutenants Chiappe and O'Rear; and the third flight, Captain Kizzire, with Lieutenants Magee and Hitt.

The 499th Squadron, with nine B-25s, was to hit the runway and both sides of the field, so as the 498th and 501st began breaking starboard ten miles south of Rapopo, Captain Loverin led them into a 360-degree turn to port, to allow the other squadrons to clear the target. Loverin and Lieutenant McClure strafed and bombed along the eastern side, while Lieutenant Baker dropped 12 100-pound bombs along the western. The

second flight, Lieutenants Cooper, Parke and Cabell, strafed and silenced an AA position which was firing at the Mitchells, then got a hit and near misses on three planes, despite a problem with bomb release and gun firing mechanism. Captain Baird, with Lieutenants Tatelman and Gath in the third flight, went along the west side of the strip, claiming hits on six or seven planes with their guns. Turning starboard after leaving the target, the crews watched shipping being bombed by the other B-25s. Fifteen Zekes made about twenty passes, but were considered less experienced and aggressive than those encountered over Wewak. The Mitchells received one 20mm hit in a left wing and another in a life-raft compartment, claiming one probable and two definite kills. A B-25 was seen over Wide Bay being engaged by fighters, and later two splashes and a fire were seen on the water. 23,000 rounds, 72 parafrags and 62 100-pound bombs were expended by the 499th.[7]

The 501st—Captains Marston, McGowan and Knoll, Lieutenants Bailey, Cather, Kilroy, Kortmeyer, Kranz and Lewis—swept in 30 seconds after the 498th, expending 43,000 rounds, 108 parafrags and 72 100-pound bombs into the west dispersal area, claiming hits on three Ki-21 Sally bombers, a Ki-61 Tony with probable hits on another Sally and two G4M Bettys, observing 30 to 40 fighters and bombers in revetments. Turning away over the sea, crews observed the 500th Squadron attacking shipping to their port. Passing Gredner Island, they saw Subchaser No. 23 blown up by bombs, but then were attacked by up to 60 Zekes, Haps, Nates and Oscars for 17 minutes. About half the fighters seemed to be waiting, perhaps for the expected P-38s. Passes were made from ahead, but not directly in front, as if the Japanese were aware of the massed machineguns in the strafers' noses. Only minor damage was inflicted on the low, fast, tight formation of B-25s, who claimed 12 fighters. At 3:30 the squadron returned to Dobodura, after a long five-and-a-half hour mission, about 45 minutes of it flown with throttles rammed to the firewall.[9]

"Moto", the diarist who witnessed the 12 October raid from the deck of *Bunzan Maru*, and in intervening days had seen more action on voyages in the area, wrote, "Today is the day that we who went to Lorengau will rest. Today, again, several enemy planes raided us. Our unit on this side need not worry, but the area around Rabaul, which is beyond us, seems to have been attacked a little again. The sound of fire from AA guns was heard and several of our planes went up to defend the vicinity of Rabaul."[10]

The 500th Squadron was to attack shipping between Vunapope and Lesson Point, just off the end of Rapopo Strip. An hour-and-a-quarter after take-off, the entire third flight turned back because of a turret failure in the flight leader's plane. The remaining six, led by

Lieutenant Mortensen, followed the other squadrons. TOT was 1:00 p.m., and as the others banked for runs on the airfield, the 500th moved on and began the final run onto their own target. Camps and supply areas on the shore ahead of them were savaged by the 48 forward-firing .50 calibers in the strafers, who broke into separate flights to attack what was thought to be the 5,000-ton *Kinkasan Maru* and the 6,000-ton *Johore Maru* both anchored off-shore. Mortensen led Lieutenants Geer and Hecox; he and Geer bombed the 5,000-tonner, seeing it overturning. Flashing over it, Hecox placed two 1,000-pound bombs just ahead of Sub-chaser No. 23, whose hull was right over the bombs as they exploded, completely demolishing the small ship. The fliers thought it was a corvette. Meanwhile, behind and to port, Captain Anacker, with Lieutenants Peterson and Wallace, were strafing their way across the water to the 6,000-tonner. One 1,000-pound bomb hit the deck and bounced off, but the other five exploded and lifted the ship out of the water. At almost the same moment fighters attacked, hitting Wallace's starboard engine, which began to smoke, vibrate and threatened to shake loose. Peterson and Anacker began manoeuvring to bring themselves back into formation on either side and behind the damaged B-25. *Johore Maru* suffered damage to the bottom starboard of Number 3 hold but not enough to sink her. No damage was recorded for the other ship.[10]

More fighter attacks followed, Peterson's port engine began to smoke, the wheel dropped and slowed the plane even more, and the B-25 fell away to a tail-down landing on the water, where it was strafed by about eight fighters. Wallace's crew had witnessed Peterson's gunner, Sergeant Korczynski, shoot down two fighters.

Mitsuyasu Yamakawa, flying number two in a three-plane flight, from 253 *Ku* at Tobera, followed his leader in an attack on the low, speeding B-25s, saw the leading pilot, Petty Officer Seki, hit the sea, felt his own Zeke shudder as it flew through the spray of upthrown water, and pulled up in shock, wondering if he himself had hit the water and if his aircraft was damaged.[12]

Anacker and Wallace flew down St. George's Channel, joining Mortensen's flight. An estimated 50 Zekes and Tonys dove on the B-25s, now in a tight defensive formation of five, attacking from all directions, screaming in to very close range. One Zeke actually flew between the planes of Anacker and Wallace, so close that the pilot's facial expression could be seen, and so close the gunners could not fire for fear of hitting the other B-25. The fighter pilot was reported as a 'mean-looking bastard'.

At the time this was thought to be a display of flying nerve by the Japanese. However surviving Japanese fighter pilots believe the Zeke was forced into the

position due to the low-level speeding flight over the sea; the pilot probably misjudged his firing pass and had to slip into the space between the B-25s to avoid a crash or collision. Takeo Shibata, who commanded both 201 and 204 *Ku*, believes none of his pilots would get into such a position intentionally. The pilot's identity is not known, and no Japanese survivor of the day's action recalls the incident.

On the coast, Peter Figgis watched the fight as the B-25s battled their way from Cape Orford past East Owen Point, out of his sight. 'It was obvious', he wrote in his report, 'that the B-25s were in difficulties, but they were still airborne when they passed out of sight . . .' Figgis, a trained and experienced observer, saw '12 Zekes, two of which were seen to crash into the sea off Cape Orford.'[13]

Meanwhile, the fighter attacks were taking effect in Anacker's aircraft. The engineer, Hardy, was wounded and crawled forward to the cockpit where the co-pilot, Migliacci, began to give him first aid and Hardy was hit again. Henderson, top gunner, was hit in the wrist. Migliacci then saw a fire in the radio compartment, used the fire extinguisher on it, and told Anacker the aircraft was on fire. Anacker saw the fire was out of control and veered away from Wallace's B-25, intending to put the plane down on the water. During the combat, Migliacci saw Hardy and Henderson each shoot down a fighter; Henderson claimed three definites and three probables.

Anacker brought the Mitchell down to a good, tail-low landing. Migliacci and Hardy almost immediately escaped through the upper hatch, followed by Anacker, after what seemed to Migliacci to be several minutes. Henderson got out through the shattered top turret, but Svec, the radio operator, was trapped in the tail and not seen again.[14]

During the long running battle Wallace's turret gunner, Murphy, ran out of ammunition, and more from the front guns was manhandled to him by the engineer, Isler, and the radio operator, Eaton. These two were also firing the waist guns, sending an SOS and clamping their hands over a punctured fuel line which was flooding the fuselage with gasoline and fumes. One turret gun and a waist gun were shot out of action.

The other B-25s pulled ahead, and Wallace was now alone, on one engine, over the sea, under attack by at least 10 and possibly 20 or 25 fighters, who kept diving, firing, wheeling around him. Staying as low as 30 feet over the waves, Wallace turned and climbed into his attackers, then swung into the dead engine to get back down to the surface of the sea. At least four attacks were met this way, and four, possibly five, Zekes were claimed to have crashed into the water trying to get below him to shoot him down. Eventually all the fighters but one turned back, and this pilot performed some slow rolls, waggled his wings, and left the battered limping Mitchell.

At 3:10, Wallace landed at Kiriwina, where Lieutenant Hicko, the navigator, was treated for a stomach wound. Hicko had been firing his .45 pistol at the fighters through the cockpit window, but had to wait till the attacks ceased before the top turret gunner could go to his aid. The B-25, Number 41-30069, *Tondelayo*, needed a new starboard engine and wing, a new blade for the port propellor, new radio and many other repairs. Forty-one bullet or cannon holes were counted.

The other aircraft suffered minor damage, and all returned to Jackson Drome at Port Moresby the following day.

The Zekes were returning to base. 201 *Ku* had launched 16 fighters, and 204 *Ku* 36, all under command of Sub-Lieutenant Fukuda. They claimed five B-25s and three B-26s, for a loss of two. Ensign Susumu Ishihara claimed the three "B-26s" among 204 *Ku's* total.[15]

Once again these figures are open to debate, as 253 *Ku* from Tobera was also airborne.

In the water around Anacker's sinking B-25, Lieutenant Migliacci was supporting the wounded, shocked Hardy who was unable to keep afloat by himself. His lifevest had been removed in the plane to give attention to his wounds. Migliacci saw Anacker about 50 feet away, and called to him to come and assist with Hardy. Anacker called back, but came no closer. After about an hour it was obvious Hardy was dead, so Migliacci released him. Anacker was nowhere in sight and was not seen nor heard of again.[16]

Japanese 4th Air Army records total the day's losses as five Navy and one Army aircraft destroyed, three and six respectively damaged, 15 KIA and 37 WIA. Shipping losses are given as one powered sampan badly damaged. Damaged were five Sallys of 14 *Sentai*, one Topsy of 20 Independent Transport *Chutai* and one Lily of 208 *Sentai*.[17]

8th Area Army issued No. 331 Information Department Communique on 21 October. "At 0830 hours on 18 October three Lockheeds made a reconnaissance flight and at 1200 approximately 100 bombers and fighters combined, with B-25s and B-26s as the nucleus, attacked Rabaul area. Total of 18 enemy aeroplanes shot down, of these, six unconfirmed. Our losses were as follows: one aeroplane self-destroyed, two did not return. Casualties among the shipping personnel were very light."[18]

On Friday, 22 October, the 3:00 p.m. Radio Tokyo English language broadcast to the USA said, ". . . about 100 enemy planes attempted to raid Rabaul on New Britain Island on Monday morning. Japanese Navy fighters rose to intercept, shooting down nine of the raiders.

Heavy damage was done to another large bomber. Three Japanese planes were lost in this encounter, but no damage was done to the ground installations." Almost certainly the "heavy damage" to the "large bomber" would refer to Wallace and *Tondelayo*.[19]

Alternately swimming and resting, Migliacci reached shore. He went across the beach and hid in the jungle till dark, watching for other crew members. None came. He turned and began pushing through the blackness.

Ten yards away was a Japanese-built road. He followed it to the south-east for a few minutes, then tried to rest in what he thought to be a safe place, but he could not sleep. The combined effects of steady rain, clouds of mosquitoes and the stressful events of the day kept him awake. At daybreak he began walking away from Rabaul and kept on for six hours. About noon, he came to a village. When he was seen, everyone except the chief fled.

This chief was Golpak, a man who remained loyal to the Allies throughout the Japanese occupation, and who played a large part in influencing other natives to remain and to support the coastwatchers. He also greatly assisted in the locating, feeding and guiding of aircrew who came down in the area. As well as Migliacci, Golpak assisted Captain Post, USAAF, Wing Commander Townsend and Flying Officer McClymont, both RAAF, to the relative security of Peter Figgis' team. If Migliacci had passed by Golpak's village, in another hour's walk he would have reached a village just occupied by the Japanese.

Golpak guided Migliacci back, all the way he had come, a seven hour hike past where he had come ashore, to Peter Figgis' camp at Wang, near Cape Orford.[20]

When Sergeant Henderson struggled out of the fuselage of the B-25 he saw the liferaft, which automatically released and inflated, bobbing some distance away. He tried to swim to it, but could not make it, so clung to an oxygen bottle and tried to inflate his lifevest. He heard Migliacci calling, but the words were indistinct. Henderson was shocked and stunned, and seemed to have no control over his voice, being unable to cry out. He drifted for a time, abandoned the oxygen bottle and took off his clothes which sank despite his attempts to hold them, then swam more easily to the liferaft.

It was badly burnt. Henderson tried to remove, and swim with, the cans of water, paddle, chocolate and fishing line, but lost them all. He began swimming to shore, reaching it about 10:00 p.m., some four miles north-east of Migliacci's landing point.

Dressed only in his underwear and lifevest, Henderson sat on the beach all night, in the rain and mosquitoes. Next morning he walked for two hours before reaching a small hut, where he was fed, had a hut built for himself to sleep in, and the day after was guided to Peter Figgis.[21]

On 19 October, Peter Figgis had been told by natives that an American airman had come ashore near Cape Kwoi. On the morning of the 20th Migliacci was brought to him. He told of the air battle, that he had been in the water about six hours, and did not know what had happened to the rest of the crew. Later that day, Henderson was brought in, suffering from wounds to his left wrist and right elbow, as well as many minor cuts and abrasions on his feet—he went barefoot.

Migliacci and Henderson remained with Figgis until 26 March 1944, when they were all evacuated. By this time Figgis was "host" to survivors of RAAF, USAAF, USN and USMC aircraft.[22]

SIB 167, for 18 October, reported a decrease in both Navy and Army activity, with 24 transport flights detected, and a possible reinforcement of 41 medium bombers to Hollandia. Eight unidentified planes arrived at Rabaul from Truk. The Navy Section contained a summary of Japanese aircraft carrier activity, and the terms used in the report indicate that "Ultra" secret information was not as exact as some of the more dramatic accounts of it purport. The carriers are "expected", "estimated", "believed" to be at certain locations or engaged in various activities.

SIB 168, for 19 October, reported an increase in Navy flights to 37 aircraft, while Army flights decreased with only 7 noted. Naval surface units reported were an auxiliary carrier and 2 destroyers "believed" arrived at Truk, and the composition of the 3rd Fleet Striking Force "believed operating from the Truk base".

AAF INTSUM 148, 20 October, reported the mission as:

"Solid overcast in some places, and a heavy front marked by many thunderstorms, stopped a large force of heavy bombers, fighters and attack bombers which had set out for Rabaul. The heavy bombers and fighters were forced to turn back. Despite the absence of fighter cover, however, the 51 B-25s slipped under the low clouds and found their designated targets at Rabaul. Bombing and strafing aerodromes, installations and shipping from treetop and masthead height, they unloaded 12 1,000-lb bombs, 404 100-lb bombs and 250 parafrags, and expended more than 130,000 rounds of m/g. Preliminary reports show one destroyer, one and possibly two merchant vessels of 6,000 tons and one gunboat sunk. One corvette was set afire. Twenty-five enemy planes were destroyed on the ground at Rapopo, and twelve believed destroyed at Tobera. Fuel dumps at both aerodromes were ignited. As the bombers left their targets they were intercepted by 40-60 enemy fighters. The unescorted B-25s shot down 24 enemy fighters. Our losses were two B-25s shot down and one missing."

AAF Intsum 149 reported in its Situation Review:

"An increase in enemy fighter and bomber strength in the Rabaul area is established by photographs of 19 October showing 211 airplanes on Lakunai, Vunakanau, Rapopo and Tobera. It is expected that reinforcement will continue. In New Guinea, although photographs of the same day showed only 48 airplanes on the four Wewak aerodromes there is also evidence of substantial reinforcement."

The review described recent Japanese air attacks in the Finschhafen area, their losses on 15, 16 and 17 October, ground operations in the Satelberg, Wareo and Ramu areas and the Allied air monopoly in the Solomons.

However, the day after the B-25s were apparently credited with destroying 25 planes at Rapopo, 12 at Tobera and 24 in combat, for a total of 61, 211 are still counted on photographs. Excluding attacks made prior to 12 October, in two raids on Rabaul targets some 200 aircraft were claimed shot down or destroyed, of which at least 140 should have been littering the airfields. These wrecks together with the normal wastage of operational flying, should have been very noticeable and were so at Wewak and Hollandia. AF Reports continue to speak of reinforcement to explain the large numbers of Japanese aircraft, though SIBs say nothing of such flights. Mitsuyasu Yamakawa, 253 *Ku*, has said that radio communications were so good that Rabaul could be contacted almost as soon as aircraft left Truk.

Before the next mission, SIBs provided their usual information on aircraft activity.

SIB 169, for the 20th, reported another increase, to 29 Naval flights, Army flights further declined, with six noted and 'no flights of any special significance'.

SIB 170 reported a sharp decline in Navy flying near Rabaul, with a total of 17 flights noted, while Army activity increased to 13 flights, mainly between Rabaul and Wewak. Navy surface activity reported was that there was no change in the locations of the Japanese Fleet Commanders, and the arrival of two battleships, possibly used as troop transports, at Truk.

Notes

A. Much of this Chapter from W. Cather's "Gunfight at Rabaul".
1. MacArthur Archives
2. tape 1982
3. AWM radio transcript file
4. tape, 1983
5. ATIS EP 270 & mission report
6. mission report
7. mission report
8. mission report
9. mission report
10. CICSPF Item 938

11. ATIS Bull 1985
12. letter 1983
13. Figgis Report 1944
14. Migliacci Report 1944
15. Takeo Shibata 1982
16. Migliacci Report 1944

17. ATIS EP 270
18. ATIS Bull 884
19. AWM radio transcript file
20. Migliacci Report 1944
21. Henderson Report 1944
22. Figgis Report 1944

10

Service Squadron Scene III

The groundcrews knew nothing of MacArthur's appreciation of their efforts, and nursed a deep-felt contempt for their commander, still evident long after the war. For them, it was a daily round of work in the heat, mud, diseases and discomfort far from home.

An example of the manpower problems faced by some of these units is provided by 482nd Service Squadron. It had 272 men, from which it was required to find personnel to run a mess hall, be medics, man the orderly room, the motor pool, fuel dump, supply office, all the shops to support the flight line, and also provide men for base supply, the wrecker service and aircraft mechanics for other tasks. Only about 20 to 25 men were available for the flight line.

The never-ending quest for a better way to get something done was a feature of the Allied Air Forces, and there were many men in the 5th who gave of their own time to do this.

Cy Stafford, 482nd Service Squadron: "I talked with many of the mechanics about some way to fasten the landing gear of the P-38 in the down position, then we could tow the plane in and not damage it. They always said fine, but how can it be done?"

Working with the welder and machinist, Cy produced a unit which could be carried easily by one man. "After about one week working on the project when we had time, the towing unit was finished. A P-38 that had broken one of the drag struts on the left main landing gear, and collapsed, was hoisted up with a C-2 wrecker, the bars were installed and the plane towed to a place to be repaired. The maintenance officer thought it was a very clever way to save time, instead of using a 30-foot flat-bed to haul the plane on. He talked to Major Summers about getting the squadron photographer to photograph each step in installation of the bars, and he had a

draughtsman draw, show the size and give a description of the material used to make it." The plans and pictures were sent to 5th AF HQ for their approval and to let the P-38 outfits have the information. This never happened, as HQ lost the plans.

"Some of the planes would land and the pilots would forget to turn the guns off, you would hear a burst of gunfire, and bullets ricocheting down the runway—man, you hit the deck quick!"

Cy decided to tackle the problem and worked with a man the 482nd was fortunate to have. He had graduated from three electrical schools before entering the service. "Many laughed at him as he would walk along the road through the shop area, talking to himself, memorizing the electrical systems of the different fighter planes."

The idea was to place either a red light or buzzer to warn the pilot of loaded guns when he either throttled back to idle or extended the landing gear. After about three weeks Cy, the electrician and an instrument man had an almost foolproof system.

"The plan was sent to 5th AF HQ and we waited and waited. About nine months later I was called to the orderly room and handed a sealed package about one and a half inches thick. It was the plan, with pages of endorsement, all the way to the Pentagon. I slowly went through it until the last page, which held the answer: the idea is a good one but it would cause the pilot to relax too much, and for that reason it is rejected. Man, that made me mad. I knew what they were going to do. Steal my idea and let some of their friends sell it to the government and make money out of it. Sure, later it was put on the planes. I never spent any more time with such ideas to send in, just kept it to something we could use in the squadron."

11

Low and High: 23-25 October

Almost as though in alliance with the Japanese, bad weather again made large-scale operations impossible in the Rabaul area for five days. Single B-24s monitored developments and F-5s of 8th Photo Squadron recorded activity on the ground. Gradually weather over the Solomon Sea and New Britain improved, seeming to confirm longer-range forecasts of the HQ meteorologists. Reconnaissance reports indicated that the Japanese had replaced losses and repaired damage inflicted in the previous attacks.

After the problems and losses of the 13th and 18th October, General Whitehead decided to limit the use of heavy bombers to daylight attacks supported by fighter sweeps.

SIB 171, to midnight 22 October, reported usual floatplane activity around Rabaul, with a comment that the decrease in medium bomber activity over the past two days may have been due to local weather there. The Navy Section indicated possible assistance given the enemy by publicity released in Allied nations.

"1.There is strong evidence that the Japanese are conducting a large-scale joint anti-submarine reconnaissance operation of the entire north-eastern, eastern, and south-eastern outer defence perimeters. The reconnaissance is extending from the Kuriles, Marshalls and Gilbert Islands, and extending as far as the Aleutians, Hawaii, the Solomons, New Hebrides and eastern New Guinea areas. At least some of the submarines engaged in these operations are carrying aircraft for reconnaissance purposes.

"*Comment*: Such a move on the part of the enemy is to be expected in view of the publicized future plan of action of the US Naval forces in the Central Pacific as well as the publicized increases in US Naval and Naval air strength and the recent raids by US Naval carrier task forces."

23 October—High Level

The intention was to launch the 90th Group against Lakunai and the 43rd against Vunakanau, with a six-squadron force of P-38s as escort: three squadrons sweeping ahead of the bombers, one with each group and another as top cover to the entire formation.

Fifty-seven B-24s rendezvoused with 100 P-38s over Kiriwina and set course for Rabaul.

Bill Martin, in the 321st Squadron, watched "all those P-38s over Kiriwina. Wow, it felt good to have them up there."[1]

But again weather interfered. Both primary targets were covered by cloud up to 20,000 feet. There had been no pre-arranged secondary target, but the bomber commanders conferred by radio and decided to hit Rapopo. The change resulted in confusion in the formations, which led to poor bombing runs in some cases and no bombs released in others. A large number of 500-pound and 100-pound bombs as well as fragmentation clusters were dropped on the runway and dispersal areas. Some squadron reports did not list results.

As Bill Martin puts it, "There were B-24s all over the place, heading for Rapopo. Various planes bombed various parts of the airfield, and we came off the target into the fighters."[2]

Fighter interception was persistent, with four Zekes claimed by the B-24s and 13 by the escort, for the loss of one: Lieutenant Edward Czarnecki, of the 431st Squadron, who managed to locate friendly natives with whom he lived for three months before rescue.[3]

The 319 Squadron launched six B-24s on the mission, one turning back, but the other five put 60 500-pounders onto the target, though did not report any damage. They sighted eight enemy fighters but no passes were made, and crews reported three victories by the Lightnings.[4]

The 9th Squadron, with 14 P-38s, met about 20 Zekes at 25,000 feet over Rapopo, claiming one destroyed and one as a probable.

The 320th arrived with ten bombers, one other returning to base, and they dropped 60 500-pounders plus 100 20-pound frags, reporting two fires in the western dispersal area, claiming two fighters destroyed and two more probably destroyed, while crews saw two others destroyed by P-38s.

The 432nd Fighter Squadron, with 16 planes, claimed two Oscars destroyed and three others as probables, reporting two Oscars, a P-38 and a Hamp going into the water.

Six B-24s of the 321st dropped their 960 20-pound frags short of the target when the lead aircraft had bombsight trouble, but claimed a Zeke as a probable. At 1320 hours, at the southern end of St George's Channel, a Zeke and a Hamp attacked, the Zeke coming in from the 10:30 position, below, to within 100 feet when it was hit and fell away smoking, while the Hamp attacked from 11:00 o'clock above but was intercepted by a P-38. One 400th Squadron bomber also returned early, but the other five dropped 1,032 six-pound frags, seeing four fires below but reporting that most of the dispersals seemed empty, and claiming one Zeke. The 64th Squadron put nine Liberators over the target, dropping 190 100-pounders, of which 37% were reported on target, crews claiming two fighters destroyed, two probables and seven damaged. The 433rd Squadron's 16 Lightnings had three turn back for Kiriwina, but claimed three Zekes and an Oscar destroyed, reporting about 50 vessels of all sizes in harbor and two convoys, of nine and four ships. Most other squadrons reported the large ship concentration.

Two of the 65th Squadron's nine bombers returned early, one with mechanical trouble and one with a pilot affected by altitude. The seven which did bomb Rapopo placed 320 frags onto the airfield, reporting a large fire at the north-west end of the runway, seeing three of four fighters destroyed by the Lightnings going into the water off Praed Point, and claiming four fighters damaged.

Danny Roberts was leading the 433rd Squadron at 25,000 feet. He held them there as the other squadrons bounced ten Zekes at 15,000, then took them diving into another gaggle of 35 Japanese. Speeding in behind one, firing the short bursts of an experienced pilot, Roberts banked right after it, his fourth burst bringing flames from its wing, then swung into a frontal attack on another which went down burning.

The 403rd had one Liberator return with nose turret trouble, but the others with intense AA bracketing them dropped 84 500-pounders on target, claiming one Hamp as a probable and four Zekes damaged.

Most squadrons reported the large concentration of shipping in the harbor, including four cruisers and destroyers.

One P-38 came right for Bill Martin's B-24, with a Zero chasing it. The fire of massed .50 caliber machineguns drove off the Japanese and the P-38 slid under Martin's left wing, with one Allison feathered, sitting there, to add his four .50s and 20mm cannon to the outgoing fire when any head-on attacks were made by the Japanese. "He remained there all the way to Kiriwina, rocked his wings, saluted, and went down to land. It was a good feeling, as we usually didn't get too close to them.

"There were times when the intercom was just screaming with 'Jap fighters' in all directions . . . some coming down from above, diving down through, some trying to sneak in from underneath, because we only had that one .50 pointed down through the lower hatch, and really if the Japs had used their heads that would have been the place to come from. But mostly it was quite aimless. One on the left, and one on the right, both swing in at the same time. (They would have) regular columns out there, a little game they played.

"I've actually seen 'em between my right wingtip and the left wingtip of the B-24 on my right. Not many came through like that, sideways. And the strange thing is, we didn't hit them and they didn't hit us half the time. It puzzled me: with all those machineguns going how you could possibly go through a space 13, 14 yards to my right, with the nose guns and the turret on top working on this guy and not get him. And why didn't he put a bullet in us? Aerodynamics and speed of the airplane, I guess."[5]

Paul Stanch of the 39th Squadron, Charles King's P-38 outfit, engaged several Zekes in combat even though his right engine was malfunctioning and overheating, and made a head-on pass at a Zeke which was confirmed by a bomber crewman, Staff-Sergeant Price, as going into the sea and exploding, after which Stanch stayed with the bombers for another 20 minutes before going on to land at Kiriwina.

Five 431st Lightnings turned back, but the 10 which did arrive claimed two destroyed and a probable for the loss of Czarnecki and two more damaged.

Marion Kirby: "It was a 4 hour 30 minute mission, escorting the heavies at 27,000 feet, and I have vivid memories of freezing feet. My head and torso were in sunlight, but my feet were in shadow under the instrument panel. I would take the hot air hose and put it in my socks. Most of us wore GI shoes. The glamorous furlined Aussie flying boot was not worn after several pilots baled out and the opening shock of the parachute slid the lovely boots right off their feet. That day there were extremely high clouds and the escort thought they would clear the target without fighter opposition. Looking down they could see the Japanese fighters climbing hard. Then off to the right, out of one of the tallest clouds, came a string of Japanese fighters, and they came and they came, about 25 or 30, and all hell broke loose. We got into one hell of a dogfight. One Zeke was directly in front of me and coming head-on. We'd heard all this about "how willing they were to die for the Emperor crap", so I just decided to see. I headed straight towards him and started firing—I wasn't planning on him getting too close for I was in hopes of hitting him beforehand. He flew right through all of my gunfire and thank goodness he broke off at the last minute and swung up to my right. I do not think I put a bullet hole in him. A few minutes later I shot down a Zeke, but he must have committed suicide, as I was such a poor shot."[6]

Twenty bombers and fighters were claimed as destroyed on the ground, but Japanese records list four Army and three Navy aircraft destroyed, with nine and two respectively as damaged. 14 *Sentai* counted nine Sallys and 208 *Sentai* four Lilys in the Army totals, along with 250 drums of fuel "burned".[7]

Sub-Lieutenant Fukuda led 32 planes from 204 *Ku* and 16 from 201, claiming 14 P-38s as "certain" kills, another as probable, and losing two, with one more pilot wounded. Japanese Naval HQ in Tokyo recorded claims for a total of 24 US aircraft down.

Eighth Area Army's *Frontline Newspaper* told its readers, "On the morning of 23 October 43, approximately 120 enemy airplanes, bombers and fighters combined, were intercepted by approximately 40 fighters of the Navy Fighter Unit outside of Rabaul Harbor. Air combat results: 24 P-38s shot down, of these 5 unconfirmed; two B-24s shot down; one P-38 shot down by ground-fire. Two of our airplanes did not return. One of our airplanes was set afire on the ground and one of our medium bombers destroyed. No other damage."[8]

Just after 6:00 p.m. that day, some of Peter Figgis' work paid off. Since 10 October he had been reporting Japanese shipping and aircraft movements past his position near Cape Orford. As seen in the SIB reports, much Japanese reconnaissance was done by floatplanes. Figgis wrote: "I had been reporting this movement for some time, and on 23 October four Beaufighters were waiting and made short work of the one Jake which appeared. The Japs did not try the movement of floatplanes after this episode."[9]

Flying Officer Drury, with Flight Sergeant Beasley as his navigator, in Beaufighter A19-111, shot down the Jake.

"Whilst patrolling over Cape Orford as White 4 at approx 2,500 feet course 045 my observer reported 'Bandit 6 o'clock, one mile 1,000 feet'. I peeled off to starboard, noticing White 2 peeling off also. I ranged myself No. 2 to White 2 and gave chase to the enemy

plane which I noticed to be a twin-float single-engined monoplane and identified it as a Jake." After a chase and some maneuvering over Cape Orford, Drury was on the floatplane's tail.

"I closed to 200 yards, the Jake's rear gunner opening fire in short bursts, which were accurate and appeared to be point 5 with much tracer. One shell exploded in my port engine exhaust. I slightly walked the rudders as mild evasive tactics giving the enemy a short burst each time he came onto the dot, closing to 150 yards. After the third burst thick black smoke began pouring from under the engine, the rear gun stopped firing and the plane pulled upwards to about 100 feet apparently out of control. I passed underneath and my observer reported that the enemy plane had burst into flames and slowly winged over to starboard, crashing into the hillside. I turned and made a photographic run over the burning plane. I used approx 120x20mm cannon."

SIB 172 reported a decline in both Navy and Army aerial activity in the Rabaul area, but in the Navy Section, "The two light cruisers reported attacked by 10 Beauforts near . . . southeast coast New Ireland are believed to have been the *Tama* and *Kiso* which were arriving in the Rabaul area in connection with convoy movements. The indications are that the *Tama* arrived in Rabaul yesterday, 23 October, alone, and suggests the possibility of a mishap to the *Kiso*.

Comment: The report of the attack by the Beauforts indicated that one of the two ships had been set on fire."

Early in the darkness of the 22nd, 27 Beauforts from the RAAF 6, 8 and 100 Squadrons searched for, found and attacked the Japanese ships. No. 8 Squadron, led by Wing Commander Nicoll, attacked first with five torpedoes, but no results were seen. The rest attacked with bombs and saw three flashes on the port side of one of the ships. No. 8 Squadron crews saw a fire on the rear of the vessel and men in boats. Flying Officer Vincent did not return from the mission. One of the pilots, Flying Officer Hales, dived to 1400 feet and put a bomb "right down the funnel".

24 October—Low Level

First Air Task Force planned a low-level strike on the airfields again: Rapopo, Tobera and Vunakanau. Time Over Target was to be 10.00 hours, almost two hours earlier than previous attacks. However, take-off was delayed for an hour, and then the 3rd Group's formation became fragmented over the Solomon Sea and time had to be sacrificed forming up again over New Britain. The defending fighters were up and waiting.

Gordon Thomas, civilian prisoner: "The Nips

knew sometimes three quarters of an hour before the actual warning sounded, and occasionally we would hear them talking about it. They were beginning to realize that the Nip army was not omnipotent. And nothing was making them realize it more in Rabaul than the regularity of the Allied air-raids, which showed the ineffectiveness of their aerial defences, despite the fact our airmen told me afterwards Rabaul's defences were recognized as being something pretty solid."[10]

Captain Sen, 5/2 Punjab Regiment: "The Japanese used to get fair warning of air raids. They had time to take off and circle about for ten minutes before our planes appeared."

All available non-fighter aircraft were flown out of the target area to nearby fields such as Kavieng, on New Ireland. At Vunakanau, Lieutenant Kiyoshi Yagita was in charge of this aspect of his unit's flying, and from mid-October to early November he "flew almost every day".[12]

So at 11:07 the 13th Squadron of the 3rd Group, with eight B-25s at 50-100 feet began the attack on Tobera, striking perpendicular to the strip, south-east to north-west, dropping 69 bombs on the strip and revetments and 12 into the plantation. Results were unobserved. Only four single-engined fighters were seen on the ground, two of them obviously damaged and unserviceable. Crews noted a fighter, possibly a Zeke, explode in the air at the mouth of the Warangoi River, and a fire, possibly a burning aircraft, near the mouth of the Kabanga River. After they left the target area, a P-38 was seen chasing a biplane to the south.

Meanwhile, the 8th Squadron was fighting its way to Rapopo. Speeding along at 500 feet south of Kabanga Bay, they were first attacked head-on by six or eight Zekes which dived from 1,000 feet, concentrating on the leading Flight. The new CO, Major James A. Downs, turned the flight up into the attack, firing his nose guns. One Zeke was hit, passed below Downs and either collided with, or shot the wing off, Lieutenant Bob Miller's plane, both fighter and bomber crashing into Kabanga Plantation—the fire reported by other crews. Downs called for fighter support, the 80th "Headhunters" swung to their aid, but Miller had already gone down.

At 11:12 nine B-25Ds of the 90th hurtled across, dropping 85 100-pounders with 8 to 11-second delay fuses onto the runway, AA positions, personnel shelters and dumps and 25 to 30 aircraft, claiming half destroyed or seriously damaged. Four large fires were seen in the dump area south of the runway. Two Zekes and a Hamp made high passes over the target and B-25 fire was seen to enter all three. Crews saw a Japanese pilot bailing out and Miller's B-25 burning.

Concurrently the 500th Squadron struck Vunakanau at minimum altitude, its nine B-25s placing 108 100-pound bombs and 27,000 rounds of machinegun fire into parked Bettys and Tonys, a radar station and AA positions. Thirty Japanese fighters which tried to get at them were held off by P-38s, and only two enemy were able to make passes at the low, fast Mitchells.

Simultaneously the 499th roared across the airfield, having been chased all the way from the Warangoi River by six or seven Zekes. One hundred five 100-pound bombs and 14,000 rounds were thrown at revetments, buildings, dumps, repair shops, AA and searchlight positions. Two bombers were seen burning before the strafers reached them, and ten of the Bettys and Sallys seen in almost all revetments were claimed destroyed. Fighter escort was deemed 'excellent' only six passes were made by enemy fighters.

The P-38s were busy keeping Japanese fighters off the backs of the B-25s. The 431st Squadron of the 475th Group reported the mission:

"On 24 October 1943 10 P-38s of the 431st Squadron took off at 0830L to escort B-25s to Rabaul. Our formation rendezvoused with the bombers over Oro Bay at 0900L and proceeded on course. As we did so we sighted a B-25 headed into the sea off Buna. The bombers approached the mouth of the Warangoi River very low (100 feet) in order to avoid being picked up by radar. As they neared the coast, Nip shore batteries opened up on them hoping to frighten the planes and break their formation, or to cause such huge splashes and geysers that the planes would be brought down. We observed a large fire near the mouth of the river.

"We dropped our belly tanks and climbed to 8,000 feet, S'ing across the bombers as they made their run from the north. At that altitude and at 1110L we saw approximately 20 Zekes, Hamps, Oscars, Tonys and a Nate at about 4,000 feet. These were intercepted by the 432nd and 433rd Squadrons. Over Vunakanau, we climbed to 14,000 feet to intercept another formation of about 30 or 40 enemy aircraft which were at about 15,000 feet. The squadron led into one Zeke. The leader made a steep diving turn to about 9,000 feet and got a good rear shot at the Zeke, which exploded. The enemy planes continued milling around above us, and we made several individual passes, but their formation remained generally above, unable to come down and get at the bombers because of our cover. We did not go to a lower level, for we considered it our job to keep the enemy aircraft from attacking the bombers. Not one of the enemy aircraft attempted to come down through our formation. When the bombers had completed their run and were on their way home, we were directed to clear the area, which we did at 1130L. As we parted, the enemy aircraft were still milling around high. As a result of our engagement, we definitely destroyed one Zeke and one Tony-type enemy aircraft, and probably destroyed another Zeke. We sustained no losses or damage. No anti-aircraft fire was encountered during the engagement; only one puff was observed to burst over Vunakanau. As we flew over the harbor we noted that it was jammed with shipping; many small barges were seen along with larger cargo vessels and possible warships.

"The enemy pilots were described as determined, eager and aggressive. It was noted that the Tony we destroyed was black and did not have the usual red circles on wings and fuselage. It was definitely an Army plane."

The 8th Bomb Squadron, with Zekes making passes, pressed on to Rapopo. Six Zekes attacked the second flight, coming in from the 10- to 2 o'clock angles through AA fire bursting around the formation. Another six fighters attacked the rearmost Mitchells, shooting away a turret canopy and wounding the gunner, though the B-25s claimed two Zekes. Roaring over the airfield, seven of the bombers strafed their way along the west side of the strip, and one took the east side, combining to drop 81 100-pounder and fire 9,000 rounds. No aircraft were seen on the ground, but large amounts of supplies were dispersed west of the runway, among many newly constructed buildings and parked trucks. Four Zeros attacked from the rear, closing to 800 feet before breaking away. Several fires broke out in the target area, with one column of smoke rising to 1,500 feet.

The 'Headhunters' had gone to the assistance of the 8th Squadron B-25s, battling their way to Rapopo. The dozen P-38s noticed pairs or larger formations of enemy fighters all over the area up to 10,000 feet, and dived on the Zekes attacking the B-25s.

"Corky" Smith: "A turkey shoot. We hit them hard from above and they cut and ran. I don't believe they saw us until too late. It was a brief scrap—nothing spectacular—we shot down 11 or 12 before they gathered their senses and took off . . . at an altitude of about 3,000 feet over Rapopo."

The 80th squadron claimed another as a probable, for five P-38s damaged, of which one crash-landed at Kiriwina and three others had to be left for repairs.

Pilots reported seeing a B-25 shot down into the water off Cape Wanat by enemy fighters.

The "Headhunters" credits for 12 victories were by Lieutenant Jay Robbins, four; Major Cragg, two; Lieutenant Freeman, two; Captain Smith, one; Lieutenants Burnell Adams and Paul Murphey, one each; and FO Willis Evers, one.

At 11:15 the nine strafers of the 501st came spearing into the dust and smoke at Vunakanau left behind the leading squadrons, adding 91 100-pounder bombs and 20,000 rounds to the chaos. Four bombs were dropped on Tobera, with unseen results. Seven Bettys, another bomber and a Mike were claimed destroyed. Mike was the recognition name given the Messerschmitt 109E, at one time believed to be in Japanese service—this was probably a Kawasaki Ki-61 Tony. Five miles south of Vunakanau, that is, about two minutes from target, the squadron was intercepted by a mixed formation of Zekes, 'Mikes' and Petes, about 20 in all. Pete, the Mitsubishi F1M2 Observation Seaplane, was a biplane with two forward-firing 7.7mm machineguns and a top speed of 200 knots. The pilots must have been very confident or very hopeful, trying to take on a B-25 or P-38! The fighters did not press their attacks, and a Zeke was claimed probable. AA was inaccurate, ranging from slight to heavy throughout the area. As they passed through the target area, crews saw a Zeke going down in flames near Kokopo, another shot down by a P-38 two or three miles north of Vunakanau, and a small cargo vessel burning off Kokopo.

The 432nd Squadron passed through the target zone from 11:45 to 12:10. Fifty Zeros and Oscars were met at 4,500 feet, and fighting surged up to 14,000, all over the area. The squadron claimed four Zekes and two Oscars as definites, three Zekes as probables, and reported seeing three fighters hit the ground in flames, as well as the large fire at Vunakanau and several smaller ones. Three damaged P-38s were left at Kiriwina.

One minute after the 501st came the 498th, hounded by 20 Zekes, attacking the stores dumps and direction-finding station with 72 100-pound and 12 300-pound bombs along with 26,000 rounds of ammunition. Half a mile north of the north-west end of the runway a large fire was started, smoke climbing to 1,000 feet and visible for five minutes after leaving the target and several small fires were seen in revetments containing Bettys or Helens. The 300-pounders were dropped on the towers, buildings and hangars at the northern end of the field. Twelve Bettys and Helens were claimed destroyed at the south-east end of the strip, and an estimated two dozen others were machine-gunned. By this time the AA gunners had settled down and were firing more accurately, but no B-25 was brought down by them. Two Zekes were claimed destroyed and one damaged in the running battle, and an unidentified aircraft was seen to crash east of Kabanga Bay.

Southeast of Tobera about 60 Zekes and Tonys were seen circling. The 9th Squadron's 12 P-38s dived on them, noting the Japanese seemed experienced but unwilling to fight, claiming six Zekes destroyed plus one more and a Tony as probables. Lieutenant John O'Neill scored a double.

Six Lightnings of the 39th Squadron swept the area from 11:00 to 11:30, engaging 30 to 40 Zekes and Oscars at heights from 500 feet to 10,000, claiming two Zekes and two Oscars as definites and four Zekes as probables, while two P-38s were damaged and another crash-landed at Kiriwina.

B-25s reaching Wide Bay reported a single bandit at their 3 o'clock, and when Lloyd Shipley of the 39th turned towards him, the Japanese broke for Rabaul. Six P-38s chased him, and after Shipley ran out of ammunition, seeing one explosion on the Japanese plane, James Walters so damaged it that the pilot bailed out. The plane went into the sea, and Shipley reported that "the pilot was strafed and killed."

Japan's 4 Air Army recorded damage as two army bombers damaged, ten navy fighters missing, three burned and nine damaged. But a report by 18th Army for 24 October stated damage was two army aircraft destroyed, ten navy "not returned," five burned on the ground, five damaged, 160 drums of fuel burned and no damage to shipping.[11]

Once again Sub-Lieutenant Fukuda led the combined 201/204 *Ku*, with 16 and 26 Zekes respectively being launched. They claimed six and 12 P-38s respectively, for a loss of six and one pilot wounded. Warrant Officer Kenichi Takahashi, 204 *Ku*, claimed his first victory, but among the losses was Warrant Officer Shizuo Ishii. He had been credited with 29 victories.

"Moto," of the Shipping Engineer Unit, noted, "it is our second large one in Rabaul. The enemy airplanes dropped bombs and fired machineguns furiously, while our warships retaliated with their AA guns and several of our fighters went up to intercept them, resulting in dog-fights. In the first raid our planes were not very active, but today, because they put so much effort into the combat, fewer bombs were dropped in Rabaul by the enemy planes. During the air battle the enemy planes could not be driven off and they came towards our unit at least three times. On their last sortie they strafed us with their machine-cannon and we hurriedly rushed into our air raid shelter. Enemy planes flew around Rabaul for about an hour. There were about 60 enemy planes which raided us. I suppose the air battle has ended since our planes have returned."[12]

Criticisms of staff planning were voiced by some crews who took part in the attack. It was obvious that the Japanese were ready and waiting; timings and routes into the attack were hardly changed; and Japanese were intercepting the B-25s before they reached the target. If the P-38 escort had not done such a good job, B-25 losses could have been much higher.

On 19 October, Peter Figgis had reported the establishment of a Japanese observation post at Baien, where warning of the approaching squadrons could be radioed to Rabaul.

Also, coconut groves surrounding the airfields at Rapopo and Tobera concealed runways, dispersal, dumps and other facilities from low-flying attackers to the extent that some crews believed low-level attacks against targets of that type were impractical. The small

number of planes seen at Tobera by the 13th Squadron indicated that their part in the operation had been almost a waste of time and effort.

However, HQ Intsum 581 declared, "Saturday's Allied raid, which destroyed 20 aircraft on the ground and probably destroyed a further 7, was met over Rabaul by approximately 50 fighters. Of these 15 (or 30%) were shot down, while 13 (or 26%) were probably destroyed—a most disproportionate loss in comparison to only two Allied P-38s. A late report shows that our medium bombers in yesterday's heavy attack further punished the enemy's air force by destroying 45, and probably destroying 10 more, light and medium bombers on the ground. In the air, 43 enemy fighters were shot down and 15 probably destroyed, out of an intercepting force of 60-70, for an Allied loss of two attack-bombers. Thus, in two days, 123 enemy planes were destroyed, plus 45 probables. Regardless of the marked flexibility of his air services, the enemy will be exceptionally hard-pressed to rebuild his strength on these aerodromes. His carefully-husbanded reserve of aircraft has been seriously weakened. His capability for offensive action has been correspondingly diminished."

SIB 173, to midnight 24 October, reported a "very low level" of Navy aerial activity at Rabaul and low Army activity of eight flights. The Navy section reported the confirmed use of destroyers on nightly transportation runs along the coast from Rabaul, information of value for the forthcoming invasion of West New Britain.

The reported effectiveness of the one-two punch by heavies on one day and strafers on the next aroused admiration in many quarters.

25 OCTOBER 1943

'GENERAL KENNEY

PLEASE ACCEPT MY HEARTIEST CONGRATULATIONS FOR YOURSELF CMA GENERAL WHITEHEAD AND ALL FORCES INVOLVED ON THE SUPERB DOUBLE STRIKE AT RABAUL STOP (XC-7653) IT GIVES ME A SENSE OF GREAT SECURITY TO HAVE SUCH AN INDOMITABLE UNIT IN MY COMMAND

MACARTHUR' (13)

25 October—High Level Again

So far, the large fighter concentration at Lakunai had been barely touched in this series of raids. Takeo

Shibata's unit had borne a charmed life in that regard. Twice heavy bombers had it as their objective and both times weather forced a change in plan, literally at the last moment on 23 October. As one of the major aims of the bombing offensive was to smash Japanese aerial power operating from Rabaul, Lakunai had to be struck hard. Also, after inflicting such damage, an attack on shipping in the harbor would be easier. The other air fields had already been hit, and on the 25th, the third successive day of attacks, General Whitehead sent the B-24s against Lakunai first and shipping second. Once again the weathermen had forecast poor conditions.

Two groups of B-24s were to be supported by the six P-38 squadrons. Two fighter squadrons were to sweep the target area ahead of the bombers, which would be protected by the other four Lightning squadrons. The lesson of fighter escort for these raids had been learned early. In Europe, admittedly against a more heavily armed adversary, the Eighth Air Force was still recovering from the blood-letting of the 17 August mission to Regensburg-Schweinfurt, 55 bombers; 6th September to Stuttgart, 45; 8th October to Bremen, 30; 9th October to Gydnia, 28; 14th October to Schweinfurt, 60; a total of 218 four-engined bombers.

Saturday Evening Post correspondent Charles A. Rawlings had been with the 90th Group, "to soak up a little Rabaul-strike atmosphere" for his story of the mission. He had attended the open-air movie with some of the groundcrews who loaded and fused the bombs for the 90th's B-24s and stayed in Colonel Rogers' tent until they were roused for the departure of the bombers.

Rawlings described it for *Post* readers: "Takeoff was up the crisp valiant dawn, north-east. The planes came out, lumbering and lazy and slow. Yachts under a soft jib, coasting out to the line, swaying heavily and ungainly in the swell, taking things easy before they get the mainsail up. Bomber men loll like yacht crews. In the navigators hatch there are always two or three elbows on the coaming, head and shoulders out, watching the scenery go past. Harry Bullis was poised at the runway end. Suddenly his four props beat into life. Slowly, the big, muddy-coloured bomber started to squash its great tires ahead, started to whine as the props fought for air. Then she went past, a tremendous hurtling giant of a thing, and you could hear her voice, the great deep organ voice of 4800 horsepower, unleashed and free and crooning with joy. Bullis held her nose down until she had her 60,000 pounds covering the ground at 120 miles an hour, and then let her fly. She went up steadily as if there were a perfect grade, ballasted, tied, and tracked up the sky, and she was mounting it. Halfway up, she made her last clumsy gesture, a ludicrous spreading of her landing gear like a cow spraddling to empty her bladder, and then the legs and wheels were gone up into

their recesses in the wings and she was a creature of the air, supple, graceful, unafraid.

"The strike followed the leader, one plane every minute, on the exact second of the minute. Bullis brought the first squadron over the 'drome when the takeoff was half over, flying at 4,000, the assembling altitude. He had them in a javelin of V's, and they droned south like a flight of cruising geese and slowly swung and came back, and when they were almost out of sight to the north the second squadron swung in astern."[14]

Rawlings and the colonel went back to wait, through the New Guinea heat, until the formation would be over Rabaul, when they would listen to radio chatter on the radio of the surgeon, Captain Will Mitchell.

The 61 B-24s rendezvoused with 81 P-38s over Kiriwina and set course. However, the weather worsened quickly and 45 minutes later the fighter leaders announced they could not continue. Apparently neither B-24 leaders heard this message, and the bombers continued on their way. Seventy-three P-38s and eleven B-24s turned back. But Major Charles MacDonald, leading the 432nd Squadron, 475th Fighter Group, decided to press on and give what support he could to the bombers. He took his squadron higher, enough to fly through the storms at that height, and was able to reach the target with the bombers.

The Japanese AA defences sent up a fierce fire from shipping and ground positions, forming a barrage between 20,000 and 25,000 feet, through which the B-24s would have to fly their runs over the harbor and airfield. About 60 Japanese fighters attacked, while Major MacDonald weaved his eight P-38s in an effort to make the defenders think more Lightnings were in the area.

Meanwhile, the bombers were also preoccupied:

"Before the bomb run was well under way, the B-24 flown by Lieutenant Charles Showalter, *Tear-Ass (The Bull)*, took a direct 20mm hit in the left outboard engine, which began to smoke, then burn. The right outboard was also hit, stopped, but started again. The propellor was nicked in one of the good engines and started vibrating. Showalter's plane dropped out of formation and he radioed Bullis, asking him to reduce speed. The formation slowed down to shepherd the cripple.

"Sergeant Harry Clay, photographer on *Tear-Ass*, will never forget what it was like in a crippled plane over Rabaul by itself. Those Zeros actually lined up to get a shot at us. I estimate there were 35 giving us their undivided attention but it may have just seemed that way. Every gun we had was going and as close as they pressed their attacks I don't know why they didn't shoot us all to pieces. They did a pretty good job of it anyway. The nose turret took a head-on shot from a 20mm cannon but the shell exploded on contact and just blew glass in on the gunner. Cut him up some but he kept on shooting. They came in on us from every angle.

"Clay grabbed a walk-around oxygen bottle and began using the belly guns. He saw some of his tracer bouncing off the belly of a fighter but didn't know if he got him or not.

"Showalter kept plugging away at it, feathering number one, fire went out, trying to keep number four going, doing what he could for the engine with the nicked prop, trying to keep what speed and altitude he could and still heading for that damn target. What the hell else could we do? Those Zeros weren't going to go away, no matter which way we went. Colonel Rogers got us all a DFC for continuing on to the target but I really don't see that we had any option. The co-pilot kept calling off the incoming shots, and he certainly didn't lack for calls. The more that came in, though it seemed to me, the calmer he got, until it sounded like a yawn would be next."

"Between the stream of urgent fighter calls Harry Bullis' voice came over the radio: Where's Showalter? Bullis to flight. Where's Showalter? Can anybody see Showalter? Bullis' left wingman answered, Bearskin to Bullis. Yes, yes, yes. Showalter's here. I am with Showalter on the wing.

"The bombs tumbled down from the B-24s and the squadron leaders reported in. Bullis radioed Showalter to ask if he was still carrying his bomb load. Salvoed bombs right on target, was the answer, Showalter adding, Thank you for slowing up. That's all right, baby, answered Bullis. That's fine.

"The six B-24s of the 400th Squadron were credited with destroying eighteen of the thirty-eight enemy aircraft claimed by the bombers—Showalter's crew in *Tear-Ass* got four, and Lieutenant Sidney Webb's crew in one of the two aircraft closely protecting *Tear-Ass* got another four.

"Although at long last there was nobody shooting at her, *Tear-Ass* was still in deep trouble, trudging along with only one engine operating perfectly.

"They threw everything out of the plane that was not tied down. The camera, the guns, canteens, what little ammunition was left—anything to lighten the load as they slowly lost altitude. Harry Clay thinks it might have been his imagination, but some of them seemed to be eyeing their photographer and wondering what weight difference he might make. They made it to Kiriwina, shot to pieces, but Showalter landed the plane on the strip, although there wasn't twenty feet of it to spare when they stopped rolling."[15]

AAF Intsum 153 included a reference to this combat in the part devoted to enemy tactics.

"A B-24 was on the left wing of a third flight and while passing over the target had 3 engines shot out. It fell behind the formation, and interception was made from all directions totalling 75 passes. Attacks were pressed to 50 yards. Passes were made in rapid succession with attacks individual at first, later developing into two-and four-airplane simultaneous passes thrusts. Most common attack was two airplanes coming in tight formation at waist and then breaking in opposite directions. Tail gunner reports several Japs went down 3-4,000 feet smoking and then came back up to make passes. One Jap pulled up into a stall to fire at the tail. Two definites and one probable are claimed.

Comment: Enemy Tactics—co-ordinated attacks 1-2-4 airplanes simultaneously. Stall to fire."

Meanwhile, there were problems in Bullis' own plane. A flak burst below them sent fragments into the plane, causing some clusters to drop and others to hang up in the racks. As this was the lead plane, several others in the formation released bombs when they saw those dropping away. Bombardier Lieutenant Tom Fetter went back into the bomb bay with engineer Oscar Sjolin and carefully made the fuzes safe on the remaining bombs, then manually released them, a dangerous hour-long job on the catwalk of the open bay at 15,000 feet.

The 64th Squadron, at 21,200 feet, dropped its 500-pounders, reporting 90% in the target and a large explosion plus four or five fires, claiming four Zekes as probables and confirming destruction of another Zeke by a P-38. Eighty more 500-pounders fell from the 65th Squadron at 20,600 feet, crews watching 12 explode in the revetments and three in the water, possibly hitting a ship, but smoke covered the runway area, making observation difficult. An enemy fighter, possibly hit by AA, exploded ahead of them.

The hit on the ship's stern was noted by 2nd Class Petty Officer Masayoshi Iwai, who thought 20 casualties resulted, that many landing craft and fishing boats were sunk close by, and damage done to Navy buildings.[16]

Down below the formations, "Moto", the shipping engineer, observed the action and wrote in his diary, "Today, again, a large formation of 52 enemy planes raided us, and it looks as though they have bombed the vicinity of the naval airfield, for a billow of smoke was rising from there. Our warships opened fire at them, but none made a single hit and the enemy planes circled around unconcerned. Again, there were quite a few dogfights. Everyone is filled with trepidation because of these daily air raids."[17]

The 320th Squadron, 90th Bomb Group, had 12 Liberators over the target at 12:28, at 24,500 feet. They dropped 60 bombs on the eastern half of Lakunai, plus 240 frags on the southern half of the runway and dispersal area, but heavy black smoke and dust prevented damage assessment. Two Zekes were claimed destroyed and one damaged for damage to one B-24. Fighter interception lasted 20 to 25 minutes, diminishing during the bomb run when AA was heaviest, but few attacks were pressed in close.

The 319th was represented by six B-24s at 23,000 feet, and their 72 bombs carpeted the western end of the target, while another six from the 400th at the same height showered 1,400 20-pound frags, 670 exploding across the strip on a bearing of 290 degrees. Six more Liberators of the 321st, under attack by 20 Hamps, Oscars and Tonys, put their 120-pound frag clusters onto the Toboi wharf area, reporting five Bettys seen low down over Keravia Bay, claiming five fighters destroyed, nine probables and three damaged, for damage to three B-24s.

An unknown diarist recorded the attack, writing at 9:00 that night:

"The high humidity makes one feel as though taking a bath. The water appears as though it were a sea of oil. The glare of the white wood of the Nippa Hosu can be seen through the coconut grove. How quiet it is! A feeling of uneasiness is written on each sun-burnt face throughout this ominous silence. At 1010, at 4,000 meters altitude, there appeared over an extinct volcano south of Rabaul tiny specks which turned out to be B-17s. (Author: really B-24s) Out of the dark clouds they came! Ten—twenty—and more! They had come! In a flash our machineguns and dual purpose guns spoke! All hell broke loose in the skies! From several thousand feet, the accurately aimed bombs dropped away from their planes and demolished our oil tanks! When our airplanes came into view over our air field the enemy airplanes were gone. It was a recurrence of yesterday's happening. Through the smoke can be seen the glittering reflection of the sun on the ocean. Except for the placid image of the volcano on the water, the whole scene had been changed. I had witnessed an attack by B-17s. I had also seen a counter attack by Zeros. It had all happened in a twinkling of an eye!"[18]

The 400th, under attack by about 35 fighters, including two black-painted Tonys since passing the island of New Ireland, sailed over the target, counting 30 fighters taking off from Rapopo. The Japanese would fly in line abreast past the formation, get ahead, then peel off individually to make their passes, diving under the bombers, who claimed 18 destroyed, and four probables. One crew member reported seeing 11 crash into the sea.

Probably realizing the eight Lightnings were the only escort, and mainly occupied with the leading B-24s, the Japanese concentrated on the hindmost bombers, the 403rd of the 43rd Group. They came on

in, and soon aircraft Number 800 was unable to keep up, one engine shot out and another useless. The 403rd arrived over Lakunai to find it a "seething, boiling mass of bomb dust" through which their normal aiming points could not be seen. However, the bombardiers switched to alternates and put all but four of 108 bombs in the target area, despite the attention of about 30 Zekes trying to disrupt the runs, counting 75 explode across the southern dispersals, 12 in the northern dispersals and six on the runway.

Sister Catherine O'Sullivan: "Planes came in at the back of our mission, behind the huts. They were preceded by twin-engined fighters which we called "double-engined fighters" as our education then was incomplete. The four-engined B-24s, we used to watch coming in, count them, and check them as they sailed majestically down St. George's Channel home. We were filled with hope that the Allies were beginning to pick up. We saw planes falling. We were saddened and disgusted to see Japanese Zeros machine-gunning Allied pilots and airmen parachuting or whose planes crashed. Our missionary priests gave Absolution for these men, and our prayers were with them."[19]

Tom Fetter, 90th Group bombardier, "was a little surprised at the interception at Rabaul on October 25. The fighters flew right into the flak and made repeated head-on passes. We were under the impression that the quality of the enemy fighter pilots was falling off because of the losses they had taken. I believe this was more evident by the spring of 1944, but over Rabaul the enemy gave a good account of themselves."[20]

Number 800 was joined by two other B-24s who attempted to provide some protection. They dropped behind the formation, and fighters pressed in, persistently trying for the damaged Liberator. The flight claimed eight fighters before the two left the straggler and flew on.

Now, over New Britain, was enacted an example of the small tragedies so often part of the European heavy bomber campaign. The damaged straggler, alone in the sky, sole prey for hordes of enemy fighters. The Japanese fighters were lining up, waiting their turn to shoot at the lumbering target. For fifteen minutes the limping bomber stood against the darting fighters attacking it from all directions in quick succession. Fuselage and wings riddled, on two engines, bomb bays awash with petrol and hydraulic fluid, top turret jammed, out of ammunition except for a few rounds in the nose . . . still it flew on. Gradually the fighters, perhaps out of ammunition or fuel, turned away, leaving six or seven which remained, probably waiting to see the B-24 fall. Then they also banked away to the coastline, leaving '800' alone in the sky.

A few minutes later, the engines cut. The pilot

brought it down for a water landing . . . the nose touched and went under. The fuselage snapped at the bomb bay and the five men gathered at the rear of the cockpit escaped . . . though the flight deck and cockpit were full of water, . . . the navigator, engineer and radio operator, all injured, struggled out of the escape hatch. Sadly, the pilot and co-pilot went down with the plane.

The other B-24s had called for a flying-boat, and a Catalina arrived on the scene, located the survivors and picked them up.

This was the only US loss in the attack. The bombers and fighters claimed 39 Japanese shot down. Mission reports did not specify damage, but later photo-reconnaissance revealed at least 21 planes destroyed on the ground.

Takeo Shibata's combined 201-204 *Ku* force was able to launch only 29 Zekes this day, compared with 42 on the 24th, 48 on the 23rd and 52 on the 18th. The cumulative effect was beginning to tell. Breaks in the attacks caused by weather were greatly to the Japanese advantage. Sub-Lieutenant Fukuda again led, but no claims were made, though one Zeke was lost.[21]

"Wada", a naval stoker First Class, arrived on 20 October, aboard *Kanamasan Maru*, with a cargo of beer, rice wine and cider for the Rabaul garrison. Ashore, he was employed building air raid shelters, dug into any rise in the ground. He worked on a tunnel being excavated half-a-mile north-east of Lakunai, camouflaged with bushes and shrubs, because it had been noted that the attacking planes approached from the north-east, along the western side of the mountain. "Wada" also recalled the warnings. 30 minutes before an attack a red parachute flare was fired, and sirens sounded 10 minutes before the enemy arrived. Many casualties were caused from falling shrapnel, as people stood about watching the raids. The troops were irritated by the timing of the attacks, at noon, as this meant the food was spoiled and the meal ruined. "Wada" never saw an aircraft shot down.[22]

Gordon Thomas: "Contacts with Indian and Chinese soldier-prisoners at this time gave us the information that the Nips were preparing to go to earth beneath the hills surrounding the town. Working parties were concentrating on the excavation of deep tunnels. Talk of another power plant beneath the hills and huge shelters for army and navy personnel and food supplies was common, and gave us one idea: the imminent possibility of full-scale air attacks on our people."[23]

After the war, in his interrogation about the Rabaul bombing campaign, Vice-Admiral Kusaka recalled this attack as the only occasion when airfield facilities were badly hit, as they were not well-protected. Nearly all the 20mm ammunition was blown up. Lakunai was hit by almost 200 bombs, with 30 on the runway. A labor force of Indian and Chinese coolies, with 1,000 navy and 2,000 army troops, was used to repair airstrip damage in the area. Even though no modern construction machinery was available, only shovels and a few trucks, the runway and taxiways were ready for use in 2 days. But Kusaka admitted if the attacks had been maintained, the Japanese could not have coped.[24]

Japan's 18 Army recorded the attack as,

"At 1000 hours a mixed force of about 120 P-38s and B-24s attacked Rabaul. We shot down 16. Our losses: burnt on the ground—22; damaged moderately—8; not returned—2; total 32."[25]

Imperial Japanese Navy HQ recorded 32 fighters and two bombers intercepted the 52 enemy planes, but no victory claims.

4 Air Army recorded losses as one aircraft destroyed and nine damaged, all from 10 *Sentai*—the Dinah reconnaissance unit—five killed and one wounded, and Navy losses as 21 Navy aircraft "missing", 22 burned on the ground and eight moderately damaged. In addition, eight ships were damaged. Destruction and damage to the airfield was ordnance stores of both 10 *Sentai* and 6 Navigation Aid Unit, radios of 48 Airfield Battalion, a "large part" of the repair facility of 14 Air Repair Depot was "burned and destroyed", along with repair, starter and supply trucks, and five ammunition and fuel dumps burned.[26]

The Japanese victory claims and propaganda messages may have been believed by people at home, but the real situation was painfully evident to the Japanese on the spot.

Soldiers of 5th Company, 2nd Battalion, 54th Regiment witnessed the repeated attacks and the effect of massed bombs from US heavy bombers. They were impressed by the numerous fighters destroyed and damaged on this day.[27]

The Japanese lacked the heavy machinery employed by the Allies to construct and maintain bases, and were forced to rely on mass human labor. The Chinese civilian population, Chinese and Indian military prisoners and local people were used in the building and improvement of fortifications, as well as the repair of bomb damage. The hours of work were long, food poor and discipline strict. Local villages had to provide a quota of men for a month of labor-duty, in which the day began 7:00 a.m. and ended at 5:00 p.m., with 45 minutes for lunch. Any slacking was punished by beatings. Theft was punished by beatings or shooting. At Tobera, only wheelbarrows and shovels were available to repair damage and materials had to be carted from over half a mile away.

Charles Rawlings: "All through the white-hot,

chromium-plated afternoon they came straggling home, for they had put down at Dobodura for gasoline, and broke formation there and crossed the range on their own. Showalter and Bearskin came in together. The pictures were very late, but the colonel waited for them, and at midnight he awakened the snoring Bullis next door and brought out some scotch, and they looked at them. They were fine pictures. They showed a devastating blow at Lakunai."[28]

In Intelligence Summary 582, Allied HQ assessed the effects of the bombing campaign on Japanese air strength. "Probably as a direct reflection of plane losses at Rabaul in the past two weeks, the enemy has almost closed down his air offensive throughout this theater. Only Finschhafen is getting attention and the attacks there, with few exceptions, are by such a small number of planes as to be ineffective. After the reported destruction of more than 350 planes in Allied raids on Rabaul 12-25 October, the enemy's total strength in the Northeast Sector (estimate) is 167 fighters and 186 bombers, a total of 353 planes. It may be doubted that the enemy, until and unless reinforcements are brought in, is capable of sending a striking force which would be commensurate with the opposition it would probably meet, whether in New Guinea or the Solomons. However, the daily, light raiding by the enemy against the Huon Peninsula must continue, if only for the purposes of reconnaissance."

Summary 583: "At least 70 enemy fighters heavily engaged the Allied strike against Rabaul on 25 October. This is the largest reported fighter opposition since our attack commenced 12 October. A portion of this element (those engaged by the small cover of eight P-38s) was reported to be interested more in locating Allied aircraft for A/A than in making interception. It is noteworthy that so large a fighter defence would be in the air; assuming 50% serviceability it would appear the enemy, before the attack, had not less than 150 fighters at Rabaul. The estimate of air strength on New Britain, as of yesterday, put fighters at 89. The point is that fighters are based in strength now only at Rabaul, having been largely withdrawn from the Solomons and with New Guinea almost denuded of aircraft. Bombardment aircraft is split (sic) with Army Air Service bombers largely based at Hollandia and Wakde, and Navy Service bombers at Rabaul. It is probable that the enemy must now despatch fighters, as well as bombers, from Rabaul for either New Guinea or Solomons missions. This is another reason why his offensive is sketchy. His air defence of any point other than Rabaul either does not exist or is too small in numbers of aircraft to disrupt Allied bombing."

The effect of the bombing is well expressed in a letter from Mr. Tajino, a civilian employee at Rapopo Airfield, to friends in 6 Mobile Repair Squad at Hyane airfield:

"To the entire advance party of 6 Mobile Repair Section, Hyane Airfield. I thank you for your service. I presume you are proceeding with your daily work in spite of the innumerable hardships and desperate battles. Due to your frequent communications, I am quite familiar with the situation in your area and I understand your difficulties. I presume you are quite familiar with this place. However, I shall give you an outline of our situation. We have had enemy air raids in formations for the past five or six days and night air attacks are still continuing. In spite of more than ten bombardments by large enemy formations, the damage sustained in the vicinity of South Airfield was less than expected. Consequently, aside from the first air attack, there has been no interruption in our work. At present, aside from the photographic unit, there are absolutely no effective planes on this South Airfield. Particularly in 14 Air Regiment (Author: a *Sentai* of Sallys) there are only one or two planes left. The place is very deserted. Total planes now left in 14 Air Regiment can be counted on both hands. The rest have been either destroyed, burned or damaged. Early next month, 14 Air Regiment is to move to South West Pacific Area (sic) for reorganization and changing of types of planes, and is now busy preparing to move. Also 14 Repair Depot is to advance to Hollandia, New Guinea. A part of it has already left. We greatly grieve the death of Technician Mihashi. The name of his illness is not known, but contracting dengue fever and heart complications, he became delirious and died. As for the casualties from the first air bombardment, the late Mr. Kaneshige's remains are on the way to Japan. Mr. Ozaki, who was wounded severely, is thought to be near Manila. Mr. Kimura has recovered and was discharged from hospital on the 16th. Please excuse the poor form. I pray for your health."[29]

To Koichi Owada, civilian in 8 Naval Munitions Depot, the air raids were so common that they were called "regular runs". The effect of the bombings began to tell and when the Japanese guards would leave at the sound of the air raid warning, Captain Sen's Indian Army soldiers would lag, to "get a few things from their ration stores."

The salvage tug *Nagaura* had come from Hankow, China. Takeo Ohara preferred Hankow, as the food was plentiful, bombings rare and life in general better. Sakura Toya, a shipmate, was worried by the bombing, but later came out to watch the actions.[30]

But at Vunakanau, Kazoyoshi Yokoyama, 751 *Ku*, was disgusted to be on the defensive, as the Imperial Forces made their gains by offensive action. Hideo Tani thought China more exciting and interesting, as the Chinese would attack the airfield guards. At about this time he assisted in the warrior burial, with full honors, of five or six Americans killed when their plane crashed near the airfield.[31]

SIB Report 174, for 25 October, reported Navy flying activity at Rabaul sharply increased to 20 flights, a slight increase in Army activity, and several Army flights to Rabaul were disrupted by the Allied raid. In the Navy Section on surface units, it was noted that "Intensive anti-submarine measures have been noted off Truk on the 24th suggesting either (a) an important sinking of some enemy ship, or (b) preliminary clearing the way for a sortie from Truk of important Japanese fleet units." An example of the value of "Ultra", warning of possible moves by the powerful Truk fleet units.

Photo-reconnaissance on the 26th showed 113,000 tons of shipping in Simpson Harbor. First Air Task Force dispatched 82 B-25s to execute a low-level strike on the ships. But again weather near Kiriwina foiled the P-38s and the Mitchells, which returned to base.

Weather was again the Japanese ally. For the next four days no large effort was mounted.

Notes

1. tape, 1983
2. tape, 1983
3. AAF Study
4. This and other squadron reports from mission reports
5. tape, 1983
6. tape, 1983
7. ATIS EP 270
8. ATIS Bull 884
9. Figgis Report, 1944
10. ANU PMB microfilm 36
11. ATIS Bull 715 & EP 270
12. CICSPF Item 938
13. MacArthur Archives
14. Saturday Evening Post Oct 1943
15. Birdsall p. 121-122
16. ATIS Intg 410
17. AWM
18. AWM Bull 877
19. letter, 1983
20. letter, 1983
21. Takeo Shibata, 1982
22. ATIS Intg 306
23. ANU PMB 36
24. USSBS
25. ATIS Bull 715
26. ATIS EP 270
27. AWM 779-3-29
28. Saturday Evening Post, Oct 43
29. ATIS Bull 838
30. letter 1982 & AWM 779-3-29
31. AWM 779-3-29

12

Four-Day Break

On the 25th in its 9:00 p.m. Japanese-language news broadcast, Tokyo Radio included the war report of Navy Minister Shimada, in which it was claimed that in the night naval battles of Kula Gulf and off Kolombangara, Japanese forces had "sunk six enemy cruisers, six enemy destroyers and six enemy transports." The report made other claims for battles in the area, going on to state that since September "enemy ships sunk in this region totalled 18 transports, 4 cruisers, 2 destroyers, and 21 transports, 4 cruisers and 4 destroyers damaged or set on fire and many other small vessels." After giving claims for sinkings by submarines, Shimada went on to total results of Naval actions since July 1943, which were alleged Allied losses of 17 cruisers, 18 destroyers, 22 Submarines, 320,000 tons of merchant transport shipping, 73 other warships and numerous smaller vessels; Japanese losses were claimed to be 6 destroyers and 12 other ships lost. Aircraft losses were said to be 1,813 Allied for 415 Japanese. But Shimada then went on to say, "The war is now increasingly severe. Since September the enemy has raided Marcus Island, the Gilbert region and Wake Island. It must be expected that other raids will be made in various regions. The situation is such that we cannot relax for a moment."[1]

AAF Intsum 150, 27 October, contained a "Situation Review":

"The air offensive against the Japanese Air Force at Rabaul, begun on 12 October, continues. On three successive days, 23, 24 and 25 October, strong daylight raids were carried out by 49 B-24s, 61 B-25s and 61 B-24s respectively, and only weather prevented our medium units returning in force on 26 October. On the first two occasions fighter escort was large but was considerably less on the third. These raids were distributed evenly among the principal aerodromes and destruction to installations was widespread; airplanes, grounded or airborne, were, however, being sought primarily and the assessment of over 80 destroyed on the ground and 95 in the air during the three attacks indicates that they were successfully found. Enemy interception was consistently heavy, from 50-70 fighters being airborne on each occasion. As the enemy has not permitted his losses to halt the flow of reinforcements into Rabaul, it may be assumed that many pilots green in this theater took part. Reports indicated that, speaking generally, the eager pilots were not experienced and the experienced not eager. Only six Allied planes in all were lost, although a number were damaged. As these raids can be read only as a final notice of an Allied intention to tear down whatever he may choose to build up at Rabaul, the enemy may feel forced in the near future to withdraw his bombers to the less exposed bases of New Ireland and the Admiralty Group. The fact that they are almost equally convenient as Rabaul as operational bases for shipping strikes in the Solomons and off Finschhafen may fortify him in such a decision. In this respect the Naval Air Service is in a more fortunate position than the Army Air Service, which, when it withdrew its bomber strength to Hollandia and Wakde, removed not only its peril but some of its sting."

Tokyo Radio, on the same date, gave its version of the recent raids in its English-language broadcast to the US:

"Another spectacular war result was reported by the Japanese Naval Air Force from a South Pacific base. On the morning of October 23 and 24, a total of 200 enemy planes attempted to attack the Japanese base at Rabaul. Japanese Navy units immediately intercepted the raiders and shot down 58 of them, while Japanese ground batteries shot down two others. The 60 planes thus accounted for included P-38s, B-24s and B-25s. In the aerial combat of the two days, 20 Japanese planes were lost."[2]

SIB 175, for 26 October, reported in its first paragraph that "The enemy suspects that coastwatchers were recently landed at various points in the New Britain-New

Ireland area; all bases were alerted to watch for and capture these men." Naval air activity in the Rabaul area again increased slightly while Army activity decreased, with flights noted between Hollandia, But, Wewak and Rabaul. In the Navy Section, it was reported that the Japanese Main Battle Fleet from Truk was believed to have sortied twice in the past month but returned to base, adding that similar action could be expected if the Japanese suspected Allied attack along the eastern defence perimeter.

Information from SIB 176, reported that radio traffic from Tokyo to Rabaul had increased, navy flying in the area was constant and army activity declined. For the 28th, both army and navy flying activity decreased, but army flying noted was between Wewak and Rabaul, while in the "Adjacent Areas" section it was noted that two vessels capable of carrying aircraft had returned to Truk from Rabaul, but the ships' names and details were not given. In the Navy section: "A group including two light and two converted cruisers is believed to be arriving at Truk today, 28 October, from Shanghai transporting troops, some of which are to be carried to Rabaul in the near future."

HQ Daily Summaries continued to accept and report the huge losses of aircraft. Summary 584: "In view of the enemy's recent heavy aircraft losses, both on and over his Rabaul dromes, the native report of strips being constructed on Duke of York Island, in St. George's Channel, is not surprising. Although the report must be treated with reserve until photographic reconnaissance either confirms or nullifies it, the construction of additional satellite fields is a most logical development. Hav-

ing suffered well-nigh crippling blows at Rabaul since 12 October, the enemy may look to further dispersals as the cure for his current ills."[3]

Again weather prevented a continuation of pressure on the important targets at Rabaul. General Whitehead intended to follow the airfield strikes with one against shipping, and on 26 October 82 B-25s set off, but the fighters could not join them due to an equatorial front developing near Kiriwina. The B-25s returned to base.

Though no daylight attacks were made, the pressure was maintained as well as could be with night raids on the New Ireland airfields in an effort to convince the Japanese that aircraft removed from the Rabaul complex were not safe elsewhere in the area. Australian Catalinas of 11, 20 and 43 Squadrons kept up a nightly round of attacks.

A four day break was more than enough for Japanese aircraft reinforcements to arrive and for repair to any damage caused in the raids of the 23rd, 24th and 25th. Rather than send in strafers at low level once more, heavies were tasked to hit the airfields again on the 29th, but even then the weather was not promising. The forecast was deep cloud, moderate to heavy rains over the sea and deep clouds with heavy showers over the ranges.

Notes

1. AWM radio transcript file
2. AWM radio transcript file
3. RAAF HO R7

13

29 October

The planning for fighter cover had been badly disorganized at Kiriwina. Due to a mistake, the 39th Squadron began taking off between flights of the 432nd Squadron, while the 431st, assigned top-cover position, found other P-38s above them, but no-one between them and the bomber formations.

Both B-24 groups passed over Vunakanau, all squadrons reporting good bombing results, with many fires and much smoke throughout the airfield area. An estimated 50 fighters opposed the attack, but few pressed on in, rarely coming closer than 300 yards. The lack of aggression was neatly summed up in the phrase "the eager pilots were not experienced and the experienced not eager." AA was a different matter, with seven of the 64th Squadron (43rd Group) receiving shrapnel holes and Captain Mulligan's bombardier killed by the only piece to hit the big bomber. The aircraft had to be transferred to the 90th Group as the bombardiers "complained of the smell of blood."

"Takagi", a diarist in the South Seas Administrative Unit, wrote:

"Number of enemy airplanes attacked us from the south. Enemy air attacks are growing intensive. Saw our fighter airplanes in action for the first time. Went to see the road work being done by the Hanabusa Force Detachment Unit at Vulcan volcano."[1]

The 433rd had five Lightnings return to base, but the remainder attacked 35 to 40 Japanese fighters at 20,000, who proved eager and aggressive, diving away from the P-38s, then turning back to attack, using the clouds as cover, but only damaging one US fighter for the loss of six Zekes claimed. The Lightning pilots reported large fires at each end of the airfield and the dispersals covered in dust clouds.

The 319th, 321st and 400th Squadrons of the Jolly Rogers sailed over, dropping 156 500-pound bombs, claiming three fighters destroyed, four probables and three damaged, reporting "weak", "not aggressive" fighter passes and fires of burning planes in the dispersals below, up to 15 counted by the 321st, which also reported a large plane, "possibly a B-24", hitting the water below.

The 43rd Group's 64th, 65th and 403rd Squadrons, which had five bombers failing to attack for various reasons, showered 5,538 frags onto Vunakanau, crews also reporting feeble fighter defense, and the large number of fires in the area, the 65th reporting 20 in the fighter dispersals, the 64th four planes burning and a twin-engine fighter exploding, the entire revetment area dotted with many fires. Six B-24s were damaged, two landing at Dobodura with an engine out, while claims were for six destroyed, three probables and 17 damaged, and the 64th confirmed a Zeke shot down by a P-38.

Sister Berenice Twohill: "We could hear the planes coming, and we would look out over the harbor and see the magnificent sight of hundreds of 'ships' floating along towards Rabaul. We always counted them, and were sad if any were hit. They would drop their bombs and easily, calmly, turn south. We rarely saw one hit and were speechless if one was. They never broke formation, never. We watched the fighter combat, but could not tell which was which, so when a plane came into Blanche Bay we did not know whose side it was on."[2]

Several crews reported a Zeke exploding in mid-air after attack by a P-38, and one Lockheed was apparently hit by AA. The bombers deemed the fighter escort excellent, keeping most of the Zekes at a distance. This was achieved due to the quality of the men and machines in the fighter units. The P-38s claimed 18 enemy, for the loss of one, Lieutenant Bartlett.

The 9th Squadron had two of its 15 abort with mechanical problems, but in the target area claimed five Zekes destroyed and a Zeke and a Hamp as probables, for the loss of three P-38s. The claims were updated to seven confirmed.

Dick Bong, leading US fighter pilot, claimed two

Zekes: one in a head-on pass, the other from astern, plus one more damaged. These kills ran his total to 19.

Claims by the "Headhunters" were one each by Major Cragg and Lieutenant Allen Hill.

The 433rd Squadron of "Satan's Angels" recorded six kills, including CO Danny Roberts' 13th.

Charles King, of the 39th Squadron, claimed two Oscars, his fourth and fifth kills. Lieutenant Gordon Prentice also scored.

A roll of color film had been sent to the 39th for use by Tommy Lynch in a test comparing the use of black-and-white and color film in assessing combat claims, as the black-and-white film was proving inadequate for coping with the contrast between the dark jungle and bright sky, However, it was not until this mission that the film was used, by Charles King, as Lynch had returned to the USA. King's two Oscars were confirmed by other members of the unit, but the color film also recorded the action "very well". King retained the film until he returned to the US, and handed it in at Hawaii. Later in 1944 he reviewed the film in the Pentagon with a major on the staff of the AAC magazine. Despite a promise to send King a copy, that was the last seen of the roll of color combat film taken over Rabaul.[3]

These two victories of King's made him the last Lightning ace of the 39th Squadron. Conversion began onto the P-47 after the 5th AF turned its attention away from Rabaul.

An 8th Photo Squadron F-5 over the area at 35,000 feet between 12:25 to 1:10 reported on the shipping in the harbor, plus "eight large fires S end of Vunakanau."

The GHQ FE Command report, produced by the Military History Section, lists the *Kiku Maru* sunk at Rabaul on 29 October.

Under the headline "Heavy Daylight Raid on Rabaul", the *Sydney Morning Herald* printed a report by correspondent H.I. Williams: "In a heavy daylight raid on Rabaul on Friday, Liberators destroyed 20 bombers on the ground, blew up an underground ammunition dump, and with their Lightning fighter cover, shot down 25 enemy planes and probably destroyed 13 more. One bomber and three Lightnings were lost. Pilots in the first wave over Vunakanau Aerodrome, the primary target, were intrigued by gay flower beds along one edge of a runway. When high-explosive bombs hit the garden, however, it blew up, revealing itself as camouflage for an ammunition dump. The bombers accounted for a large share of the enemy fighters shot down, claiming nine of the definite kills and seven of the probables. 'The Zeroes came a little closer this time,' said Staff-Sergeant J.E. Callaghan, of Connecticut. 'They do not really want to mix it. Their passes are only half-hearted.' But one Zero pilot did show determination and made 15 head-on passes at the bomber in which Sergeant John Fratto, of West Virginia, was the radio gunner.

"Captain Richard I. Bong, leading US fighter pilot in the South-West Pacific, shot down two Zeros on Friday's raid on Rabaul, and increased his score to 19. His nearest rivals among American pilots are Major Tom Lynch and Lieutenant George Welch, who have shot down 16 each. Lieutenant Welch opened his score in the raid on Pearl Harbor, when he destroyed two Japanese planes."[4]

On the same page of war news, published on November 2, readers were informed of Allied victories in Italy and South Russia, a diplomatic defeat for Hitler at the Moscow Conference, and the derailing of the Paris-Marseilles Express by French saboteurs.

18 Army noted the attack and listed losses as 13 KIA, 14 WIA, 4 Navy aircraft "not yet returned", five attack aircraft on fire and two seriously damaged. However, 4 Air Army also listed the above four, five and two, plus two Ki-61 Tonys of 68 *Sentai* burned, four more Navy land attack planes (Bettys) burned, two more Tonys of 18 *Sentai* and a Ki-43 Oscar of 13 *Sentai*, plus a Ki-46 Dinah of 74 Independent *Chutai* as damaged.[5]

The value to the defenders of the four-day break can be seen in the numbers airborne from Takeo Shibata's 201/204 *Ku*: 32 and 23 respectively, claiming five P-38s and a B-24 for 201, and four P-38s and a B-24 for 204 Ku, for no losses.[6]

Imperial HQ was not idle in the claims field: "From the first part of October our Naval Force in the South Pacific achieved the following results: 2 aircraft carriers, 28 cruisers, 19 destroyers, 67 transports, 4 submarines, 131 other boats used for military purposes, all sunk, totalling 2501."[7]

The view from Allied HQ is expressed in the Daily Summary for 30/31 October, Summary No. 587: "Rabaul and the Buin-Faisi bases were again blasted over 28/29 October with heavy Allied raids. While 40/50 fighters were aloft at the former, there was no interception at the latter. Nor did the enemy make any attack, contenting himself apparently with his intense reconnaissance. Considering the accelerated scale of Allied air activity throughout the North-East Sector as against the enemy's puny defense and offense, it begins to appear that he, at least temporarily, so far as utilizing his air power in retaliation, is helpless. Photographic coverage of the Rabaul dromes has not been successful since 19 October, so it is not possible to estimate to what level his air strength has been reduced by the Allied raiding. At the same time that the Solomons and New Guinea bases are being denuded of planes, reinforcements obviously must be pouring into Rabaul to fill the draining losses reported there. Nevertheless, so long as the enemy cannot adequately put an air cover over Rabaul, it is doubtful if, elsewhere, he can make a show of activity strong enough to count. There is every reason, however, to expect that main and accessible targets, such as Finschhafen and Treasury Island, will get some attack attention, probably by way of reconnaissance. It is also possible that the enemy may be dispersing unknown numbers of aircraft in this theater, such as on the New Ireland dromes, to meet with an amphibious Allied force [closer than in the Central Solomons]."

SIB 178, for the 29th, again included usual reports of floatplane activity from the Rabaul area and Army transport flights Wewak-Rabaul, plus, in "Adjacent Areas": "Substantial air reinforcements are indicated en route from Japan to Rabaul." No information was included as to numbers, types, units, dates of arrival and so on, but the Navy Surface Units Section reported that "Number 2 Transport Group, originally consisting of *Gokoku Maru*, *Kiyosumi Maru* and destroyers *Yamagumo*, *Nika* and *Isuzu*, engaged in transporting materials and troops from Shanghai to Rabaul, is believed arriving at Truk on the 28th and is scheduled to reach Rabaul about 1 November. *Comment*: Present indications are that this is a troop convoy and that the transporting vessels are all warships and converted warships. If this is so, it is probable that the troop carrying capacity would be between 3,000 and 5,000 men."

The Japanese themselves began to adapt to the constant raids. At Vunakanau, with 751 *Ku*, Iwao Matsuda began to take things as a matter of course. He still feared the strafers—eight .50 caliber guns in the nose of each B-25 commanded respect, if not outright fear—but began to watch the attackers, assessing the flying skill and personal bravery of the Americans. At this time the men were constantly told of a large counter-attack force of aircraft being gathered in Japan, titled the Dai Kessen

Butai. Privately, he believed this to be "mere boasting."[8]

Yukio Omura, also a member of 751 *Ku*, began to arrange his duties around the expected noontime attack. In all the time he was on New Britain he had no leave, and the only location outside his unit area that he visited was the brothel. He did not have any contact even with any other units.

On the night of the 30th-31st, Bill Martin took his B-24 to Rabaul on a night weather flight. It was decreed that these planes would not bomb, but Bill could not see himself flying all that way, 500 miles, without dropping something. So, as takeoff was after dark and no one could see what they were doing, he sent his crew to all the nearby revetments to collect any spare bombs, and any rifle grenades. "There were always rifle grenades, but I could never figure what the Air force had to do with them!" So they went up to Rabaul, "buzzed back and forth until the lights came on", and went on to the next airfield, just keeping people awake.[10]

The 5th Air Force as a whole had lost 27 P-38s in October, ending the month with 186 on hand. Sixteen B-24s were lost, but 234 were on hand, while 16 B-25s were gone, but 264 remained.

Notes

1. ATIS Bull 880
2. tape, 1983
3. letter, 1983
4. SMH 2 Nov 43
5. ATIS Bull 715
6. Takeo Shibata 1983
7. ATIS Bull 585
8. AWM 779-3-29
9. AWM 779-3-29
10. tape, 1983

14

Service Squadron Scene IV

Hygiene required large quantities of hot or boiling water for mess kits and kitchen utensils. Firewood was in short supply, so the sheet metal shop of the 482nd Service Squadron made a petrol-fired water heater and rinsing tubs from several 55-gallon drums in which the water was heated and allowed washing in one and rinsing in two successive drum-halves. A washing machine was constructed from another 55-gallon drum, with wooden vanes to agitate the water and clothes, a five-eighths horse-power motor fitted with reduction gear from a P-39 flap motor providing the power source.

Ringworm was endemic in the area, and all personnel were required to wear something on their feet. One day, Norilla of the 482nd was walking barefoot and was caught by Major Summers, who asked why he did not have shoes on. Norilla replied his old ones were worn out and the supply sergeant would not give him new ones. The Major took Norilla to supply, and "got all over the sergeant", then told him to issue Norilla new shoes. Norilla put the shoes on, thanking the departing major. Then he pulled off the shoes and handed them back to the supply sergeant, who said, "I have always given you shoes when you need them! What's this all about?" Norilla confessed it was the only way he could think of to stay out of trouble with the Major. The Sergeant got hot under the collar, then said, "That's so ridiculous it is funny," and they laughed together about Norilla pulling the wool over the major's eyes.

Films were almost the only source of entertainment, and the 482nd was stuck with an old, worn out, patched-up projector that rarely got through a film without a breakdown. One of the 482nd, on a work detail, was at base supply. He saw a new projector delivered, noted the part number, the building number and the number of the bin into which it was put, then called the squadron with the information. At once the paperwork was made out, and sent along with the old projector to base supply. The soldier on duty denied having any projectors in stock, but after some argument went and looked in the building and bin where the visitors told him there was a projector. And what a surprise . . . the supply man "was stumped. People who did not work there knew more about what he had in supply than he did!"

The chaplains sometimes received new converts in usual ways. Cy Stafford: "Sometimes fighter drop-tanks would be damaged or holed and sent to the welding shop for repair. The pickling compound used to prevent them rusting in transit could result in an explosion in the presence of flame, so the tanks were supposed to be rinsed out and partly filled with water. However, a ready water supply was not always available in the field conditions, so in the 482nd the welder, Elliot, would take the filler cap off and leave the tank overnight, then in the morning pass the welding torch over the hole. Sometimes a four- to six-inch-long flash would result, and the flame would go out. Then, Elliot did it to a 200-gallon tank, and when he put the torch to the opening to burn off any vapor we heard a roar like a 500-lb bomb had exploded. We ran to the welding tent to see what happened and who got hurt. The tank was blown into two wadded-up pieces and Elliot was walking around in the shrubbery in a daze, mumbling about getting blown over the side of the tent. The medics rushed him to hospital but could not find any broken bones or damage other than being addled by the blast. About three days later he was released from hospital. Elliot before this was a rough cookie, drinking, gambling, looking for women and what else he could find. He said when that blast blew him over the edge of the tent it was like he was looking down into the depths of hell. He went right to the chaplain when he got out of hospital, talked to him, confessed his sins and was saved. Many of us were a little skeptical about it, but he went to chapel service regularly after that, stopped drinking and gambling, and when he left New Guinea had not gone back to his old ways." As Cy comments, "possibly the only person that one might say was blown right into heaven."

15

Living There—I

The Allied forces in the Pacific, in 1943, were advancing into many areas rarely visited by Europeans, except on the fringes. Maps were often non-existent or rudimentary, covered with large blank spaces marked 'Unknown' or 'Not Explored'. Further north, but still in the tropics, it was the Japanese who had exploded the myth that Europeans could not perform heavy physical labor in the tropics by putting to work the thousands of prisoners taken in their swift advance. A strange discrimination in the use of these prisoners was recorded in a notice from the Japanese Chief of POW Administration, dated 7 July 1943: It directed that where possible on POW work details, the right person for the job should be employed, but that "those of Indonesian blood, Dutchmen and those of relatively low . . . abilities should be assigned as far as possible to simple tasks such as public works, mining and freight handling, etc. Positions requiring comparatively high technical and mental capacities . . . should be filled by Americans and Englishmen."[1]

On the coastal areas of Australia's North Queensland, labor on the sugarcane fields had been native, but more recently had become European, mainly Italian, Spanish or Basque migrants who were prepared to endure the tropical heat performing hard physical labor to build a new life there. It was still generally accepted that Europeans could not perform continuous heavy physical work in the region and retain their health. Now the Allies were to advance into that part of the world. They themselves would have to fight, and to carve out the airfields, roads, harbors and minor cities necessary for prosecution of modern war. A period of acclimatization was necessary for all Allied personnel, and the climate itself was debilitating for them. Diseases, particularly malaria, would inflict more casualties on either side than their respective firepower. Almost all food for the thousands of military had to be imported, and preservation techniques were in their infancy. Relaxation, recreation

and leave for most of the personnel had to be taken in the area, merely in a quiet sector. Civilization was days away by ship or hours by air. Because the European war was to be won before the Pacific, transportation space was always at a premium and travel to the populated locations in Australia was mostly reserved for combat flight crews.

While flight crews faced a combat tour of so many missions or combat hours, and return to the USA when the tour was completed, other personnel literally stayed with their units in the tropics for years.

The complexes of airfields established in the Allied advance were, of necessity, transitory in nature. (Perhaps if the conservationists and "greenies" of the 1980s were about in the '40s nothing would have been built.) Personnel accommodation was generally in tents, though individual efforts resulted in some palatial tropical "residences", where and when time and materials could be put to use.

Dennis Peterson, of the 90th Group's 319th Squadron, thought the four-man tents quite good, as "they were cool and kept the rain out." Bill Moran, flight crew photographer in the same Group's 321st Squadron, accepted the basic tent and bed as "adequate", but it was a matter of the extras which made a difference, such as footlockers, "depending on who failed to return from a mission". Harry Young, of the 43rd's 65th Squadron, lived in a 16x16-foot tent at Port Moresby, but decided to build a house at Dobodura. As he was one of the pilots of the "hack" B-17 and was able to make runs to Sydney, he was in a better position to bargain than many other people in the area. An Australian engineering depot at Oro Bay received "something in bottles" and Harry received some lumber and sheet metal. Twenty-one gasoline drums, in rows of seven, provided the feet of the building, logs were laid across them, a floor and walls were erected, roof laid, fox-hole dug underneath, and three crews moved in.

No-one looked after the fighter jocks. "Corky" Smith: "the living conditions were poor. We lived in tents, were subjected to continual harrassment by mosquitoes, ants, assorted bugs and numerous flies. Mess tents, mess huts and cooking facilities were protected by screening, to some degree, but the flies always won out." Yale Saffro, crew-chief to the 80th's Ken Ladd, thought the living conditions "miserable. Our tents were all 3 1/2 or 4 feet off the ground because of the dampness and rain. We used four coconut trees as corners and then laid beautiful white pine boards as floors." Clint Solomon, 3rd Bomb Group, was appreciative of the air mattresses provided for combat crews, and does not know how any of the personnel would have lived without mosquito nets.

Like their American counterparts, RAAF living conditions were primitive. On Goodenough Island, base for the Beaufort bombers which operated around Rabaul, the crews had two-man tents which Ted Dorward remembers as "like ovens in the heat. The mandatory mosquito nets did not assist in keeping cool. There was absolutely no entertainment. The only electricity was provided to the messes and the darkness was deep indeed after the sun went down. The only hot water was for the kitchen, and as the water supply came from a six-inch pipe laid from a mountain stream, and was very cold, shaving was a hardship."

Charles King: "Then there was malaria. Not too many came down with it because of the quinine and later the atabrine. I for one could not take quinine, as it made me dizzy and I was afraid to fly after taking it, so I didn't. After a trip to Guadalcanal I came down with a classic case and spent a couple of weeks in a Moresby hospital and several weeks in Australia on sick leave."

Australia, the major base area for the SWPA, was settled only in 1788, first as a penal colony for the British after North America was lost to them. While the south-eastern area of the continent was reasonably developed, the north had a very poor system of roads, ports and airfields. In addition, it was sparsely populated.

Australia was suffering from the short-term effects of the great Depression of the 1930s, and the longer-term effects of being subject to the industrial domination of Britain: the empire (or commonwealth) sent raw materials to Britain where manufactured goods were produced, then shipped back to the colonies and dominions for purchase by the locals. Any attempts to establish manufacturing or industrial concerns outside Britain were fought by every means, fair and foul.

In particular, Australian attempts to establish an aviation industry were resisted strongly. Then in 1940 the British had to inform Australia that no modern combat aircraft could be spared and the best that could be done was to arrange for the Bristol Beaufort to be produced in Australia.

Australia had raised and sent overseas a force of four army divisions, cruisers, destroyers, fighter, bomber and flying boat squadrons to aid the British military operations in the Middle East, Europe and Malaya. In December 1941 nothing in the way of combat units remained at home.

The huge complex of bases, facilities and major and minor industrial firms required to support a modern military force such as MacArthur's (and Kenney's 5th Air Force) was not conceived, gestated, born and developed in the normal span of decades, but rather cobbled together and force-fed like some huge Frankenstein's creature. The selfish attitude of some unions, particularly the Communist-dominated, and more particularly waterside or longshore unions, did little to actively assist the war effort unless it suited them.

Australia's war effort may be gauged by the differing situations there during the years 1939-45. In 1939, with a population of about 7 million, the male population between 18 and 26 (combat age) was 492,000. Only 20,000 tradesmen—qualified mechanics, etc—were available. The army had no formed regular combat units; the 14 squadrons of the RAAF had no modern combat aircraft; the navy had six cruisers, five old destroyers and two sloops.

By mid-1941, the army had seven divisions overseas or training to go, the navy had 68 ships in commission, factories were producing artillery, machineguns and (obsolescent) aircraft, while ships up to destroyer size were being built. The RAAF performed mainly a training role, all combat units being overseas.

In 1943, 840,000 women were employed either directly assisting the war effort or contributing in a supporting aspect. All available manpower was in the armed forces or those occupations deemed necessary to the war effort.

As well as food and supplies for Britain, Australia was required to provide many of the basics for the US military as well as her own. The country was big and provident enough; there just was not the number of people required to extract the produce.

The tremendous engineering effort in the period 1942-45 involved works of all types from Melbourne to Japan, and is well reported in the series of official volumes telling the story of engineers of the South-west Pacific. Volume VI describes airfield and base development, and concludes:

"nine things were common to most Southwest Pacific operations:

1. The tremendous distances involved, in both combat and supply operations;
2. The particularly adverse conditions of adverse

terrain, primeval jungle, and torrential rainfall;

3. The complete lack of existing facilities adaptable to the military requirements of a theater of military operations;
4. The primary tactical importance of the air arm;
5. The primary logistical importance of waterborne transportation;
6. The prime dependence of both shipping and air efforts on construction to provide operating facilities;
7. The continual critical shortages of construction material and forces;
8. The continuing paramount necessity to improvise;
9. The single pattern of tactical operations: the stepping-stone advance."

The report goes on to say that "utilizing its wide experience in the field of civil works construction in the 1930s, the (US) Corps of Engineers had made a great effort to modernize its military construction techniques and to change troop construction methods from employment of hand labor to use of mechanical equipment. Considerable improvement was made in the field of research and development during that pre-war period, in devising suitable mechanical military engineer construction equipment. However, very inadequate appropriations and staff decisions emphasizing a high degree of mobility in equipment at the expense of effectiveness and durability prevented the Corps of Engineers from obtaining proper construction equipment objectives.

"Military engineering practices, doctrines, training, organization and equipment at the beginning of World War Two were, therefore, based on the condition that many of the tasks to be performed by either engineer combat or engineer construction troops would be largely accomplished by hand labor, supplemented in special cases by a small number of highly mobile but light machines. Actually, the contrary became true in most Southwest Pacific operations. The construction program was necessarily undertaken and completed by mechanical means whenever possible. Picks and shovels served mainly when equipment could not be provided."

The air forces were the primary tactical weapon in the SWPA, and over 200 runways were built from Australia to Okinawa, with numerous supporting facilities. Before 1942, design standards for military airfields stipulated a 1,000-foot-wide clearing with paved runways 300-400 feet wide along the center-line, three intersecting runways in the direction of the three prevailing winds, with runway length appropriate to the type of aircraft designated for the field: 3,000 feet for fighters, 4,000 for medium bombers and 5,000 for heavy bombers. In addition, the pavement was to be able to withstand the stress of an aircraft landing on one wheel, that is, the entire weight into the area of a wheel tread, plus 50% for impact. In the 'real life' of the SWPA all these were radically modified. For example, it was found that at the instant of landing, most of the weight of the aircraft is still supported by the wings, and that most severe stresses on pavement were suffered near the end of the landing run, on taxiways, aprons, dispersals and so on.

The best tribute to the largely unsung work of the engineers in the SWPA is probably the words of the chief engineer, Major General Hugh J. Casey, in his foreword to Volume VI:

"In terrain and climate anomalous to military experience prevailing at the time, modern engineer doctrines were applied and improved upon in stride. Much had to be learned, and past training and present experience were practically the only available textbooks for reference. From their backgrounds and through keen observation, these technically trained men devised the means to conquer and harness some of nature's most rugged and violent outposts. Their persevering efforts produced masterpieces of engineering ingenuity on barren islands, on mountains, and in swamps and jungles.

Such accomplishments could only be achieved by exceptionally proficient men."

Flight crews were given fairly frequent leaves out of the operational area back to Australia, for obvious reasons. Ground crews received less leave. John Brogan, of the 8th Service Group, spent 34 months in the SWPA, during which he had one leave in Sydney and one 14-day rest at a Red Cross camp near Mackay, on the central coast of Queensland. Cy Stafford, also of the 8th—the 482nd Service Squadron—had one week's leave in 27 months in New Guinea.

It soon became obvious that it would be more convenient all around for units to rent continually a house or similar in Sydney, to which personnel could go and be assured of accommodation. John Stanifer, of the 80th "Headhunters", returned to Sydney in 1983, and took a cab to Bayswater Road, looking for the old leave house, but nothing seemed the same . . . "things were always a little hazy then as I was mostly drunk in Sydney . . ."

Marion Kirby: "Sydney leaves are still the subject of reminiscences. Each pilot paid five pounds towards the rent of a place in Sydney, each lot paying the rent for the next party coming down. Fighter pilots had to hitch down as the units did not have a multi-engine plane for this purpose. On arrival in Sydney, the pilots would go to the apartment, clean up and go into town, collect food and clothing coupons, buy up a big stock of booze, head into David Jones' department store to buy fresh pants and shirt, back to the flat to change and store the goodies. That evening it was head on down to the Australia Hotel. At 5 pm the beautiful Sydney ladies, dressed in their best, would come in and take a seat, first in the leather-covered seats in the middle of the lobby, then in the chairs around the wall, and after all the chairs were filled they'd start standing. After the place was quite full, the pilots made their entrance. You would merely walk around, we referred to it as window-shopping, until you came to the young lady who most appealed to you. Then it became routine. 'Are you waiting for some-one?' 'Well, yes, I am, but it doesn't look like he's coming.' 'Would you care to have dinner?' 'Well, we might as well, it doesn't look like he's coming.' Each time, same questions, same answers. We would then retire to a nearby bar, have a few drinks and make reservations for dinner, usually at Prince's or Romano's. After a nice meal, lots of drinks and dancing, we'd all end up back at the flat for a real party. The girls would spend the night and next morning they would be up preparing breakfast for those able to eat, then about 10:30 or 11 o'clock they would excuse themselves. About 4 o'clock that afternoon they would return, having been to their own flat to get enough clothes to last them for the duration of our leave. Some pilots were surprised to find the same thing was happening in the States, when they returned there. When the leave was up, the pilots put their clothes in storage, gave unused food and clothing coupons to the girls and went on back to Port Moresby. It was a great life, made only for the young."

Charles King: "As far as I know the 39th never had an apartment. For some it was a seven-day drinking bout, but for many like myself it was a time of rest, good eating and a couple of nights at one of the two night clubs, Prince's or Romano's. There was supposed to be rationing of food but the hotel restaurant waiters always sensed who we were and we never had less than we wanted. Next to the fresh salads the best memory was of steak and eggs for breakfast, something unknown in my part of the US. I remember one leave when I met a very nice and proper doctor's daughter with one of those British double names. I of course asked her for a date, but the weekend was coming up and she had to go to the family beach home north of Sydney. However, she was able to get me a room at a nearby inn and I had the unusually good fortune of having dinner and a pleasant evening with a real family. I didn't get to see very much of her but the hospitality they showed made the long bus ride each way well worth while."

Harry Young: "Sydney was heaven. Or probably, more accurately, what is said by the Moslems to be Paradise. The people were the friendliest, most hospitable I have ever met. The girls, well, you Aussies all went to war in 1939 and we were there in 1943. A girl, if she was 14 when the war broke out, was 18 in 1943 and chances are she never had a date. I jokingly asked an Australian Brigadier at the bar of the Australia Hotel, 'How do you like our American Army of Occupation?' He replied, 'You mean bloody army of seduction, don't you?' Brisbane was MacArthur's headquarters and Sydney was a leave place.

"Our squadron leased a four-bedroom house in Rose Bay. It cost us 20 pounds a week, but that was only five pounds an officer and we kept a crew on rotation, R and R, for a week at a time. Romano's Nightclub was another attraction, as was King's Cross. I regret I never found time to visit Bondi Beach or Manly. I remember beef and chutney sandwiches for tea at the Hotel Australia.

"One day a lady asked my co-pilot and myself to a cocktail party that she was giving for her son who was a major, home on leave. This was in David Jones' store. At the cocktail party a friendly Aussie gentleman was complaining about the austerity, et cetera. I told him about the fine steaks and chops that we had gotten for just one carton of cigarettes. The girl at my side nudged me as the gentleman got really mad. He was the Collector of Customs."

Larry Tanberg, 38th Group: "Leave to Australia was about the only thing we had to look forward to. Rotation of aircrews and maintenance people was very slow to almost nonexistent. We knew Europe had first priority on just about everything. We were second in priority and hence a leave was 'the thing'. More specifically, a leave to Sydney! Sydney, more so than Brisbane, Townsville or elsewhere was more like one of our US cities and the place to stay had to be the Bondi Beach area. We were treated royally by the people of Sydney and it gave everyone an opportunity to forget the war for a little while, anyway. While it was R&R to Sydney, we used to say we had to go back to New Guinea for the 'rest' portion of the R&R. Away from bully-beef, powdered eggs and the like, we gorged ourselves on just about everything and laced this with liberal quantities of Australian beer (in quart bottles packed in a straw covering in a burlap bag) along with Old Corio whisky (if I remember correctly) not to mention the company of the lovely Australian gals. This, of course, before the latter part of the war when Sydney became overrun with 'Ugly Americans'. I remember Sydney as the first place where I watched a horse race in which the horses ran clockwise—where we really learned of and appreciated Australian hospitality—where we couldn't go back to New Guinea without flying under the Sydney bridge—and where we were made to feel that the hardships of New Guinea were all worth it. It was probably the only factor that made the tour there somewhat 'bearable'. At our last reunion, Sydney got a great share of the 'remember-whens'."

John Shemelynce of the 3rd Attack Group spent 2 1/2 years in the SWPA, went on leave to Sydney several times, staying in the King's Cross area, and still remembers "the lounge at the Wellington Hotel." John also still recalls a "wonderful" small town on the coast south of Townsville—Mackay. "What all the Yanks enjoyed in Australia was steak and eggs. Also surprising, the first thing many Yanks wanted when they came on leave from New Guinea was fresh milk."

Bill Martin, B-24 pilot: "Oh boy, it was like going to heaven! Things like fresh tomatoes! We ate salads like crazy, because we were so starved on the bland diet we were living on. It was great, the Australian people were real friendly. And of course there were the Aussie girls to date, there were places to eat, wonderful places to go dancing . . . we'd even do things like go to the zoo, as it was so different."

On 12 October the Sydney theaters were showing, at the State, Abbott and Costello starring in *Pardon My Sarong* ; at the Victory, Ray Milland and Betty Field in *Are Husbands Necessary?*; the Lyric had Joan Crawford, John Wayne and Philip Dorn in *Reunion in France*; Rita Hayworth, Victor Mature, Carol Landis and John Sutton were in *My Gal Sal*; at the Empire, it was *Down Argentine Way* with Betty Grable, Don Ameche and Carmen Miranda; the Embassy had *First of the Few*, with Leslie Howard and David Niven, and at the Savoy the crowds were seeing *Gone With The Wind*. People also went ice-skating at the Glaciarium or to the amusement center at Luna Park—"A riot of fun and merriment!" as the ads described it.

In the more mundane things of life, The House of Peapes at Wynyard Station, George Street, Sydney, was advertising gaberdine rain coats for six pounds sixteen shillings and sixpence—and 40 coupons; David Jones' was advertising lipstick refills "in all Elizabeth Arden's beautiful shades"; tobacco was available from Carreras Ltd—20 "Craven A" costing two shillings and twopence, or "tuppence" in the vernacular.[3]

On 21 October, along with articles on the Calcutta street population, a new government for India, the future punishment of war criminals, an exchange of prisoners through Barcelona and the arrest by the Gestapo of priests in Northern Italy, the *Sydney Morning Herald* printed an American article about Australian girls.

"Australian Sheilas. American View on Sydney Girls. New York, Oct 20. In an article in the *Saturday Evening Post* headed 'The Sheilas of Australia', George Moorad, Columbia Broadcasting System correspondent, says that Americans returning from the South West Pacific give an 'enthusiastic endorsement of the beautiful sheilas who comprise an attractive and preponderant segment of Australia's inhabitants.' The Americans en-

tered Australia on an almost unbelievable wave of popularity, he says. I recall arriving in the exciting lobby of the Australia Hotel, Melbourne. The foyer was jammed with uniforms and comely sheilas, and over the din a young officer told his pal, 'Comrade, this is as close to heaven as we will ever again come.' The sheilas and their families are hospitable and not inhibited by British shyness, and this has inevitably led to romances, though since the adoption of strict regulations marriages have dropped off, says the correspondent. He points out that this 'open-hearted, mutual admiration did not apply universally.'

"I have heard some of the prettiest girls in a warm debate on what anyone could possibly see in the Americans, but the majority, unabashed, said they found the Yanks an amusing novelty, well-dressed and gentlemanly, he says. Moorad claims that the Australian swain is not disciplined from childhood in the little considerations which the Americans accord to women. He is apt to let his 'sheila' get in and out of cars under her own power, sometimes forgets to send flowers, and his affection may be expressed with a brotherly thump on the shoulder. The unfailing good manners of our troops were a surprise to everyone, he adds.

" 'The Australian sheila, particularly the Sydney model, is much like the American stenographer—the best. She is slim, tanned from surfing and tennis, perky, her dresses follow the Hollywood style, and she dances like an angel, he says. To be truthful, there was a period when American popularity aroused some misgivings among the members of the AIF stranded in the Middle East, but this feeling was largely dissipated when the Ninth Division, the heroic 'Rats of Tobruk,' marched home and completely out-glamored the callow Yanks. The Aussies have always contended that their men are bigger and tougher than anyone else, inured as they are to the outdoor, pioneer or ranch life, and the Yanks who fought with them in New Guinea admit that it is pretty comforting out on a creepy jungle front to see hard-bitten Diggers moving up on your flank. But not in a Sydney cocktail lounge."

"Moorad adds that an infallible method of detecting a South Pacific veteran is to approach and say confidentially, 'Australia'? A bona-fide veteran, if a quiet contemplative sort, will answer, 'Yum-yum.' If he is an honest extrovert, he will say 'Yeeeow.' "[4]

Notes

1. ATIS EP 321
2. all personal quotes from letters or tapes 1982-84
3. SMH 12 Oct 43
4. SMH 21 Oct 43

16

'Bloody Tuesday'

Simpson Harbor 2 November

4 NOVEMBER 1943

LIEUT GENERAL KENNEY
CG, 5TH AIR FORCE

THE HISTORY OF WARFARE SHOWS NO MORE VALIANT CMA NO MORE DETERMINED CMA AND NO MORE EFFECTIVE BATTLE THAN THE ONE WAGED BY YOUR MEDIUM BOMBERS AND FIGHTERS YESTERDAY AT RABAUL PD PLEASE EXPRESS TO EVERY OFFICER AND MAN OF THE FORCE MY UNBOUNDED ADMIRATION FOR SUCH A MAGNIFICENT PERFORMANCE

MACARTHUR

2 November

Yet again after 29 October an impenetrable weather front formed a barrier between the American strike squadrons and their targets, and yet again the effect of the raid was lost as the Japanese were given time to repair damage and prepare for the next attack. Both sides knew attacks would be made, and the stress of waiting to fly a low-level strike into the harbor bore heavily on the crews of the B-25s.

Despite claims put forward in official summaries of the raids, it was obvious that strikes on airfields were having less success and now were not worth the effort. Instead of the cumulative effect of chaos caused by raids over three or four days—say, 12 to 15 October—the attacks had been strung out over 17 days, giving the Japanese defenses and supply system ample time to adjust.

The Japanese fighters were not being caught on the ground and the remaining 40 or so bombers were well dispersed and protected. The target promising best results was shipping in Simpson Harbor. A successful strike against them would provide great assistance to the series of landing operations scheduled in the area, particularly Bougainville on 1 November.

But around Rabaul were the heaviest AA defenses in the South-west Pacific. The natural shape of the harbor, oblong, almost completely surrounded by hills, was nearly perfect for defence against low-level attack by aircraft and weapons of the time. As well as shore-based guns, shipping would add a great weight of fire to the volume thrown at the attackers. In addition, fighters would be there.

While some P-38s could sweep ahead to disrupt defending fighters, and others could accompany the B-25s, the dense AA defenses were the most formidable problem. One solution would be to blind the gunners. Experiments showed that white phosphorus bombs with instantaneous fuzes could be safely dropped at altitudes of 100 feet, and it was decided to use this tactic to confuse the gunners and render them impotent.

So Fifth Air Force's plan for the attack was for fighters to sweep the harbor ahead of and with the bombers; the first wave of B-25s would attack the AA defenses and the second would attack the ships. The overall fighter leader would be Gerald Johnson of the 9th Squadron, with Captain Dick Bong as deputy.

Three minutes before the bombers arrived, the 39th and 80th Squadrons of P-38s were to sweep Lakunai and Simpson Harbor.

The 345th Bomb Group, led by Major Ben Fridge, and protected by the 431st and 432nd Squadrons, 475th Fighter Group, were to arrive from the northeast, covered from view until the last moment by the hills and volcano slopes. Passing along the sides of the harbor, they would neutralize the AA gunners with phosphorus and high-explosive bombs plus strafing, but leaving a gap in the smoke through which the following B-25s would hit at the ships.

Fridge's force would attack as follows: nine B-25Ds of the 499th Squadron would drop 108 100-pound white phosphorus smoke bombs on buildings and AA positions in the Rabaul town area; nine more from the 501st would shower 443 23-pound parafrags; another nine from the 500th would drop 96 phosphorus bombs on AA positions; eight from the 498th would release 378 parafrags behind them.

Major 'Jock' Henebry would lead the 13th and 90th Squadrons (3rd Group) to begin the attack proper, covered by 9th Squadron P-38s. Four minutes later the 8th (3rd Group), 71st and 405th Squadrons (38th Group), protected by the 433rd's Lightnings, would sweep in as the second and last wave of shipping strikers. All five squadrons would drop 1,000-pound demolition bombs armed with 4-to 5-second delay fuzes. The state of the tide had been taken into account, and the ships would be swung broadside to the direction of attack.

For four successive days the strike force and escort were warned for the mission. Each day, at the last minute, First Air Task Force cancelled the strike because of weather. High tension in the crews was increased by the knowledge that all the time the Japanese were repairing damage and replacing losses.

SIB 179, reported "aircraft are indicated moving from Tinian to Rabaul". In the Navy Surface Units section, it was reported that "light cruiser *Kiso* arrived at Truk on 30 October. *Comment*: It is believed that this is the light cruiser, which, in company with the *Tama*, was attacked on the 21st off the coast of New Ireland. The *Tama* subsequently anchored at Rabaul, but the *Kiso*, apparently having been damaged in the attack, returned to the fleet repair facilities at Truk."

SIB 180 gave a warning note: Navy flying activity greatly increased, and the accompanying comment was that the increase related to the Allied landing operation taking place on Bougainville. It also reported that "Fighter reinforcements, which were brought in by sea to the Bismarks on 15 October, were divided between 201 and 204 Kokkutais operating under the 6th Air Attack Force."

Admiral Koga had sent 300 fighters from the Combined Fleet at Truk.

On 1 November, "Moto", the army shipping engineer, wrote that he and other members of a newly-formed special unit were embarking at Kokopo with infantry of 17 Division to go to Bougainville "to annihilate the enemy who have landed." They sailed through the night on *Yunagi*, one of the destroyers transporting

the counter-invasion force, but early on 2 November re-entered Simpson Harbor. He wrote, "According to the sailors, the situation on Bougainville was unfavorable, therefore we had returned to Rabaul. After having been in such high spirits, we were very disappointed. However, there are rumors that we will set out again."[1]

Makoto Ikuta, the Dinah reconnaissance pilot, watched the reinforcing Zekes lined up along the sides of Lakunai as there were no revetments to spare, and thought, "Dangerous! What if the enemy attacks now?"

In the harbor, Captain Tomeichi Hara commanded three destroyers, *Shigure*, *Samidare* and *Shiratsuyu*. He knew Rabaul had been attacked several times recently and was alert to the possibility of another raid at any time. He was uneasy at being trapped in such a target area as this harbor, and had his ships as ready as could be for anti-aircraft action.

SIB 181, for 31 October, distributed on 2 November, reported a high level of Navy flying activity around Rabaul, and that four separate indications of reinforcements for Rabaul were noted: "31 October, *Chuyo* brought 45 fighters and 15 reconnaissance planes to Truk; 30 October, *Lyons Maru* aircraft transport arrived at Kavieng; medium bombers from the Kuriles were to go to the Bismarks and a new fighter unit, 231 Ku, may have been joining 11 Air Fleet at Rabaul."

Early on the morning of 2 November, as on the previous days, the Allied force was alerted for the mission. Takeoff began, but with four squadrons actually airborne, First Air Task Force again cancelled it. The bombers returned to base. Two F-5s of 8th Photo Squadron sent out later reported clearer skies and smoother flying. In the harbor they photographed 28 ships: 7 destroyers, a tender and 20 merchantmen. On the airfields were 230 planes, including 170 fighters.

While the F-5s were over the target, the strike force was ordered off, but after the F-5s left, an Imperial Navy force of cruisers and destroyers had entered harbor, from a night engagement off Empress Augusta Bay, Bougainville. A formidable addition to the defenses.

At low-level, the Mitchells and Lightnings formed up off the New Guinea coast and turned on course for Rabaul. Lee van Atta, war correspondent, had spent some time with the 3rd Bomb Group and flew in Dick Ellis' B-25s:

"Our flight position was on Henebry's wing, and our Mitchell was *Seabiscuit*. With all due respect to the horse of the same name, *Seabiscuit* was a rank exaggeration in the case of the bomber Ellis, my host, had decided to fly. It was, and remarkably enough still is, the slowest attack plane in the Southwest Pacific."[2]

Marion Kirby was by this time operations officer of the 431st Fighter Squadron and would lead on this mission. After the inaction of the previous days, they were told to "get the hell to Rabaul", to "occupy the Jap Air Force", as a diversion to the landing taking place. Marion could not start his engines and lead the Squadron take-off, due to nervousness "and to be honest there was plenty of that in my cockpit", but he did get off after the others were airborne. Making straight for the rendezvous, he thought his plane was not gaining speed quickly enough, so tapped the air-speed indicator—too hard. He knocked the glass out and damaged the indicator itself. As he had no ASI, when he joined the squadron he slid onto the wing of Lowell Lutton, who was to have been his wingman, but now would be leader. Clouds were right down on the water.[3]

John Stanifer, 80th "Headhunters": "This was my first mission to actually encounter enemy fighters. I had made a couple of routine patrols in the Port Moresby area, but they were milk runs with no interception. I recall the absolute radio silence and the minimum altitude approach to the target, the B-25s so low that their propwash was like that of a ship and the P-38s S-ing above them so low that their wingtips seemed to be scraping the bombers."[4]

Correspondent Lee van Atta: "It was 25 minutes after 1:00 when we reached our initial point off Lord Howe Island and we were up to our necks in trouble from then on. I knew action was imminent when I noticed the Lightnings were gone from above us. Far ahead at 10,000 feet plummets of silver followed by geysers of water showed they were dropping their bellytanks. They don't do that unless there's interception ahead. We were running parallel to the coastline near Rapopo, and there was anti-aircraft all over the skies. Most of it was being thrown up by a Jap destroyer flotilla we encountered in a staggered line about fifteen miles from the entrance to Keravia Bay. They were running directly at us and I could see the pungent flashes of their heavy guns. They were coming too damned close for my happiness, but the spectacle of destroyers at 30 knots chasing Mitchells at 200 m.p.h. was ludicrous enough to make even a tense Ellis and a shaking war correspondent join with Dean in a hearty, if slightly forced, laugh."

John Stanifer: "As we entered St. George's Channel, radio silence was abruptly ended with the signal for the fighters to drop tanks and scream for altitude. Shortly afterward someone called out, 'Bandits 12 o'clock high,' then all hell broke loose."

At Lakunai, Guard Petty Officer Kikawa was watching the south, the direction assigned to him, using a 20-power telescope. He had a reputation for good eyesight and a sense for finding enemy aircraft faster than anyone else, so was given the most important direction: the south.

Kikawa was anxious when he could not see the enemy scout planes which normally appeared around Cape St. George on their routine flights. His tension grew. After awhile, Kikawa looked between the mountains, a direction he rarely checked, and saw a large formation of enemy aircraft flying at extremely low altitude to the north.

Kikawa gave the warning, and it took five or six minutes for the aircraft to takeoff. Just as Kikawa was into a shelter, the raid began. Kikawa was given special praise by Commander Shibata for his feat in discovering the enemy well in advance.[5]

The 39th, led by Captain Ralph Bills, swept across the harbor first, and saw little opposition, but the following 80th, led by Major Ed Cragg, engaged 60 to 100 fighters, claiming 14: Lieutenants Schriber and Hill three each, Captain Jones two, and Major Cragg, Lieutenants Hailey, DeGraffenreid and Hanover and Flight Officer Evers, one each. Some of these were later discounted and a total of eight awarded.

Allen Hill of the 80th joined Hamilton Salmon of the 39th, attacking Zeros hounding the B-25s. Twisting and turning through the shoals of Zekes, Hill got two and Salmon one, the last P-38 victory scored by the 39th Squadron.

John Stanifer thought if he had been estimating the Japanese fighter opposition it would have been about 2,000. "They were everywhere" and his reaction, as the first Zeke with its red meatball on the fuselage flashed by, was the classic, "What am I doing here? I could be in training or transports!" He was impressed with the aggressiveness of the Japanese pilots and found himself in a head-on pass with a Zeke, closing each other at about 700 m.p.h. "We blazed away at one another until the last possible second. It was I who broke away with a violent push-over to avoid a head-on crash."[6]

Escorting the approaching 345th Group, Marion Kirby in the 431st Fighter Squadron saw the destroyers firing at passing B-25s, putting their big shells into the water ahead of the formation in the hope that aircraft would run into columns of water and crash, but to no effect. Lowell Lutton salvoed his drop tanks and began to climb. Marion thought it too early, but followed and the 431st climbed to 7,000 feet, now on internal tanks. Below them the 432nd was at 4,000 and they entered the battle area.

The 499th Mitchells roared across the target, .50s drumming, bombs falling away, and 'thoroughly' strafed the town, AA positions, supply buildings and barracks areas, as well as parts of Lakunai airfield, where Hamps, Nates and Zekes were shot at while taking off. Fifteen Rufe floatplanes were strafed at the seaplane anchorage, as well as targets on Matupi Island and Raluana Point. At least 30 Japanese fighters were seen around the low-flying squadron, and 10 to 15 attacked over Matupi, engaging for 20 minutes. Four fighters were claimed as destroyed and four more as probables, for three B-25s damaged and three crewmen wounded. Crews reported unusual 'skyrocket' AA bursts from warships in harbor, but saw no B-25s lost to these weapons.

At Lakunai the Zekes were scrambling to takeoff. Photography from B-25s shows some actually lifting off the end of the runway, under the arching tendrils of burning phosphorus, turning starboard into the onrushing strafers. Makoto Ikuta, Dinah pilot, was waiting, engines running, to get a chance at the runway, but the fighters were intent on getting themselves airborne. He had never been caught on the ground before, never seen any of the previous attacks. His duty was to preserve the aircraft and he had been airborne and climbing hard to safety out of the combat area before the American bombers arrived. This time he was to have a ringside seat. Still in the cockpit, he saw the fighters and strafers coming toward him and knew it was too late. He jumped from the Dinah and took shelter nearby, watching a P-38 diving across Lakunai hit by groundfire, roll and crash into the mountain slopes, exploding in a burst of flame and smoke.[7]

The 500th Squadron sped over the town, reporting all bombs dropped into the target area and smoke covering it entirely. Six to eight Zekes attacked, making 'weak' passes from ahead and above over Rabaul and across country to south of Vunakanau. Two Zekes were claimed destroyed for the loss of one B-25 to AA plus one other damaged. Crews reported the harbor 'jammed with shipping' and a 'heavy crossfire' of AA achieved by guns on ships and on the heights around the harbor. The 498th's parafrags were seen 'well dispersed throughout the target.'

By this date, Masao Mori, of 2nd Battalion 53rd Regiment, had become used to the fact that raids occurred around midday, but in this case bugles sounded 'Alert' and the B-25s were over them immediately. Though his unit had only three killed and ten wounded, he was told that hundreds of casualties were suffered in the nearby area. "Wada", stoker on the *Kanamasan Maru* which arrived on 20 October, and who had been building shelters nearby, was irritated at the lunchtime disruption and glared at the white walls of smoke billowing up.[8]

Behind a hail of 28,000 rounds of .50 caliber, the 498th released its parafrags, reporting all bombs in the target area. AA positions in the pass between Mother and North Daughter and in the north and west part of town were hammered into silence, and two freighters unloading at docks on the north edge of the harbor were 'thoroughly strafed'. About 25 Zekes, Hamps and Oscars were reported attacking over the target, making single passes from all directions. Four were claimed

destroyed, three as probables and one damaged. Crews saw two submarines in harbor and aerial burst bombs which threw out 'long red streamers' were dropped without effect by the Japanese.

As the alarms went, Superior Private Sadao Iwaoki, 2nd MG Company, 53rd Regiment, and the rest of the company went into the shelters. When the first wave of B-25s had passed, the soldiers came out to look at the spreading white clouds and departing twin-tailed bombers. Behind the spectators the next squadron roared in, machinegunning and bombing, killing or wounding between 50 and 60.[9]

The 501st thundered over the saddle, across the town and Lakunai, trailing parafrags and firing 26,000 rounds. They crossed over Sulphur Creek and the airfield, strafing a flying boat, seeing Zekes scrambling through the descending parafrags, claiming a twin-engine bomber destroyed on the ground and three 'new twin-engine fighters on Rapopo', strafed on their way out of the area, plus a Betty claimed destroyed there and a launch. Over 50 Zekes were seen at heights up to 500 feet, and three were claimed in air-to-air fighting, plus eight more on the ground, for the loss of one B-25. A large fire was seen burning north of the center of Lakunai, and a cruiser and two transports seen 'densely smoking' in harbor.

Along the harbor shores and over Rabaul town great billows of smoke, white tumbling masses, long arching tentacles shooting out from exploding phosphorus bombs, were rising and spreading, tinged with black and gray where houses, buildings and supplies began to burn. Among it all detonating parafrags added to the confusion and danger for the AA gunners.

Lee van Atta: "We were in battle echelon and only a few yards from Henebry's wing as we strafed the ack-ack spouting coconut islet and began climbing for altitude to get over the volcanoes around Rabaul."[10]

John Stanifer: "The thing that knocked me out of the fight was kind of a fluke—a single bullet into the left engine's prop junction box which caused the Curtiss electric prop to run away. I was in a steep dive trying to get away from a very persistent Zeke and the sudden torque of a runaway prop caused me to roll a couple of times before I could regain control. The prop went into the full low pitch position and would not feather due to the damaged circuitry. With the vastly reduced performance of a windmilling engine I headed for Kiriwina."[11]

Marion Kirby, with the 431st over the harbor, dived to get below the clouds, watching fighters of 253 *Ku* taking off from Tobera, to his right. He suspected that the Japanese would fly down the harbor and pick up the Americans as they left the target. Climbing away from Tobera was Takeo Tanimizu, a young pilot on his first operational mission, later to become an ace.[12]

The 431st turned left and began a sweep across the area. Kirby saw the B-25 of Robert Fox with its right engine on fire, flames streaming back to the tailplane, five or six Japanese hounding it, taking turns to fire, banking away and coming in for another turn. Kirby dove on one and shot it down—the pilot was seen to parachute by other P-38 pilots—and began swinging around for another pass, when his attention was taken by the mass of "anti-aircraft fire coming from the slopes of the volcano, the gunners shooting down" at the US aircraft. Continuing the turn, he fired at another Zeke and shot it down, but when he came out of the turn this time "the B-25 was gone . . . it had crashed". Now there was a Zeke on his tail, but Lieutenant Fred Champlin chased it off.[13]

Lowell Lutton, alone, attacked a gaggle of Zekes, sending down one on fire, but two others swung behind him. Ed Wenige and Franklin Monk intercepted, destroying one and making the second break away. Banking back and forth over the B-25s, the three interfered with the firing passes of the Zekes. Two made a head-on attack on Lutton, but again Wenige got one and Monk forced the other away. Out of ammunition, Wenige dodged under an attacking Zeke and Monk destroyed him. Lutton, alone again, twisted and turned in a swarm of Zekes, and all three tried their best to break the attacks on the B-25s.

Lee van Atta: "A solid curtain of black anti-aircraft puffs lay over the craters, broken by spitting fire and exploding phosphorus shells. It seemed as if the rumbling volcanoes had come to earth-shaking life. Our airspeed had dropped to barely 150, climbing at 2,000 a minute, and we were a sitting duck if the Japanese in the volcanic pass positions had not been harried themselves by the lead we were hurling on our own hook and the anti-personnel bombs Fridge had dropped seconds before. Henebry was slightly ahead of us and the rest of the formation slightly behind. They were holding a little lower, apparently to get the full benefit of their .50s without endangering our two lead Mitchells. And suddenly, amid skies which seemed if they must suddenly be aflame, Simpson Harbor was before us—a bathtub-shaped anchorage barely two miles wide and with an unparalleled defensive machine surrounding its deep water-filled tub."[14]

Around the mountain mass came the strike force, into the confusion and pandemonium inside the harbor. The cruisers and destroyers were unaffected by the smoke and put up a barrage of flak in the faces of the B-25s. Makoto Ikuta climbed out of the shelter, up onto its top, 'never so excited'. All around were smoking aircraft, speeding B-25s, Zekes on their tails firing, AA exploding, water columns thrown up by bombs, machinegun bullets and crashing planes, mixed with 'dark red smoke and flames'. Zekes slipped in to land, having shot away all the 100 rounds of 20mm they carried. Past Ikuta hurtled the second wave, going for the ships.

Lee van Atta: "The whole harbor was filled with ships—warships, cargo vessels and freighters, big fleet tankers, and the omni-present barges and luggers. They were maneuvring as I had never seen vessels maneuver in such limited waters. A pall of smoke and fire lay over the township and Lakunai. The ack-ack neutralizing force had done a superb job, only the sky road down the mountains and into the harbor remaining clear. But the smoke had failed to jolt the Japs as much as we hoped, and black stains of anti-aircraft poked through the phosphorus smoke pattern.

"Then we were diving down the slopes into the harbor. Jock lined up a 3,800-ton transport which crowded our Mitchell out from the run Ellis had planned, and we drove onto a 6,600-ton destroyer tender. Howe, meanwhile, had cut sharply to the left and was aiming for a 2,000-ton transport. We were low on the water and all guns were firing with a monotonous rythm. Dick was throwing all the lead he could as fast as he could get it out.

"The first bomb was away when we were perhaps 50 feet from the tender. One minute it loomed before us and the next was gone. Dick started to put us back on the water and open an attack on an 8,500-ton transport he had already picked out. But between us and the transport lay a 10,000-ton cruiser of the *Nachi* class, Japan's most formidable."[15]

Overhead, slipping in and out of the clouds, the 432nd Lightnings struggled with attacking Zekes. Hedrick and Rundell dodged a ramming attempt, but Leo Mayo sped in on a Zeke, battering it from so close the disintegrating Zeke knocked a wing off his P-38. Mayo jumped, parachute blossoming, protected from strafing Zekes by Fogarty and Rundell while the lone Hedrick gave top-cover. With one engine out and four Zekes howling after him, scenting a kill, Hedrick destroyed a careless Japanese which slid in front of his guns. The others turned away.

All guns firing at the waves of American planes streaking overhead, Hara's three destroyers headed for the open sea. Few passes were made at them, only *Shiratsuyu* being damaged slightly by a near miss. Normally, fire from surface ships had little effect on speeding aircraft, but this time they were passing close and bunched. Hara believed at least five planes went down to his ships' guns and that his fire was breaking up the attack formation. He did not take into account the spreading smoke clouds, fighters and a storm of AA as being the real reasons.

Amid the confusion, a typical B-25 pilot's view of the attack:

"Henebry lined *Notre Dame de Victoire* up on three ships in a row—a freighter, a transport and a cruiser. The heavy fire from the warships at water-level threw up huge waterspouts in front of the attackers. The forward firepower of the B-25s again bewildered the Japanese, and some hid behind their armor plate and never attempted to return the fire. Henebry strafed the freighter and thought he saw some fires before he bombed. He pulled up sharply directly amidships and dropped a 1,000-pound bomb. He thought he got a hit as he sped on. Then the freighter was there, and a second bomb definitely hit, setting fire to the ship. But Henebry had made what he called the arch mistake. When he pulled up over the second ship, he found the cruiser a lot closer than he thought and he couldn't get *Notre Dame de Victoire's* nose down to get his guns on the deck of the cruiser. He saw the Japanese pom-pom guns following him but could not retaliate. He could feel hits and knew they were shot up pretty good. The tail was badly damaged and both he and the co-pilot had to fly with both feet on the right rudder. There was no way to hold a formation in the confines of the harbor, and Henebry knew they were on their own. He had to get out as fast as possible."[16]

Not only warships and fighters were claiming American planes shot down. The merchant ship *Hokuyo Maru*, 4,200 tons, claimed two planes brought down with her 7.7mm guns. But photographs show clearly that many merchantmen did not fight back. Their guns can be seen still under canvas covers or pointing fore-and-aft, unmanned.[17]

Lee van Atta: "The cruiser, speeding at full speed out of the harbor, was ablaze with belching anti-aircraft guns. The eight-inch turrets, four in all, were pointed dead at the incoming flights. We held to 50 feet, our Mitchell swaying and bouncing crazily with each concussion. We knifed across the bow of the cruiser a bare ten feet above the forward turrets. The figures of the warship commander and his staff were clearly visible. That cruiser was big, terribly big, and it looked like a floating fortress.

"We were hardly off it when another blast from the forward batteries whipped our tail up and pointed us toward the water. Ellis and Dean fought the controls together, Dick on the wheel, Johnny neutralizing the rudder and stabilizer. It was a critical moment, and we were a bare ten feet above the water. But already our .50s were chattering again, and looking ahead I could see Ellis had once more deviated from his course and was making the approach on the transport.

"The flaming tracers cartwheeled into the wheelhouse, then into the decks, then into the open portholes. We were banking, climbing, diving and skidding in evasive action and I had to grab the armor plating behind me to keep from being pitched to the floor. The vessel loomed ever bigger before us; Ellis appeared oblivious of it. He held his left index finger firmly on the machinegun trigger, his right poised on the bomb release. The only thing I could see was the mid-ships of the vessel; the sky, the bow and stern, everything was blocked and blacked out. The two remaining bomb lights went out. Simultaneously, Dean and Ellis pulled back on the controls with a stomach-thudding heave. If they had waited an instant longer, our Mitchell would have been a torpedo instead of a bomber. We were down on the water in a dive as rapid as our climb. Our bombs were gone, but Ellis was strafing a gunboat which lay in the path of our escape out towards Vunakanau strip and Wide Bay. Then we were up and over the gunboat, seeking altitude. Again our airspeed dropped and *Seabiscuit* groaned as Dick rammed everything forward. We were barely indicating 135 when we reached the top of the volcanic ranges and clipped along the valley-punctured plateau where Vunakanau lies."

Flight Officer Harold Prince: "I moved into close formation with Major Henebry as we started our run on a 10,000-ton transport. We dropped two 1,000-pound bombs on this vessel, one of which the gunner reports landed in Number 2 hold. The whole side of the vessel appeared to blow out and fire could be seen to spread over the ship and water."

The 90th Squadron dropped 16 1,000-pounders and a 500-pounder, fired 19,000 machinegun and 60 cannon rounds, claiming direct hits on a freighter which left the entire midship aflame, on an unidentified vessel which was left enveloped in black smoke, a 2-3,000 tonner last seen smoking heavily, a freighter which appeared to blow up, one with unobserved results on a 3-4,000 tonner, on a cruiser which "appeared to roll over on its side with a large amount of flame and smoke coming from it", on a freighter with the entire midship burning fiercely, another blowing part of another freighter away, a direct hit causing smoke and explosion amidships of a destroyer, another causing explosion and fire forward of the stacks on a freighter, one amidships on a submarine chaser, and another amidships on a destroyer "causing a large explosion". Other near misses were reported. AA positions, the harbor, town area, radio station and revetments were strafed; three fighters and four or five bombers were "believed" to have been damaged.

"*Here's Howe* had started a 230-mph run on a freighter. At eight hundred yards Howe opened fire with his eight .50s. He kept up the constant stream of bullets until he was forced to pull up to clear the masts. One of his thousand-pound bombs was dropped early and skipped into the side of the ship and the other banged off the decks. The ship sank immediately."[18]

Above it all, Danny Roberts kept the 433rd low, snaking through the clouds, AA bursts and hordes of Zekes, giving what protection they could.

The 13th Squadron set off with ten B-25s, but two turned back 20 minutes after takeoff. The remaining eight carried 16 bombs, which were dropped on four ships off Malaguna and luggers off Toboi Wharf, plus two other ships off Sulphur Creek. They strafed their way across the harbor as far as Vulcan Crater, and shot at two twin-engined bombers in the south-west dispersal area of Vunakanau as they passed. Fighters attacked from all directions while over the target and after leaving it, but did not press in closely. Two Zekes were claimed destroyed and three damaged. The squadron reported the AA positions on the slopes of North Daughter as 'particularly vicious,' and that the shipping appeared undisturbed by any previous attack. Crews reported the numerous warships and the effective smoke over the BP Wharf area. One B-25 failed to return, last seen with the port engine on fire, losing height near Vunakanau. This may have been the one later seen to crash between Vunakanau and Tobera, the crew of which were given a warrior's funeral in which Hideo Tani took part. Another Mitchell, hydraulics shot out, crash-landed at base without injury to the crew. The 13th took still and motion pictures of the attack.

Clint Solomon saw a speeding Zeke very low on the water chased by a P-38—the Zeke exploded. Later, talking to the Lightning pilot, he was told the Zeke put a wing into the water and crashed.

Lee van Atta: "As we reached the summit of our climb I went back into the navigator's dome and surveyed the wreckage of Simpson Harbor. Only three of the five squadrons had completed their runs, but already the harbor was a flaming mass of mortally-wounded shipping. Etched against a background of smoke and fires from the township was a sight to gladden the heart of any American. A Mitchell scored a direct hit on the after turret of the *Nachi* cruiser, even as I watched, and the two vessels we had attacked were both afire. One was sinking, split nearly in half by the force of our two bombs; the first transport hit by Chuck Howe was sinking by the stern; Henebry's initial objective was spouting flame and rocking with explosions; probably 11 ships were fatally blasted.

"Dick was trying desperately to gain speed, and I saw why. We were all alone—every other ship in our flight had long since steamed past a limping *Seabiscuit*. Our wing was ripped into silver gashes and our right engine was throwing oil. We had been hit by two 20mm shells. With everything wide open and the three of us pushing mightily, *Seabiscuit* rebelled at 170. And as we came out of a local rain squall, we ran into ten Zeros

idling at 3,000 feet. They were waiting for a set-up, and it became painfully apparent we were it.

"Over the interphones, Mullenhour announced, 'Ten Zekes at three o'clock.'[19]"

Lieutenant Bob Murphy had been shot down by fire from a cruiser.

Behind the first wave of strikers came the second: the 8th, 71st and 405th Squadrons. The 8th was led by Major Raymond Wilkins, pilot of the sole surviving A-24 from a catastrophic mission in July 1942. That he was the sole survivor led him to believe that he was destined to live through the war.

On the way in, the 13th Squadron had made a change in the approach route close to the mountain mass. Behind them, Wilkins radioed a query about the alteration, but followed, turning away to the north, then swinging sharply back into the harbor. Both sharp turns broke up the 8th's formation, and as they speared down into the harbor there was only a 300-foot gap between the smoke walls. The B-25s could not attack line abreast, but had to jockey through the opening. Wilkins was reported to have hit a destroyer, claimed to be 'a mass of flames and definitely left sinking,' while the other aircraft reported the squadron's 16 bombs contributed to direct hits on a 19,000 ton tanker, a freighter or tanker, a direct hit and a 'very near miss' on another ship, probable hits on a freighter, and cruiser, a near miss to a freighter, and two near misses to a cruiser. Only a small amount of strafing was reported. As well as two missing B-25s, one other had AA damage to hydraulics, turret, trim tabs, engine and tail, and gunner wounded. AA was reported as inaccurate from the ridge-line, but intense and accurate from the warships, the cruisers being reported as "a mass of flame from AA fire." Crews reported about 60 ships in harbor, three large unidentified ones were burning, a cruiser was observed "to explode," a large freighter was seen down at the stern and two near-misses were seen close to another 6,000-tonner.

Hemmed in by the smoke and other B-25s, damaged by AA, Wilkins had been forced to head right for a cruiser, whose fire shot the Mitchell out of control, and Wilkins died at the mouth of Simpson Harbor. The cruisers also shot down Lieutenant William Mackey just south of their position. Wilkins received the Congressional Medal of Honor.

Eight B-25s of the 71st, carrying 11 1,000-pounders, hurdled the pass between Mother and North Daughter, bombing four merchant vessels of between 3,000 and 10,000 tons, a 3-4,000 ton tanker and two destroyers, plus a 'village between Rapopo and Cape Gazelle.' Some 19,000 rounds were fired at ships, other targets and 15 blue-colored Zekes which made ten weak passes over the target. One was claimed as destroyed, but all eight B-25s were badly hit, one being "unaccounted for", one crashing into the bay, and another crash-landed at base due to a blown-out tire. Crews reported one vessel sinking rapidly just off the old wharf, the bow of the vessel sticking out of the water, and many fires burning throughout the harbor. Warships in single file were steaming out to Blanche Bay. The P-38 cover was deemed "excellent" by the crews, and the smoke "effectively covered the shore batteries," but was drifting west and the planes were forced to fly through it.

Six 1,000-pounders were dropped by the 405th Squadron, claiming four direct hits and two near-misses, a submarine chaser sunk by strafing, a flying boat set on fire, a Rufe floatplane, a cruiser and a destroyer all hit with 11,000 rounds expended. A dozen Zekes attacked from ahead but not too closely, as "the enemy tries to avoid the nose guns." Two Zekes were claimed destroyed and one as a probable, for the loss of one B-25 "not accounted for," three moderately damaged by AA fire, with one crewman slightly wounded. Crews reported four ships burning and one broken in two; two burning planes were seen between Mother Mountain and Duke of York Island and a P-38 seen to crash into the water east of Kabanga Bay.

Over their heads, Danny Roberts' 433rd Squadron had lost three, claiming two from the enemy hordes, but neither was confirmed.

For both sides it had been a whirlwind of smoke, planes, AA fire and explosions, a kaleidoscope of flashing B-25s, roaring engines, darting Zekes, tracer, speeding twin-boomed P-38s, flak bursts, Japanese flags on sternposts, small motorboats scurrying for cover, wreckage and survivors in the water, muzzle-flash of cruisers and finally clear skies to the south.

"Mitsui", diarist in the 53rd Regiment, arrived on the *Okitsu Maru* on 13 October, was in a shelter during the attack, and wrote, "As I came out of the air raid trenches an appalling sight met my eyes. Through the palm trees I saw one of our ships enveloped in black smoke and a moment later I saw a pillar of flames shoot up to the sky and the ship exploded and sank. All other ships must have suffered the same fate, as columns of black smoke were emanating from them."[20]

Flight Officer K.R. Ladd, 90th Bomb Squadron: "My airplane attacked a freighter from mast height dropping one 1,000-pound bomb. We scored a direct hit on the stern and my gunner reported debris filled the water and sky almost immediately. We strafed nti-aircraft positions near Vulcan Crater, a radar station and three Zekes and four medium bombers we found on Vunakanau airdrome."

Hisaji Sakai, 54th Regiment, wrote: "Air raid. The sky over Rabaul was dark with smoke. The situation was a living hell. Spoke with my comrades of the pitiful conditions of today. There were many rumors. One of our warships was burning and sinking."[21]

Major Gerald Johnson, fighter commander: "To me, the whole harbor seemed to suddenly catch fire. I could see debris from vessels already attacked flying all over the sky. The heavy cruiser was firing repeated salvos at the bombers."

Another Japanese soldier who had complained of the constant air attacks, daily rain and interrupted meal times had been aboard *Gokoku Maru*, where the sight of lumber from Japan made him homesick. "I gnash my teeth with anger at the daily enemy air activities, but this is useless."[22]

Flight Officer Jack Harrington of the 3rd Group: "I was unable to make a run on any of the merchant vessels. A heavy cruiser was sighted in the southern part of the harbor, offshore from Vulcan Crater. I was forced to make the approach while climbing because the crater was in my path. Consequently I was unable to strafe the decks and my co-pilot dropped a bomb on it when the altimeter read 500 feet. The bomb was observed by the turret gunner to hit into the side of the cruiser just aft of amidships. A crippling hit was also reported by the tail cameraman. The resulting explosion appeared to roll the cruiser on its side."

"Kasato," diarist on the *No 100 Koeki Maru*, noted briefly that, "The ship is flooded, half sunk."[23]

"Moto," the shipping engineer who returned from the abortive attempt to land on Bougainville, wrote, "Around noon, several hundred enemy planes came to bomb the harbor and city of Rabaul. Up until today, there has been no air raid that can compare with today's on Rabaul Harbor. Our destroyer, the *Yunagi*, and several other warships and convoy vessels that were anchored in the harbor sent up a fierce barrage. The enemy planes approached our warships and strafed them. This is the first time since I came to the battlefront that I witnessed such events. Enemy planes were hit by our guns and crashed into the sea and mountains. Four ships in our convoy were bombed. According to rumors, it is said our forces shot down one hundred and some enemy planes. The fact that we were able to see such a spectacular event is something we do not know how to express. While we were thinking that someday we should encounter such an event, we were already seeing it before we were aware of it. Our departure has again been post-poned until the 5th. We spent the night on the *Yunagi* again."[24]

Captain Harvey Minor, 90th Squadron of the 3rd Group: "We saw a large, undamaged freighter transport directly in our line of flight. We had begun violent evasive action immediately we entered the harbor and now we dropped lower, all the time skidding violently. It was my idea that the ack-ack on the ship was firing over us, because we were so low, and they must endanger their own vessels if they aimed directly at us. I could not strafe this vessel but straightened out just before reaching it, and, at my signal, the co-pilot dropped two 1,000-pound bombs, the second by accident. The first hit squarely into the ship at the waterline (confirmed by my wingman) while the second bomb skipped over the exploded just beyond the transport. The vessel was later beached."

Masao Mori, 2nd Battalion 53rd Regiment, did not see any American planes downed, though he watched Japanese fighters attacking. Almost all the dumps near his unit were destroyed, out in the harbor he saw two freighters and what he thought was a destroyer sunk. Afterwards, the troops grumbled about the lack of air cover.[25]

The B-25s were speeding out of the cauldron, and above, the P-38s were also disengaging. Marion Kirby's tanks, to which he had switched just before climbing over the harbor, were empty, and it was time to go. He could not see any Zekes, so flew on until he came upon a B-25, and accompanied it to Kiriwina.[26]

Sergeant Emmor Mullenhour, turret gunner in *Seabiscuit*, jumped by Zekes near Vunakanau: "They started their passes out of my range and when I would give them a couple of bursts they would pull away and not come in. The last plane I saw coming was coming in our blind spot. He came within 200 yards, firing all the way. He pulled away to the left, with his belly to me. I saw tracers entering his plane back of the cockpit. The whole tail section broke into flame and the pilot bailed out while the plane was in a 90-degree bank."

Lee van Atta, in the B-25, watched the combat: "I have never felt so lonely in my life, or so exposed. Armor plating covered the backs and heads of Ellis and Dean and was dandy for me if we were undergoing frontal attack. Unfortunately we weren't and there was only one wing and quantities of prayers between me and them. Mullenhour snared first blood. A Zeke whipped at us on a pass from right to left. His cannon fire snapped into our tail; we could feel the thuds. But as he climbed for altitude again I could see Mullenhour's tracer bullets flood into the enemy's fighter. There was a puff of orange fire, a short, telling one. And from the cockpit a figure was snapped out by a parachute."[27]

Ellis kept on through the Zeke passes until P-38s arrived and drove off the Japanese. Nursing the damaged right engine, they kept on flying.

"Yamada," machinegunner in 2nd Battalion, 53rd Regiment, heard the warning given by the Navy as the raiders appeared. The sole casualty in his company was his friend. From the slopes, he saw a cruiser apparently sinking and a destroyer down at the stern, deck almost underwater. Work began at once on deepening trenches and improving them with coconut logs.[28]

Flight Officer Jack Harrington: "Hugging the tree tops, we escaped from Simpson Harbor to the southeast. Vulcan volcano, lined with anti-aircraft guns, and heavy cruisers in Simpson Harbor and Keravia Bay kept up a steady fire. Eight Zeros attempted to intercept us near Vunakanau."

Sadagi Kawao, 8 Shipping Engineer Regiment, watched the attack, saw two transports hit and estimated 20 to 30 aircraft had crashed. After the raid, he saw about ten men in rafts on the harbor, and one captain and a lieutenant as prisoners. (Author: I have been unable to locate anything more about prisoners taken that day.)[29]

Toshio Yoshio was a petty officer on Subchaser 18, which with Numbers 16 and 17 formed 81 Guard Force. He saw cruiser *Agano* damaged and in what he thought was 'a sinking condition,' and *Haguro* apparently unhurt, sailing for Japan. Later he was told *Yamabiko Maru* sank near Truk, en route to Japan for repairs. Morio Yamanaka saw 'many' ships hit and damaged, and *Haguro* take a hit with slight damage to her stern.[30]

Dick Ellis, in the lagging *Seabiscuit*, finally caught up with the rest of the squadron, who were staying with Henebry in badly damaged *Notre Dame de Victoire*, sinking lower and lower to the waves. Henebry handed over the formation to Ellis, who took it on ahead, while Chuck Howe stayed with him. Van Atta began typing out his account of the mission on the return flight. The remainder of the squadron reached Dobodura shortly before five o'clock, and van Atta was "never so glad to see a strip of jungle in my life."

Back at Rabaul, the raid was seen by people in different situations in different lights. Captain Sen, Indian officer prisoner with 5/2 Punjab Regiment: "One day a raid of twin-engined bombers, about 80, came along in 'V' formation and bombed the whole of the harbor and Blanche Bay. We were very thankful for that raid because we had fish for four days." But Koichi Owada recalled this attack was regarded by the Japanese military as a surprise and a very frightening experience.[31]

A B-25 had crashed near the harbor shore, and from it the tail camera was removed. The Japanese were impressed by this method of obtaining accurate assessment of bombing attacks. Makoto Ikuta saw the developed film; the photos showing bombs missing the ships, throwing up huge columns of water. The Japanese regarded the Rabaul defenses as formidable, but the courage and daring displayed in the attack, defying fighters and AA, excited admiration for the fighting spirit of the Americans involved. Ikuta was "astounded at such bravery in a very low-level splendid attack."[32]

F-5s of 8th Photo Squadron were over the target area before the strike force had reached base, reporting: "Sightings: All shipping manoeuvring in harbor 1405L one approximate 4,000-ton M/V sunk offshore 1 mile Keravia Bay. 1415L large fire S part of Lakunai drome. During this time over area six unidentified planes seen to crash." And: "A/A heavy accurate to inaccurate from harbor area. Sightings: Total shipping in Simpson Harbor six unidentified M/Vs Cape Gazelle heading for Blanche Bay."

John Stanifer was flying to Kiriwina on one engine, and coming out of the target area, spotted a single B-25 heading for home so tucked under his wing, welcoming the protection of his turret and waist guns. Stanifer could not establish radio contact, and didn't realize the B-25 had suffered major damage until it was obvious it was slowly losing altitude. As they got lower and lower the crew began jettisoning all loose equipment including the waist guns in a vain attempt to remain airborne. Finally they splashed in short of Kiriwina, Stanifer called "Dumbo" and limped in for repairs.[33]

Henebry had also ditched. All his crew was collected by Catalina and at Kiriwina they hitched a flight back to Dobodura.

The circuits, strips and taxiways at Dobodura were crowded with returning B-25s and P-38s, one Mitchell and three Lightnings making crash-landings. Some B-25s had wounded aboard and stopped on the dirt strip while casualties were removed. One crashed on the strip in front of Charles King's P-38, forcing another to skim over his onto the taxi-strip.

At Kiriwina, damaged and short of fuel, aircraft were creeping in, the tired pilots arranging repairs and refueling. Marion Kirby checked the 431st. Nine set out on the mission, six made it to Kiriwina. Ken Richardson, Carl Planck and Lowell Lutton did not return. That night the six slept as they had never slept before, drained by the tension built up over the days preceding the mission, and the operation itself.[34]

Back at Lakunai, Takeo Shibata's combined 201/204 *Ku* were counting their claims. Sub-Lieutenant Oba led 21 fighters from 201, and Sub-Lieutenant Morita 17 from 204. 201 *Ku* claimed one B-25 and seven P-38s, while 204 claimed ten B-25s and nine P-38s, for a loss of two: Kaneko and Shinamoto. Takeo Tanimizu landed at Tobera claiming two P-38s. Another pilot, Sugino, who had flown in the Aleutians and at Midway, claimed three victories. Ensign Ishihara of 204 *Ku* repeated his 18 October claim of three "B-26s."[35]

During the night, Beauforts of RAAF 6, 8 and 100 Squadrons attacked Tobera.

War correspondent H.I. Williams, for the *Sydney Morning Herald*, sent an article printed under "Rabaul Air Exploits. Americans Tell of Raid. New Guinea, Wednesday. 'It was like a Hollywood version of a raid,' said Major Edward Cragg, of Connecticut, describing Tuesday's spectacular strike on Rabaul. 'There was all hell being raised over the harbor—the worst anti-aircraft barrage I have ever seen. I have never seen so many Japanese fighters. There must have been more than 100 of them.' Major Cragg led a formation of Lightnings which had a running fight for 35 minutes with three times their number of Zeros. 'It took us right down St. George's Channel (below Rabaul) And all the time we were covering 40 B-25s just beneath us.' he said. 'The channel was a mass of burning Japanese planes, but I saw only one of ours in the water.' Major Cragg shot down a Zero, bringing his total of confirmed kills to 14. All the Japanese fighters he saw were brand new. Some of them also carried belly tanks, which the pilots, also evidently new to Rabaul, forgot to drop when they began to fight. None of the fighters showed the volcanic dust which soon covers aircraft there".

"Lieutenant Louis Schriber of Wisconsin, another Lightning pilot, shot down three Japanese fighters, but escaped injury when one of his engines and his cockpit were hit. Schriber lost his wing pilot, who shot a Zero to pieces in the air and then disappeared. Finding himself alone about 6,000 feet up, Schriber dived to join in the fight and on his way down shot the tail off a Japanese fighter. Still diving at about 400 miles an hour, he got on the tail of another one, which tried to turn over the harbor, hit the water and was smashed. 'I went up to 4,000 feet, shot at a lot more and missed and then got another one,' Schriber said. 'There were so many Zeros you just had your choice. I know I fired at 15 altogether.'

Bomber crews described how the warships threw up a terrific curtain of fire and then depressed their heavy guns to shoot waterspouts in the path of the skip-bombing Mitchells. 'The spouts go up about 100 feet and if you hit one of them you're gone,' said a radio-gunner, Technical Sergeant Joseph Pugh, of West Virginia.

"Another gunner, Staff Sergeant Herbert Baker of New York, said that his pilot intended to pass between the Mother and Daughter volcanoes, but the sky was a mass of smoke from flak shells so they went around. 'Then we got over the harbor and the first ship I saw was broken clean in half,' he said. 'All over the town there was a great mass of smoke, with flames leaping 200 feet through it. Flames were rising from ships too, and we went past so close we could feel the heat. There was heavy ack-ack right down the harbor and we got the lot. One salvo from a heavy cruiser threw us up violently in the air.' Baker shot down two Zeros.

"Lieutenant Hamilton Salmon, a fighter pilot from

New York, joined another Lightning pilot in a screaming dive from 9,000 to 900 feet. As they flattened out three blazing Zeros drifted to earth behind them. They had shot them out of the sky.

"Mitchell pilots saw one of their bombers score direct hits on a destroyer, one of its bombs striking the superstructure. Then the plane was hit by an anti-aircraft shell and crashed into the harbor with its left engine burning. A Mitchell pilot coming in for a mast-head attack flashed past a burned and unconscious man drifting down by parachute. 'Unidentified,' the terse official report stated. Another parachute floated forlornly in an oil slick at the mouth of the Warangoi River."

Adjoining articles told of the intricacies of the trial for the murder of Sir Harry Oakes in the Bahamas, that there had been 200 strikes in September in Britain, with 500 since the beginning of the year on the coalfields alone. Referring to any future settlement in Europe, General de Gaulle said that France has a deep feeling that failure to recognize her rights and dignity would be "both an injustice and a mistake." The US Democratic Party was concerned at the decline in its vote attracted from the population.[36]

Damage claimed inflicted, as opposed to that recorded and admitted by the defenders, and that established by post-war researchers, has been the subject of discussion and writing since the day of the attack. The conflicting information available is included in Appendix 2.

Results of the mission are almost certainly more than what are now official records and repeated by both US and Japanese official sources. Strike photography alone shows many hits on vessels, and a vertical reconnaissance photo of 3 November shows at least 10 vessels burning or leaking oil.

"Bloody Tuesday" was the most costly attack on Rabaul mounted by the 5th Air Force. Forty-five men were killed or missing, and as well as the aircraft lost in action or ditched, others were so damaged they were written off back at base. The attack was daring in conception and resolutely executed against a determined defender.

Losses inflicted on the attackers were claimed by the Japanese Army as 13 B-25s and 10 P-38s; and for the Navy 35 B-25s, 85 P-38s and a B-26, for a total of 48 Mitchells and 95 Lightnings. The claims were later boosted to 200, and widely circulated among the Japanese forces. But even some of them were doubtful, and captured documents include skeptical remarks.[37] Actual losses were nine B-25s and ten P-38s.

Masatoshi Tsuruta, Lieutenant in 3rd Battalion 141 Regiment, was told and believed along with his men, that 205 enemy had been shot down. Goro Taguchi, a Nakajima torpedo bomber pilot, flew into Rabaul on 5 November and was told of the 200 planes claimed on the 2nd.[38]

Japanese staffs and headquarters could well have used the Allied method of photographic evidence of strike results. Their claims were becoming more and more removed from reality.

Tokyo's English-language radio broadcast to America on the 6th stated: "Comment on the Rabaul air raid, Tokyo: The enemy air onslaught on Rabaul was particularly fierce. As announced by IHQ Communique on Friday, our Navy air units, intercepting 200 and several scores of enemy planes, shot down 201 of them in close concert with our naval surface units and ground batteries. Our losses were only 15 planes. This means a ratio of losses of over 13 or 14 to one, the most glorious war result ever achieved in an aerial fight. It is recalled that some time ago, 300 planes in an attempt to attack the city of Schweinfurt in Germany lost 135 of them by German interceptors. This result at that time astonished the whole world. However, the present result attained by the Japanese over Rabaul far surpasses that German victory."[39]

However, even with photographs, some report writers on the Allied side painted overly optimistic views. Allied Air Force HQ Intsum 153 reported the attack as: "Attacking at mast-head height in daylight with 1,000-lb demos, 75 B-25s raided shipping in Simpson Harbor, Rabaul. Preliminary reports list the following: (a) Sunk: 2 destroyers, 1 destroyer leader, 6 merchant vessels, an 8,000-ton freighter, a 6,000-ton stack-aft freighter, and 4 luggers; (b) seriously damaged: 2 heavy cruisers, 2 destroyers, 7 merchant vessels of from 4-6,000 tons, and two tankers of 10,000 and 8,000 tons. Also many AA positions around Simpson Harbor were strafed and bombed. In addition, 8 F/Ps and 4 4EFBs were destroyed, presumably at their moorings, and 7 fighters and a M/B destroyed on the ground. This effective raid was covered by 80 P-38s. Interception was extremely heavy with about 125 fighters of which 67 were destroyed in combat and 23 probably destroyed. Our losses were 9 B-25s and 10 P-38s. About 8 hours after, Beauforts attacked Tobera, with all bombs falling in dispersal areas."

GHQ's PRO Communique 572 described the events in almost the same terms, showing little difference between a communique for public consumption and a report by members of th staff making a detached assessment of strike results.

"Anticipating that a counterattack on our right wing in Bougainville was in preparation at Rabaul we attacked the enemy's naval concentrations in the harbor from the air. A desperate battle ensued. The enemy's air component as well as his anti-aircraft batteries went into full action to support his war craft and merchant shipping. Our fighter cover engaged his attacking planes, and our medium bombers went in at masthead height. The harbor was practically swept clean, nearly every ship there being heavily hit or sunk by 1,000-pound bombs. Before our planes had left the scene of combat the following boats had sunk: three destroyers, eight large merchant ships of an aggregate tonnage of 50,000 tons and four small coastal vessels. In addition, direct hits were scored on two heavy cruisers, one of which was left listing with a large hole in the hull, seven large merchant ships of an aggregate tonnage of 30,000 tons and two tankers of 6,000 and 8,000 tons, respectively. The entire shipping area was a scene of utter wreckage and destruction. The air battle was of the fiercest. At Lakunai, seven fighters and a bomber were destroyed on the ground and other planes damaged. Offshore eight floatplanes and two four-engined flying boats were sunk. In the air 67 of his planes were shot down and 23 others probably destroyed. We lost nine bombers and ten fighters."

The optimistic acceptance of claims for destroyed aircraft is still evident in the Daily Intsums. The Japanese were fighting over an area with four airfields, to which a damaged plane need only stagger, for repair or salvage. Pilots were close to base in the event of going down in a damaged plane. As sustained attack over many days was prevented by the weather, the defence was well able to cope with losses. But as the Japanese continued to rise to the defense in never-decreasing numbers, though they were supposed to be shot down in large quantities, the answer seized upon was that of constant massive reinforcement. Only one reinforcement had been noted, on 1 November.

Summary 590, 2-3 November: "Photographs taken yesterday morning at Rabaul disclosed 259 aircraft, of which 171 were fighters, an increase of 37 planes, or 17% over the 222 present on 19 October. Thus, despite four heavy raids against Rabaul during the interim, which accounted for 226 aircraft destroyed, 63 'probables' and 43 damages, he has continued to flood his New Britain fortress with replacements. If we assume that 60-70% of the 171 fighters there yesterday were serviceable, our destruction of 74 means that 62-72% of his defensive airstrength has been annihilated; if the 23 'probables' of yesterday's combat are included, the debacle reaches the point where 81-94% of his serviceable fighters were lost.

"It is indeed problematical how long this present extravagant rate of attrition can continue. Though his current monthly production of combat aircraft may not be hovering near the 1,000 mark, of which probably 540 are fighters and 260 are bombers, it is doubtful if the enemy can much longer afford to pour such a large pro-

portion of his output into the Bismarks-Solomons maelstrom. Though it must be increasingly clear to him that this strategic base is becoming rapidly untenable, he will probably fight determinedly to stem the tide."

And in Int Sum 591, 3-4 November, the never-ending supply of planes is still unable to be explained away: "The 259 planes (including 171 fighter) which were photographed at Rabaul prior to the Allied raid, less a reported total of 67 destroyed, plus 23 probables, may not accordingly represent total servicable strength in the N.E. sector. Certainly the enemy has sent to Empress Augusta Bay a maximum of aircraft based on his known strength. Also, there have been no attacks elsewhere in the theater. The Rabaul strength seen in the above-mentioned photographs implies that the enemy has been moving not less than 12-13 planes daily into New Britain since our attack commenced 12 October. This reinforcement arises from the fact that about 300 planes were at Rabaul in early October, which total approximates the reported destruction and damage to enemy planes over the intervening period. With 259 planes being found at Rabaul 2 November, the daily replacement rate would be about 12-13 planes. The Rabaul total, of course, would include those planes coalesced at Rabaul from New Guinea and Solomon bases."

The 'Ultra' Special Intelligence Bulletins for the days after 2 November did not reflect the confusion and determined defence at Rabaul. Despite the major attack, Bulletin 182, for 2 November, reported Navy flying declined, with 22 floatplane and ten other flights being noted, despite the arrival and congestion at Lakunai, despite the hundred or so Zekes airborne around the battle. The Navy Surface Units section reported the southward move of a force of five cruisers, destroyers and three transports from Truk to Rabaul.

SIB 183, next day, could only report "stable" flying activity around Rabaul, and the Navy Surface Units section continued tracking the southward bound force of cruisers and destroyers, making the comment that this was probably in reaction to the Bougainville landing operations.

For 4 November, SIB 184 reported the southward movement of the Japanese ships, that Navy flying increased at Rabaul, but of the 40 flights noted, 37 were floatplanes, 16 from 958 *Ku* patrolling north and west of Kavieng. Also active from Kavieng were fighters of Airfleet 21, thought to be from 201 or 253 *Ku*, on convoy cover.

Thus the "Ultra" Intelligence Bulletins provided almost nothing of use about the attacks or the flow of reinforcements supposedly necessary to make good the great losses inflicted by every attack. Of definite value for shipping movement and some Army moves, it has been seen that they were far less useful than photographs alone, and like every other source of information, had their limitations.

Notes

1. CICSPF Item 938
2. all Van Atta extracts
3. tape, 1983
4. letter 1983
5. Takeo Shibata 1983
6. letter 1983
7. letter 1983
8. ATIS Intg
9. ATIS Intg
10. Van Atta
11. letter 1983
12. letters, 1983
13. letters, 1983
14. Van Atta
15. Van Atta
16. Birdsall p. 126
17. ATIS Bull 2087
18. Birdsall p. 128-129
19. Van Atta
20. ATIS Bull 1016
21. ATIS Bull 650
22. ATIS Bull 618
23. ATIS Bull 917
24. CICSPF Item 938
25. ATIS Intg 350
26. tape 1983
27. Van Atta
28. AWM 779-3-29
29. AWM 779-3-29
30. AWM 426-6-36
31. Lancaster Report & letter 1983
32. letter, 1983
33. letter, 1983
34. letter, 1983
35. Takeo Shibata, 1983
36. SMH Nov. 43
37. ATIS Bull 726; EP 257
38. ATIS Bull 314; AWM 423-6-36
39. AWM radio transcript file

17

Living There—II

Food is historically of interest to soldiers of all nations. The climate, basic nature of the camps and the speed with which any sickness spread due to lack of hygiene in the heat and dampness called for what would amount to a revolution in the preservation, transportation, preparation and serving of food which would sustain the ground and flight crews in the SWPA. It was one thing to acknowledge this, but the realities at the time fell far short of the theories.

The single most despised item was, and is, bullybeef. Tinned preserved beef which may have seemed adequate in the cooler southern areas of Australia, Europe and North America, became a semi-liquid greasy mess in the tropics.

Clint Solomon's phrase, "I don't know what it is, processed meat of some kind", is an apt description.

Corky Smith of the "Headhunters" believed the food "was bad—I eat about anything and am not a complainer—and our squadron cooks had no reliable refrigeration facilities. Consequently, meat was spoiled and inedible a good portion of the time, and fresh eggs virtually nonexistent. We had a lot of canned bully beef which was despised by all and sundry, no milk fresh or canned, no fresh vegetables, our drinking water was bitter from the dose of essential chemicals to make it potable, there was no ice, all drinks were warm, our butter came in gallon cans and was like lard. My main staple was peanut butter. Dehydrated eggs and potatoes were there, but terrible, nothing like today's products. Our bread got mouldy and was infested with weevils. Bomber and transport units . . . took their own planes to Australia quite frequently and came back with liquor, fresh vegetables, meat, eggs, etcetera. More important, they brought back refrigerators and associated equipment. This was beyond our capabilities, and no one looked out for the fighter jocks."

On arrival in New Guinea, John Brogan weighed 210 pounds, and 150 when he left 30 months later. "The food was very bad. We had captured Japanese fish and rice, bullybeef and hardtack. No eggs, potatoes or bread for 24 months. I blame this on our illustrious commanders. They did not want to make waves or have MacArthur look down on them. I remember after not eating eggs or bread for 22 months, someone went back to Australia and brought back two crates of eggs. We got some bread from the QM at Port Moresby. It was dark when the cooks were dishing out the eggs, so I went through the line three times and got two eggs each time. Someone recognized a ring I had on and noticed my hands going through the line. They turned me in and I had to go before the group commander—a full bull colonel—and he asked me what I had done with the six eggs I had for breakfast. I said, 'Hell, colonel, what would you have done with them if you had not eaten eggs or bread for 22 months? I ate them! What else could I do?' This colonel was a friend to me, so he arranged for us to fly to Townsville next day and he took me to a restaurant and he told the waitress to bring me as many eggs as I wanted. I guess I ate about 50 at one sitting! One time we traded some Australians some smokes for 12 hams, all packed in salt. We hid them and only cooked them when we wanted a good meal. Another thing we would do was buy things from merchant ships coming into Port Moresby harbour. We would pay $5.00 for a ham sandwich, and at this time in the States you could get a sandwich for 20 cents. MacArthur used to have a supply B-17 fly in from Australia. Every night it would land at about 7 p.m. at Seven-Mile Strip. My crew was always on duty at this time, so we would call GHQ for a truck to pick up whatever rations he had aboard to be delivered to MacArthur's HQ. One night I told a little Italian corporal to put some major's rank on his hat, take a truck, and tell the pilot he was from GHQ to pick up the rations. Well, he did just that, and in the rations was a side of beef. We had a ball for a few days until MacArthur's men began to look for that stolen beef. I was called in again by the colonel and asked where my people got the beef. By this time it was all gone. I said, 'Hell, colonel, it was a small kangaroo. We found it on the runway.' He said, 'With all the fur off of it?' I said, 'Yes, sir!' I hear MacArthur got that story and had a good laugh at it."

In July of 1942, at Port Moresby, the Japanese were coming closer and rations were short. An Australian truck would deliver food to the "Headhunters". Marion Kirby: "A truck would drop off a burlap bag at the squadron and whatever was in the bag was the rations. Fridays always meant fish, or fish was the sign it was Friday. Flies would collect on the mess tent in a black sheet. The Australian unscreened bakery produced bread that was rather like raisin bread but the black things were flies caught in the dough. You might say it was very high in protein." Army biscuits were so hard they were soaked in coffee from "many minutes" before the squadron personnel could eat them. At Milne Bay, the 80th supplemented rations by spotting the herd of cattle turned out to freedom by the departing civilian staff of Lever Brothers' plantation there, when the Japanese were landing. The location of the herd would be reported to some of the groundcrew who would take a truck fitted with a winch, shoot a beast, haul it up on the winch, dress it, then bring the carcass back to the squadron.

Robert McCandless: "I can recall the time we had fresh meat. My sergeant and I shot several wallabies, and we invited some nurses over for dinner for 'fresh meat.' It had a wild taste but all went well until we confessed how we got the meat. Then two nurses were very sick and a couple resorted to fist beating on their escorts."

In Melbourne, John Shemelynce was at the "busy train/tram station where I first tasted a mutton meat pie. Never attempted to eat another one. It tasted like wet wool."

18

5 November

Again the weather closed in, and attention was diverted to cope with the Japanese naval units and transports coming south. General Whitehead had moved the 345th and 475th Groups to Kiriwina, and the 43rd to Dobodura, as part of his preparations to hit either Rabaul or the fleet units. Admiral Halsey, conscious of his beachhead at Empress Augusta Bay on Bougainville, intended to attack the Japanese force in Rabaul Harbor when it arrived there on 5 November. Accordingly, he asked if the 5th Air Force could attack the town and airfields, while his carrier planes struck shipping.

The 5th could only manage to put 27 B-24s of the 43rd Group, escorted by 67 P-38s, over the wharves after the carrier planes had struck with great success. Halsey's pilots had hit cruisers *Takao*, *Maya*, *Aito*, *Saijo*, *Akaya* and *Nodai*, plus destroyer *Fujinami*. *Aito* was not repaired until 22 December, at Yokosuka, *Saijo* went to Kure until 18 February and *Maya* was at Yokosuka until April.

"Moto," the Army Shipping Engineer still waiting to go into battle on Bougainville, wrote: "This morning at 0700 we embarked on the destroyer *Yunagi*. At 0900 the alarm was sounded and at the same time several hundred enemy planes flew over in formation and attacked the fleet which lay at anchor in Rabaul harbour. The guns from the fleet fiercely opened fire and our planes went up and engaged the enemy in dogfights. Five enemy planes dived and inflicted damage on a cruiser. The fleet moved out of the harbour. The number of raiding planes is unknown. At 1400 we received orders to move out. We left Rabaul . . . but returned as the situation was unfavourable. We went ashore . . . I slept at the 1st Company."[1]

Max Osborn, 65th BS navigator, usually manned the belly guns over the target, to watch the fall of the bombs and report to Intelligence. On this mission they had a new co-pilot, who looked down and saw Max moving to the rear, looked away, and when he looked down again saw Max's oxygen hose flapping loosely by the open bomb doors. The co-pilot called to the tail gunner, to watch for the navigator, who had fallen out! Max called and reassured him.

For 'Kasato,' on *No. 100 Koeki Maru*, the attack resulted in "ship set afire by air attack. From today, we become mechanics at HQ." After surviving eight attacks, the ship was gone.[2]

The 43rd Group's target was the north west part of the town. The 64th Squadron went over at 19,000 feet, reporting all bombs on target, large explosions and a fire near Toboi wharf, and 3 other large fires south of the wireless station near the oil and coal wharf. The entire area was blanketed with smoke, rendering damage assessment difficult, but 20 to 25 vessels were seen scattered throughout the nearby waters.

Captain Sen, Indian 5/2 Punjab Regiment: "We were working on the Toboi wharf, there were about 40 to 50 ships in the harbor and we lost ten of our boys. They blew up a petrol dump which kept blazing for two days."[3]

The 433rd Squadron reported 30 to 35 vessels of all types in the harbor. Only eight of their Lightnings reached the target, another six turning back due to mechanical problems.

The 432nd had 13 planes over the target, while the 431st arrived with seven, four others turning back.

The 53rd Regiment had just arrived on *Kiyozumi Maru* and was ashore. The bombing impressed many Japanese soldiers, including Sensuke Takamori, especially as the ammunition, food and supply dumps concealed by the trees were destroyed despite the concealment and the trees themselves were uprooted. The devastation in eastern parts of the town at this time was memorable. He saw nine ships sunk during his stay in Rabaul but did not see the raiders as most of his unit was rattled by the attacks and fled into shelters. The only planes he did see were three Japanese ones taken for salvage.[4] Masatsuga Sato: "At 1100 'about 100' aircraft attacked, and a direct hit was made on a shelter, killing 200 men. Oil, on fire, was spreading on the water."[5] According to Corporal Shigeto Kishida, in this attack 400 men were killed by hits on the shelters of various units. He thought the AA was ineffective and that the fighters kept away, but Company morale was high, as the raid was more exciting than fearsome.[6]

Max Osborn watched the bombs fall away, becoming "giant steps walking across the hills and shore north of Simpson Harbor, and at once a large orange-red mushroom . . . we hit fuel tanks. I saw a cruiser that appeared to be hit, but a little later realized it was firing at us. What I saw were flames shooting out of the gun muzzles."

The 65th Squadron claimed "bombing excellent," with bursts observed parallel to the shore from the Burns Philip and coaling wharf, inland for 1,500 to 1,800 feet, a large fire was started 500 feet west of Burns Philip wharf, 32 ships were seen in the harbor complex, including four cruisers. AA inflicted minor damage to three B-24s.

Once again, fortunes of individuals and units varied, depending where the lightning struck. Masayuki Yoshida, of 1st Battalion 81st Regiment, was among those landing. He thought the bombing effectiveness was extremely severe, as he saw the damage to food and fuel dumps and was told of the 200 killed.[7] Shigeo Tanaka, 81st Regiment: "In order to recover the condition of our health after so many days at sea, the company commanders had their men do gymnastics on the sand. Suddenly, about 200 fighters and bombers appeared and bombed us. About 500 were killed or wounded."[8] 'One hundred Allied planes' was the number thought to attack by Hideo Morimoto, 1 MG Company of 81 Regiment, in the process of landing. The unidentified company next to his suffered about 50 percent casualties, the troops panicking and trying to burrow in the sand near Number 3 jetty.[9]

The 403rd Squadron put 48 of its 56 1,000-pounders into the target area, starting three large fires and several larger explosions behind the oil and copra wharves. Five cruisers were among the 35 ships counted in the area. Five planes received AA damage.

The 54th Regiment was also caught disembarking and Hisaji Sakai knew of ten men KIA.[10] An unknown diarist noted that the unit "suffered casualties of more than 30 men soon after we landed from enemy aerial bombardment.[11]

Saburo Sano, 23rd Field Artillery, arrived on the morning of the 5th, and was put to unloading the *Gokoku Maru*. What he thought was a formation of 40 four-engined bombers attacked, causing about 400 casualties as the unloading parties did not go to proper air raid

shelters and anti-personnel bombs fell among them. He saw a P-38 crash into the sea, and another into the mountains.[11]

Also below the 43rd Group was Masayoshi Iwai, in the pay branch of the Yoshida Unit, which had been in Rabaul since July 1942. The barracks were on fire, a transport ship was hit on the stern, with about 20 casualties, an MLC and fishing boats were sunk, and two of his friends were killed in a shelter cave-in.[12] Yoshitaka Haruna saw three guns near Number 2 pier destroyed, three transports burning on the harbor and thought the AA ineffective.[13]

Looking down through the belly gun hatch, Max Osborn "saw a Tony coming in view beneath and in front of us, so I let loose and noted him flying straight into my tracers, but he nosed up just before they hit him and shot into us. Later we found he had cut the fuel transfer hose at the top of the bomb bay, as the doors were still open."

The P-38 escort was above the bombers, mixing with numbers of apparently disorganized Zekes and Hamps. At 24,000 feet the 39th Squadron engaged 20 Japanese flying loosely, in no particular formation, claiming one as probable. The 9th Squadron lost one P-38, claiming two Zekes from a group "in very poor condition and the pilots were very inexperienced and unwilling." Dick Bong dived, coming in astern, and shot down both. The 80th Squadron swept across the area, saw Zekes in the distance but had no combat, and reported Rabaul township 'smoking and burning.'

On this day the 201/204 *Ku* could operate only 24 fighters, 201 sending 13 led by Acting Sub-Lieutenant Aiso, and 204 launching 11 led by Acting Sub-Lieutenant Isozaki. Together they claimed four P-38s and five TBFs.[14]

Charles King had the 39th Squadron engaging, bouncing 15 Zekes, claiming two probables and a damaged. Camera gun film showed the canopy shot completely off one. A claim for a definite kill of the third Zeke was not made, as a flight leader saw the Japanese pullout the badly-hit, diving Zeke just over the trees.

One P-38 was skillfully shot down right out of the middle of a formation. This was Alfonse Quinnones, on his first mission, flying as wingman in the middle of a 39th Squadron flight, when a Japanese of exceptional ability fired a deflection burst which downed him. Fortunately—or unfortunately, depending on one's view of POW life in Rabaul—Quinnones escaped from the destroyed Lightning before it hit the ground. He was one of the small group who survived both Japanese imprisonment and Allied bombs, until freed in September 1945.

The Japanese version of the attack claimed 84 US aircraft of the "148 attackers" for a loss of four. Fifty-one victories were claimed by fighters.[15] Their captured records contain differing figures, giving Army casualties of between 100 and 120 killed and the same wounded, 20 landing craft, 15 houses and 10 trucks damaged. Navy losses were "under investigation."[16]

HQs Daily Summary 593 for 5-6 November, again addressed the problem of the never-decreasing numbers of Japanese fighters over Rabaul. "The continued presence of from 70 to 100 enemy fighters over Rabaul at the time of Allied raids strongly indicates several possibilities; that reinforcements are continuing to pour in, that at the same time large numbers of aircraft may be dispersed elsewhere in New Britain and New Ireland. The Allied fighters are reported to have destroyed 50 or more fighters in intercept combat again and again, yet there is no appreciable decline in the air opposition. Photographs showed 171 fighters at Rabaul 2 November, but that afternoon Allied fighters met and destroyed a reported, probable total of 90 fighters. Yesterday, between 72 and 100 fighters were aloft. Even assuming an improbable 75% serviceability, there were certainly more than 130 fighters in the area. This would represent a replacement of 60 planes in three days. Quite obviously the enemy has no intention, within his limitations, of abandoning Rabaul to Allied strikes as he has done with his Bougainville bases. Wewak, on the other hand, got fighter protection yesterday. More likely, the enemy will continue to maintain a strong defence of Rabaul."

(Subsequent evaluation of the victory claims resulted in heavy reductions. The most shootdowns *credited* to fighters over Rabaul was 40, on 24 October.) In the night, RAAF No. 8 Squadron sent four Beauforts to attack with torpedoes. Each aircraft attacked individually. The leader, Flight Lieutenant Quinn, attacked at 10:04 pm, an unidentified ship at a jetty on the northeast corner of Keravia Bay. As the bomber made its approach, it was picked up by a searchlight dead ahead, and although the torpedo ran true, results could not be observed because of the glare from the light. The second aircraft attacked a "Fox Uncle" in Keravia Bay, making an unopposed run but the torpedo was observed to 'hook to port shortly after entering the water' and missed. The third aircraft claimed a probable hit on a cruiser near the Beehives, attacking through the glare of two searchlights from the target, and three each from Matupi and Vulcan, as well as slight inaccurate AA. The Beaufort crews reported a large quantity of smoke hanging over Simpson Harbor, and observed the bombing of other RAAF aircraft at Vunakanau, where a large fire was seen.

Michio Yamada, a driver at Rabaul Hospital, was told that torpedoes had run ashore.[17]

The Vunakanau attack was made by four Beauforts of RAAF 100 Squadron. Only three reached the target, attacking the dispersal and dump area, starting three large fires in the north and northwest dispersal area. After the first bomb exploded, the flarepath was lit and aircraft were seen to take off. At 9:54 pm 30 miles away a large explosion was observed from the location of Keravia Bay.

The SIB for the 5th, No. 185, reported Navy flying activity had increased, 26 of the 52 flights noted being floatplane reconnaissance, while the others appeared to be operating from Vunakanau, probably over Bougainville. Army activity was low, mainly between Hollandia and Wewak. SIB 186 observed that Navy flying decreased, Army activity remained low, but a long-range reconnaissance aircraft from Rabaul was noted over New Guinea. In 'Adjacent Areas,' it noted that aircraft flying from Kavieng to Vunakanau were to carry torpedoes. The Navy Section reported the 2nd Fleet Commander "is known to have arrived at Rabaul with the cruiser task force which arrived during the past week," and that it was "believed" that all the transports at Rabaul would return to Truk for more transport duties; *Gokoku Maru*, *Naka* and *Isuzu* "are believed" to have arrived at Rabaul on the morning of 5 November shortly before the attack by the carrier planes; "fair evidence" existed that heavy cruiser *Myoko* had been damaged in Rabaul during the past week; and that after the carrier plane attack, cruiser *Chokai* returned to Truk, with the *Comment*: "There is insufficient factual information upon which to base an accurate estimate as to the net warship strength now remaining in the Rabaul area subsequent to the air and naval actions of the past week."

Notes

1. Moto
2. Kasato
3. Lancaster Report
4. AWM 779-3-29
5. AWM 779-3-29
6. ATIS Intg 350
7. ATIS Intg 350
8. letter, 1982
9. ATIS Intg 432
10. ATIS Bull 650
11. ATIS Bull 617
12. AWM 779-3-29
13. AWM 779-3-29
14. AWM 779-3-29
15. Takeo Shibata, 1983
16. ATIS Bull 672
17. ATIS EP270 & Bull 716
18. AWM 779-3-38

19

The Service Squadron Scene V

Bravery was not confined to, or demonstrated solely by, combat troops and flight crews, Cy Stafford, 8th Service Group: "One day a B-24 was taking off on a bombing mission and the left engines cut out as it was lifting off. It crashed about 100 yards off the left end of the runway and caught fire. All except one of the gunners in the rear got out, but that gunner's leg was caught in the warped fuselage. Our boys driving the C-2 wrecker reeled out the tow cable and were trying to pull the metal away so the boy could free his leg. The fire spread into the bomb bay, and the trapped gunner begged the two rescuers to run for their own lives, as the bombs would blow up. They worked as long as possible, but could not free him, ran and dived flat just as the plane blew up, flying pieces of the B-24 went over them, taking out all the windows in the wrecker and damaging the radiator. The two boys were not injured, but grieved because they could not save the gunner's life."

One of the 482nd Service Squadron, Hurusich, was a good mechanic and became fairly proficient at flying the small L-19, until the CO placed a notice on the board to the effect that an enlisted man was flying an L-19 and would be court-martialled when caught. But Hurusich's adventures were not over. Alone, he was working on an L-19's engine, and pulled the propellor through manually, as required to start it. The engine began to run faster than he had intended, and as the chocks had been removed the small plane began to taxi. Hurusich ran around to climb into the cockpit, but "as he was getting in his foot slipped, and his right foot got caught in the fork of the right wing strut and there he was running on his left foot trying to pull himself up enough to hit the throttle to stop the engine. We kidded him about not having a licence to chase aircraft," Cy recalls.

20

Living There III

In contrast to the glowing spirit of international friendship in the "sheilas" item, the *Herald* carried an article on 2 November headed "Sordid Night Life" and "Immorality and Drink" by an unnamed Special Reporter: "Unseemly conduct by Servicemen and young girls in various stages of intoxication in the city streets during the early hours of the morning is causing much concern to police and volunteer welfare workers, and attention is again being given to nightclubs and cabarets which remain open until 2 a.m. It was thought that when police closed hamburger shops at midnight, a ban was placed on the hire of taxis after 12:30 a.m., except for urgent transport, and the brown-out was lifted, an effective check would be given to happenings that had been the subject of serious complaint. The closing of hamburger shops has removed some of the rendezvous of the undesirables who were robbing Servicemen, and police say the absence of taxi transport has curbed the operations of women who lured Servicemen to flats with the object of robbing them.

"But the city's night life is still marred by wanton behaviour that is causing the moral degradation of young girls and is threatening the morals and physique of young Servicemen. The ages of the girls concerned average from 16 to 21."

The article went on to describe scenes outside nightclubs and along the streets, where girls were seen resting their 'drink-sodden' heads on their knees; on the 2 a.m. tram to Vaucluse on which women from a 'low city nightclub' insult other passengers; and one girl who had discovered it was easier to make money 'meeting' soldiers at the entrance to Town Hall Station rather than going to work in a factory.

In the adjoining column of the page were smaller items describing how the organizers of a "charity dance" were fined 170 pounds for selling alcoholic drinks without a licence, and the licencee of the Crite-

rion Hotel in Liverpool Street was charged with having 15 gallons of "illicit spirits" on the premises.

The entertainment world had not yet experienced the explosion to come from LP records, television and cassettes. 78-rpm records, films and personal appearances, along with radio, were the means by which stars were known to the public. Pop tunes of 1943 were on a narrower field than today's. There was no Top 100. The Hit Parade had eight tunes. In Australia, the only Hit Parade functioning at the time was Allan Toohey's "Ashley's Choice." Australian releases were augmented by Toohey acquiring discs from Americans and so widening the variety available. It was an era when Victor Sylvester had over 200 releases—twice as many as Bing Crosby. Joe Loss had over 80, Harry Roy over 70 and the New Mayfair Dance Orchestra over 50. The great American influence on Australian music and listening tastes had barely begun. Songs popular at the time were *Praise The Lord And Pass The Ammunition* by Dick Bentley; *As Time Goes By*, Eric Winstone and his Orchestra; *Blueberry Hill*, by Glenn Miller. The Hit Parade of October-November 1943, from the local radio stations, would have been:

1. *White Christmas*   Bing Crosby
2. *Why Don't We Do This More Often*   The Andrew Sisters
3. *When The Lights Go On Again*   Vera Lynn, also Vaughn Monroe
4. *Elmer's Tune*   Glenn Miller Orchestra
5. *White Cliffs Of Dover*   Jean Cerchi (Australia's Deanna Durbin Contest winner), also the London Piano Accordeon Band
6. *Be Careful, It's My Heart*   Bing Crosby
7. *Jingle Jangle Jingle*   Gene Autry

8. *There Are Such
Things*   Harry Roy and his Orchestra

The 3rd Attack Group had two extra aircraft, an A-20 named *Steak and Eggs*, and B-25 *Fat Cat*. Recalls John Shemelynce: "These two were assembled from crashed aircraft by maintenance personnel, thus they didn't show up in higher HQ. They were used to haul fresh food, mostly meat, from Australia, along with other items. One item was a portable sawmill which someone located in Australia. It served two purposes— lumber for our own use and lumber to barter with other units who may have some item we wanted. We also acquired an icecream machine. Later higher HQ found out about these aircraft and made the unit covert them to bombers."[2]

Notes

1. letter, Lyall Richardson 15 Oct 82
2. letter, 1983

21

Final Missions: 7 and 11 November

The heavies returned on the 7th, attacking Rapopo. They had set off again on the 6th, but the old enemy, weather, forced a return. The 90th Group's B-24s pounded the airfield despite fighter interception.

From 24,000 feet eight Liberators of the leading 319th Squadron dropped 56 1,000-pound demolition bombs fitted with instantaneous fuses across the northern and western dispersal areas, noting one large and several smaller fires after bombing. Results were not accurately assessed due to heavy fighter interception over the target by 60 Zekes and Oscars. As well as claiming eight destroyed and two probables, the 319th saw three Zekes shot down by P-38s go into the water.

Aircraft identification in the midst of a bombing attack was not always perfect, and the raiders were thought to be B-17s by Sergeant-Major Chiji Ishihara of the 53rd Regiment's 2nd Field Hospital, who also believed the attack went on for 30 minutes but caused slight damage. He watched the fighter interception, and was later told that 50 enemy and 12 Japanese planes were shot down. Around the shores were three freighters beached as a result of previous raids.[1]

The 400th Squadron, following at 22,000 feet, had six planes dropping 42 more bombs across the airfield from northeast to southwest, and was attacked by fighters just after bombing. Aerial burst phosphorus bombs were dropped on the formation by Japanese aircraft circling overhead, but no B-24s were lost or badly damaged by them. The P-38s kept the attackers from making accurate passes. Though AA was heavy and accurate, mostly from warships, only the lead plane was hit, by three fragments.

The P-38 escort was busy keeping Japanese fighters away from the bombers. Some 60 Zekes were seen in various formations, some just circling. The 9th Squadron pounced in pairs, yo-yoing through the Japanese formations, losing one P-38 for one Japanese. The 9th pilots counted 50 aerial bombs dropped on the B-24s. The 39th lost two, one pilot bailing out for a single Zeke "probably destroyed," engaging new, shiny fighters.

Dick Bong and his wingman, Stanley Johnson, attacked about 10 Zeros hounding a single P-38 flown by Lieutenant Moore, saving him, but Johnson was lost. Later, alone, Bong again attacked a gaggle of Japanese who were onto another single P-38, distracting them and allowing the Lightning to escape. Takesaburo Sasaki, a member of 101 Naval Pioneer Unit, saw what he thought to be 300 B-24s and P-38s, of which he was told 60 were shot down. He saw one Lightning crash into the sea, the pilot bale out to be taken prisoner, another crash into the mountain and a third hit by 25mm flak, with no survivors.[2]

Major "Porky" Cragg led nine "Headhunters," taking them down into an estimated 100 Japanese. Soon the P-38s were maneuvering violently through the bunches of Zekes. Cy Homer made at least nine attacks, diving and climbing through the shoals of Mitsubishis, sending two down. Three Japanese were claimed destroyed for one P-38 lost. Two others limped back on one engine.

After bombing from 21,500 feet with 34 bombs, the 320th's six Liberators were attacked by 25 to 30 fighters—mostly Zekes and a few Tonys—all the way to Wide Bay, claiming five Zekes destroyed, two Zekes and a Tony probably destroyed and a Zeke damaged. Fighter attacks came from all directions but were not pressed to close range. Though smoke covered the area, bombing results were claimed to be excellent, with a large fire, possibly fuel, burning in the east dispersal area. Once again aerial burst bombs were dropped on the heavies, but no damage was suffered by the Americans.

Captain Sen, 5/2 Punjab Regiment: "We saw a lot of Jap planes come down, with Jap pilots in parachutes.

The Jap pilots got a Lightning one day and the pilot got out by parachute. The Japs machinegunned him into the sea and no boat picked him up."[3]

Last to bomb was the 321st: six B-24s from 20,000 feet, with 33 1,000-pounders into the target. Just prior to bombing, at least eight aerial bombs burst ineffectively 300 to 500 feet above the formation. Forty Japanese planes were seen over the harbor, and about 20 Zekes, Hamps, Tonys and Oscars attacked, though their fighter passes were not closely coordinated or pressed to close range. No B-24 was lost, two fighters were claimed as probables and one damaged. All squadrons reported sighting of various numbers of cruisers, destroyers and other shipping in the vicinity of the target.

Marion Kirby was "escorting B-24s along south coast, almost to New Ireland, then we turn onto the target, continuing on to the south. On this mission I came closest to being shot down." The weather was relatively clear over the target. Seeing a Zero to the right, Kirby swung and began firing. His wingman, Charles Samms, slid below Kirby as Kirby turned toward the Japanese, moving into a trailing position, right into the ejected shell cases from his leader's guns. The cockpit was struck by the brass, splintering the glass and blinding Samms, who, in shock, began firing and shouting. Samms' guns were so close to the belly of Kirby's P-38 that the muzzle blast was clearly felt in the cockpit. By talking to Samms, Kirby calmed him, and guided him out of the combat area, getting him flying straight and level, until Samms' sight returned. It was only after the story was pieced together late that Kirby realized what had happened, and "it literally scared the hell" out of him. It was his last mission to Rabaul.[4]

Japanese losses for the 7th in 4 Air Army's records are six airplanes burned and one missing, plus three people killed. Again it is doubtful if the reports are full and correct.[5]

HQ Daily Summary described the raid and again addressed the problem of accurately assessing enemy losses in Summary 595, 7/8 November. "Yesterday's strike on Rabaul was met by 50-60 fighters. Again the enemy suffered substantial losses in combat, 23 planes— 38-46% of his defending force—being shot down and eight more probably destroyed. In addition, nine bombers and three fighters were demolished on the ground. His position in these attrition actions is deteriorating. As photographic interpretations are not now forthcoming from forward echelons, an accurate estimate of his strength and allocation of aircraft among the Rabaul dromes is not feasible. Due to recent Allied air pressure at Rabaul fields, it is possible that he is now dispersing a portion of his planes to bases in New Ireland where they are more secure from Allied bomber attacks, and may be maintaining something of an air patrol over Rabaul. The fact that his air defence continues strong, in numbers of fighters sent up, is indicative that replacements continue to arrive in the area."

Claims by the Japanese include the New Guinea area:

"7 Nov—Eighteen fighters and nine medium bombers raided Nadzab and destroyed 60 small-type airplanes on the ground. On their return trip they encountered three squadrons of enemy fighters and scored the following results: five F4F and one P-40 shot down by the fighters and ten P-40s (three probables) shot down by our bombers. Our losses—two fighters and two bombers, two fighters not yet returned, one bomber made forced landing."[6]

For the same day a mission by 26 fighters claimed three P-40s and a B-26 over Nadzab, Madang and Hansa. On 9 November, four P-38s and eight B-25s were claimed shot down at Alexishafen, while on the 10th, 12 B-25s and a B-26 were claimed in th same area. Japanese losses were five bombers and three fighters burned on the ground. An Imperial GHQ Announcement of 8 November claimed 18 Allied planes were shot down and 50 destroyed at Nadzab and Marata Island, for a loss of seven Japanese planes.

An Imperial HQ Intelligence Report lists results of a Navy Air Force attack on Allied forces south of Bougainville on the morning of 8 November:

Battleships	sunk	3	Severely damaged, on fire	1
Cruisers	sunk	2	Severely damaged	3
Destroyers	sunk	3	Severely damaged	3
Transports	sunk	4	Severely damaged	1
Aircraft shot down:	12 at least		Losses (Japanese)	16 planes

Before the next attack, SIBs contained little of value on air strength and intentions, and that on surface units was contradictory. SIB 187, 7 November, reported a decline in Navy flying and Army activity constant, but commented that photography showed strength increases at Wewak. The Navy Section contained more of note. Japanese losses were "definitely determined" for the night naval action off Cape Moltke, Bougainville: Cruiser *Sendai* sunk, cruisers *Haguro* and *Myoko* damaged and these two further damaged during the air strike of 2 November. The report continued, "It is believed" that cruisers *Isuzu* and *Naka*, plus *Gokoku Maru*, departed Rabaul for Truk on 6 November. Also the report said the Commander 2nd Fleet, Kurita, may have been in Rabaul or may have been returning to Truk; "there is evidence to indicate" Commander 3rd Fleet had been at Rabaul; all shipboard bombers at Kavieng flew to Rabaul on the 6th, carrying torpedoes. SIB 188 informed that Navy flying increased, while Army declined, and further air reinforcements for Rabaul were "indicated moving southwards". Again the Navy Section contained detailed information on shipping losses and damage from recent actions in the area, though the results were admitted "not definite". At least five and possibly six, cruisers "are known" to be en route to Truk from Rabaul. While it was known that *Agano* was damaged, there was "negative information" on *Maya* and *Noshiro*, "which suggests the possibility they may have been heavily damaged or sunk in Rabaul during the period 2-6 November."

In SIB 189 naval flights increased, as did army activity. Navy surface unit information was that *Hakkai Maru*, a repair ship, was believed en route to Rabaul to assist in repairs to damaged vessels, and Cincpac believed that *Agano*, *Noshiro* and *Maya* were sunk in the Rabaul area or heavily damaged. Also it was reported that damage to *Agano* in the previous bulletin was "believed to be in error", and it was *Mogami* which was damaged.

On the night of the 8th, Beauforts of RAAF 6, 8 and 100 Squadrons attacked. No. 6 Squadron sent off eight Beauforts, three of which were forced to turn back by the weather. The other five attacked Rapopo between 2:00 and 2:25 am, starting three large fires. Ten Beauforts of 100 Squadron attacked Vunakanau between 0150 and 0219 hours, causing small fires and a large explosion, seeing the explosions at Rapopo.

Allied aerial torpedo performance had been poor throughout the war. In the US naval air strike of 5 November, 23 torpedoes had been dropped for only two hits, one of which was a dud. Air Commodore Hewitt, commanding the Australian No. 9 Operational Group, decided to launch a large torpedo attack on the shipping in the harbor. However, a naval officer, Lieutenant Greentree, flew as observer on a reconnaissance prior to the strike and reported that as well as the bad weather, the Japanese had dispersed their ships in an anti-torpedo formation. The experienced flight commanders joined him in saying that a formation attack could not succeed. A tense, late conference took place with the crews standing by. Under pressure from Air Commodore Hewitt, the squadron leader, Wing Commander Nicoll, and two of his experienced men, Price and Quinn, volunteered to make the attack. They took off and battled through a heavy electrical storm, with thunder, lightning and heavy rain. As they neared Rabaul the weather cleared and the three Beauforts made their approach at less than 100 feet. Low, at full speed, they roared over the narrow neck of land at Talili and into the harbor. Nicoll attacked a Sugar-Able class vessel in the northern part of the harbor, and Quinn pressed an attack on a light cruiser at the mouth of Keravia Bay, claiming a probable hit, though the AA and searchlights prevented proper observation. Price had gone for a line of cruisers, through a

"tremendous barrage" of flak, and a bright explosion at 2:41 am was believed to be the destruction of his aircraft and crew.

In a strike on Alexishafen on 9 November, Danny Roberts collided with his wingman while turning after a Zeke; the P-38s exploded and a fighter leader of great potential was gone. Danny Roberts had commanded the 433rd for five weeks, and in that time his pilots claimed 55 victories for a loss of three.

Gordon Thomas wrote in November 1943:

"An air raid is expected tonight. Two hundred planes will take part. The word is passed around. Individual reaction to the information is varied. . . . A laugh of bravado. . . . A careless shrug of the shoulders and a murmured 'Kismet'—or its equivalent. . . . A hunted look of fear. . . . Assumed indifference. . . . But yet, in the minds of each is working up a vivid picture of 200 black spots coming up out of the clouds, growing clearer and closer; swiftly travelling to a point overhead: 'The bomb strikes as the plane is overhead.' The phrase is remembered. What will be the result?. . . . Annihilation?. . . . Mutilation?. . . . Slow suffocation in a collapsed shelter?. . . . Or safety after they have all passed over?

"Conversation resumes its normal pitch and subject: Old days. . . . Future days. . . . Trivialities. . . . And then: I wonder where they'll come from. . . . What time?. . . . I hope it's soon, so we can get a good night's sleep. And so, throughout the evening, the thought recurs to each: 200 planes. . . .

"Bedtime arrives. More than usual care has been taken to screen the lights at *Shoto*; scarcely a light is visible. The power house watch remarks there is little load on the engine, for so few lights are being used throughout the town. . . . All ominous signs of the approaching horror!

"In bed one's ears are strained to catch any unusual drone or crump! Above, the interminable whine of the engines of the power house or the ice-plant. An engine throbs . . . a plane? No, a motorcar . . . And the watchers are well on their toes, they'll pick them up all right . . . But still the raiders shut off their engines and glide over the hilltops like they have done in the past . . . Sleep comes at last. Then awakening: 'What, no raid?' Sleep again, then dawn . . . With dawn comes relief. There now can be no night raid, which is always more tedious, more nerve-racking than day-raids, when you can see—more or less—what is going on, and not conjecturing wildly or rashly assuming dangers which really do not exist.

"There has been ten hours of mental strain, high-pitched tension for nothing! For 10 hours one has been imagining the horrors of a raid with 200 heavy bomers overhead . . . And they never came!"[8]

General Imamura, Commanding 8 Area Army, made a speech on 9 November:

"I speak to you officers and men of this army area on this occasion while our unit's stand in this battle is at its climax, and our country is faced with the most critical situation in its history. In face of physical hardships, lack of supplies and superiority of American and Australian forces, you officers and men have fought bravely and have succeeded in checking their counter-attacks. To those men who have died in action, and who have succumbed to diseases, I pay my deepest respect. Although our army and navy have met with success everywhere in this war since its outbreak, the situation has by no means eased. We must keep up our perseverance and endurance . . .

"During the fighting of the past year and a half, you officers and men have demonstrated the invincible spirit of the Japanese, especially in hand-to-hand combats, in overcoming hardships and lack of material. Your strong determination that you shall never become prisoners has been amazingly borne out by our enemy's broadcasts. In view of what I have stated, there still remains the fact that there are a few who, through the lack of bravery, have the tendency to overestimate the enemy strength, who withdraw without orders, who fail to fight to the last man.

"To obtain victory requires the serious consideration and cooperation of the officers and men of this entire unit. You must also keep in mind the pledges of those 100 millions in Japan who have firmly sworn their willingness to sacrifice their lives. Each group commander should bear deeply in his mind the histories of past wars, and should strive to improve his fighting tactics rather than adhere to obsolete methods.

"With these thoughts in mind, you must defeat all counter-attacks of our arrogant enemy and protect the Empire of Japan."[9]

AAF Intelligence Summary 155 reviewed the Japanese air strength question: "Photographs of 10 November showed 188 airplanes on Lakunai and Vunakanau alone. Exact comparison with photographs of the previous day is impossible as Vunakanau on the first occasion and Rapopo and Tobera on the second were not covered. A sharp increase of fighter strength at Lakunai within the 24-hour period is, however, established and the same may be reasonably assumed of Tobera which is also a Naval fighter base. There had been 33 fighters on Tobera on 9 November. Vunakanau too had more than its normal complement of fighters (presumably Army) on 10 November. The suspected expansion of air strength on New Ireland has now been confirmed by photographs of 9 November showing 57 airplanes on Kavieng as against 18 on the last coverage on 30 September . . . In all, it is estimated that enemy air strength in the New

Britain-New Ireland had been rebuilt to well over 300. While the source of these reinforcements is uncertain, further sightings of carrier-based, single-engined torpedo and dive-bombing types in the Solomons again suggests the possibility that carriers are also being stripped to supply fighter strength." The report went on to describe the decline in shipping seen in Simpson Harbor, and the significant absence of cruisers, where eight had been active recently.

HQ's Daily Summary also included the Japanese air strength question. Summary 598, 10/11 November: "The sharp rise (38%) in fighters photographed yesterday on Lakunai airdrome—99 of this type plane compared with 73 the previous day—suggests that:

a. Reinforcements continue to come into the area, and
b. Our estimates as to enemy losses have been high, or both.

"It is quite apparent that our current series of heavy raids on his Rabaul bastion, with the accompanying severe losses in his fighter aircraft, is goading the enemy into committing an ever-increasing portion of such planes from the production line direct to S.W.P.A. While Keravat, Rapopo and Tobera were unphotographed because of clouds, the presence of only 20 medium bombers on Lakunai and Vunakanau strengthens the belief that the enemy is probably dispersing this needed type of aircraft to less vulnerable bases in New Ireland. His gradually mounting air strength in the bismarks is indicative that stronger local defence and more frequent offensive sorties lie in the offing."

However, for 10 November IJN HQ listed combined 11 Air Fleet and Carrier Division 1 air strength at Rabaul as 170 fighters operational, 83 damaged and 16 in reserve, with 12 attack planes.

On the 10th, only Lakunai and Vunakanau were photographed, showing 147 fighters, 41 bombers and 32 floatplanes.

SIBs for the days close to the final attack in the 5th AF daylight bombing campaign contain the same types of information as they had for the duration of the offensive. SIB 190, for the 10th, told of 36 naval flights observed, 14 unidentified and 11 the usual floatplanes, while there was "further evidence" that all or part of Carrier Division 1 were land-based in the Bismarks. Cruiser *Kiso* was indicated in the Kure area, "strengthening the assumption" that it had been damaged on 21 October. SIB 191 reported 43 Naval flights observed, 10 being floatplanes, and three Army bombers of 14 *Hikosentai* noted flying from Wewak to Rapopo. There was "further evidence" that one heavy cruiser believed damaged in the 5 November attack may still have been at Rabaul or been sunk there.

SIB 192, for the 12th, included an identification of

the army's 81st Regiment, moving from Rabaul to Bougainville. Navy and army flights were reported as usual, and aerial reinforcements for Rabaul were "indicated" by flights to Truk and Tinian of a total 49 aircraft of various types. In addition, it was "indicated" that army air units from Rapopo and Alexishafen had moved to Wewak, probably because of heavy Allied air attacks. In the Navy Section, it was "probable" that Allied air action against Rabaul since 31 October had sunk one cruiser and one destroyer and damaged eight cruisers and five destroyers, with three cruisers "believed" still in the Rabaul area, too damaged to preceed to sea, awaiting repair and destroyer escort.

In the early morning hours of the 11th, six B-24s from the 403rd Squadron set off for Lakunai, reporting 50 to 60 searchlights in the area, forming cones into which the AA fired regardless of the true position of the planes. Small fires and explosions were seen.

11 November

The 11th was to be another great one-two punch, heavies and strafers going after airfields and shipping respectively, to complement a strike by Halsey's carrier planes. Rabaul was really to be on the receiving end, but once again the weather intervened. Planes preceding the main strike force reported impassable weather from sealevel to 35,000 feet, and the mission was called off. The 5th AF could only assist Halsey with an early morning attack by unescorted B-24s who reported explosions and fires on Lakunai.

The bombers, from the 64th, 65th and 403rd Squadrons, placed 459 100-pound demolition bombs and 1,920 20-pound frags across the target. Weather caused return or recall of the other Liberators.

Moving into landing sequence on the return, Lieutenant Palmer in B-24 *Jackpot* slid in front of Captain Bill Martin, in *Joltin' Janie II*, the huge white skull on *Jackpot's* vertical fin grinning into Martin's cockpit only feet away. At only 1,000 feet, Martin had to make an awful decision. To avoid crashing into a hill, he pulled back on the control column, his nose crashed into the tail of *Jackpot* and Martin pulled away. Palmer and his crew died in the explosion as the bombs still aboard detonated on impact. Martin brought damaged *Joltin' Janie II* in for a landing.[10]

Thirteen P-38s of the 432nd Squadron were over the target for 30 minutes, seeing neither B-24s or other P-38s, and engaging 40 to 50 Zekes and Oscars, though claiming none, for the loss of one P-38 last seen in normal flight near Tobera. The Japanese seemed not eager to engage, dodging in and out of the clouds, and the P-38 passes were made without results being observed.

The 433rd Squadron also could not claim any enemy, though one P-38 was hit in the nose by AA. The Lightnings dropped their tanks and weaved over the bombers during the bomb run, trying to keep off the Japanese fighters making head-on attacks.

Gordon Thomas describes a daylight raid: ". . . the sharp cry of the siren, the shooting of the rocket; yellow in color, shaped like a giant octopus. Fighters taking off in every direction, making height, and then the dull, far-off drone of high-powered engines working in unison; the puff of ack-ack fire; the detonation of the shells; the sight of dark spots, raged in order, against the cloud banks—15,000 to 20,000 feet high. Then the rush to cover as the fighters approach, and sitting in the dark, listening to detonations, then hearing the angry growl, CRUMP! of bombs falling, feeling the shudder of the earth; the corkscrew reverberation of the high explosives; the incessant bark of the ack-ack, the staccato bursts of the pom-pom guns, like worrying dogs. The roar of a plane nearer, nearer. Now overhead . . . 'The bomb strikes as the plane is overhead!' It passes, then c-r-u-m-p c-r-u-m-p-! CRUMP! How far away? Will the next lot be nearer? Almost motionless one sits in the shelter 12, 15 feet beneath the surface. Sufficient protection against AP, but not from a direct hit from HE, or anything like it! Such a bomb would mean annihilation. Well, so long as it was quick, what would it matter? Then silence. The sounds of planes in the far distance. . . . silence and waiting. Then. . . . fifteen minutes. And then the sound of the All Clear, the *Kaijo*, and the word is repeated by each one as he walks out of the shelter, with a sigh of relief. What a relief to walk about, to move freely after such long inactivity and tension!. . . . Another raid is over. . . . Life is still sweet."[11]

Japanese losses were again apparently incompletely reported. 4 Air Army lists six small boats burned or damaged and 500 drums of fuel destroyed. Eight fighters and a destroyer were lost and three ships damaged. On the other hand, Allied naval and air forces from the Solomons claimed 138 Japanese planes over Rabaul this day.

On the 12th, only 108,000 tons of shipping were in harbor. The Japanese began to realize Rabaul was a trap, and turned to Kavieng, New Ireland.

Notes

1. ATIS Intg 433
2. AWM 779-3-29
3. Lancaster Report
4. tape, 1983
5. ATIS EP 270
6. ATIS Bull 726
7. ATIS Bull 672, EP 257
8. ANU PMB 36
9. ATIS Bull 856
10. tape 1983
11. ANU PMB 36

22

Perspectives

SONG OF RABAUL

GOODBYE RABAUL
TILL I RETURN.
FAREWELL TEARS WILL FLOW FOR SOME
    TIME.
I COULD SEE THE SOUTHERN CROSS BETWEEN
    THE COCONUT TREE LEAVES.

LET'S TALK ON DECK THROUGH THE NIGHT
    WHEN YOU
CANNOT SLEEP BECAUSE OF THE NOISE OF
    THE WAVES.
WHEN I LOOK AT THAT TWINKLING STAR
THE CIGARETTE IN MY MOUTH TASTES
    MILDLY BITTER.

THE RED SUN SETS BETWEEN THE WAVES.
IF YOU STAND UP ALL AROUND YOU SEE THE
    HORIZON.
TODAY AGAIN WE ARE STILL FAR AWAY ON
    THE SOUTH PACIFIC ROUTE.
A SEAMAN IS JUST LIKE A SEAGULL.

Japanese Song from the War

It has often been said that comparisons are invidious, and it would be easy to compare the hardships and fortunes of war in the various theaters. But a little comparison is inevitable. The resolute German air defence of Europe is equalled only by the resolution of the USAAF and RAF to triumph. Flying conditions over the "Hump" in the CBI are generally agreed to be the worst in any WW II theater, closely followed by the Aleutians.

Every theater had its own set of conditions—enemy, terrain, weather, particularly tough targets, resupply priority, etc. For the 5th AF it was a merciless enemy, primitive living and working conditions, danger-ous weather and a hostile, little-known environment in which survival was, at this time, due to a set of circumstances classed as "luck."

The 5th's planners, groundcrews and flightcrews did their best but the weather intervened to the advantage of the Japanese and the intended series of hammerblows in rapid succession was broken up into separated strikes. The courage of the 5th, through all this, is undoubted.

It has been seen how intelligence staffs relied on photography for their most accurate assessment of Japanese aerial strength. SIBs did not provide the detail necessary. Their indications of aircraft reinforcements for Rabaul and the Solomons were general in nature, though surface unit activity was much better reported. When weather precluded photographic reconnaissance of the target area, Staffs were almost literally blinded.

The weather, regarded by pilots and staff alike as possibly a greater enemy than the Japanese, was perhaps the best ally of the defenders of Rabaul. Despite crews pressing on through dangerous flying conditions, the longest sustained period during which attacks could be made on consecutive days was three—23, 24 and 25 October—and the remainder of the attacks were single days squeezed in between slabs of foul conditions.

There were no efficient networks of agents and resistance workers as in Occupied Europe to assist the Allies with information about their enemy, despite Japanese preoccupation with weeding them out. The coastwatchers made an important contribution to campaigns in the region, but apart from teams such as Peter Figgis', to the south, there was no Allied team operating close enough to add eyewitness accounts to mission and photo reports as to the effectiveness of the attacks. Their operational life and chances of survival in close proximity to the targets would have been minimal.

So the staffs were forced to gather information from signals intercept, crew reports, mission reports and photography, with the results being their intelligence summaries included above. Damage was generally over-estimated, but in this they were no different from their counterparts in Europe, or the Germans or Japanese. History repeated itself in Korea and Vietnam.

During November, the 5th would lose 38 Lightnings, ending the month with 165 on hand; 20 B-24s were lost for 225 on hand, and for B-25s, 21 were lost leaving 243 on hand to fly December missions.

The Rabaul raids should be kept in perspective with the rest of the 5th Air Force effort in 1943. The Statistics Book for that year gives such a view. In that time the 5th flew 170,477 sorties, of which fighters flew 34%, bombers 9% and the unsung transports 54%; the remaining 3% being reconnaissance flights. 1,976 bomber and 3,156 fighter sorties engaged the enemy in aerial combat.

The target receiving most attention was Cape Gloucester, with 3,671 bomber and 1,237 fighter sorties, followed by Madang, Wewak and Salamaua. In fifth place was Rabaul, with 1,740 bomber and 504 fighter sorties.

By comparison, transport tonnage lifted in the year by 5th AF planes alone was 186,925.4 tons, with most sorties flown into the Markham Valley: 19,194, with 1,904 fighter escort sorties. Dobodura received 13,023 transport flights, which had 235 escort sorties.

Bomb tonnage figures for the year are a total of 21,177 tons dropped, with the targets receiving most being: Cape Gloucester 5,671 tons; Madang 2,851; and Rabaul 2,136 tons.

Aircraft replacements flowed in throughout the year, and the 5th was 154% stronger in December than it had been in January. It had lost 179 P-38s to all causes and gained 291, while 123 B-24s had been lost but 310 gained, and the 117 missing B-25s were replaced by 291.

The hazards of operating a wartime air force in the theater are shown by figures breaking down the total losses:

	fighter			heavy bomber			attack bomber		
cause:	enemy	accident	other	enemy	accident	other	enemy	accident	other
Oct	27.6%	37.8%	34.6%	40.9%	31.8%	27.3%	40%	35%	25%
Nov	32.7%	35.6%	31.7%	29.2%	37.5%	33.3%	68%	16%	16%

When it became obvious that Rabaul was neutralized, the Japanese applied themselves to defining the lessons learned and forecasting future Allied moves. One paper prepared by Major-General Inada, of 2nd Army in West New Guinea-Moluccas, accurately describes General MacArthur's future advance to the Phillipines and the Central Pacific offensives.

"1. Evaluation of enemy situation and terrain.

After neutralizing the effectiveness of 8 Area Army, US forces will launch a drive along the entire Pacific Front towards the Japanese mainland. From New Guinea they will thrust to the Phillipines and cut Japan off from the south. The enemy will exploit fully his sea and air supremacy in his attempt to recapture the Phillipines. His route of attack will be along the Northern New Guinea coast; from the Arafura Sea and Northern Australia to the Moluccas, thus seeking to bring the operations to a swift climax. Only secondary offensives or diversionary movements will be made against areas where resistance in several phases is anticipated. Further flanking routes will be planned from Western Australia northward. These will be mainly air attacks on Java to destroy petroleum resources. Judging from experiences in the southeastern operations, the enemy will intensify his leap-frogging operations, gradually increasing in strength. Out strongly held key areas along the coast will be cut off from the rear. Starvation tactics will be applied. Main strength will land on islands and along the coast, deep in our rear to facilitate the rapid development of operations. Therefore, each key position must be made as independent as possible. The principle of defense lies in lightning air-sea counter-attacks. For this purpose, adequate air and sea bases must be established. We must recognize fully that air and sea fighting can break out at any time in the vast Pacific. This is characteristic of naval warfare. It is necessary to abandon the concept of a single front as in land warfare."[1]

The rest of Major-General Inada's paper describes recommended measures the Japanese should take to prepare Western New Guinea and particularly the Geelvink area, for the expected Allied moves.

The Japanese also analyzed the attacks on airfields in 4 Air Army's area, in their Intelligence Report 102, which stated in part:

"in attacks on airbases in the south eastern area heavy bombs are not used, but great numbers of parachute bombs are to inflict casualties on personnel. The horizontal burst effect is very great and very effective against objects which have inadequate cover. A substantial number of parachute bombs have proved to be duds which points out the need for thorough experimentation beforehand."

In the section titled "Raids," the report said:

"it is important to take note of the comparatively small losses incurred by the enemy. The reason for this lies in the manoeuvrability of the B-25 and its ability to fly at a slow speed which gives difficulty to our combat planes and AA guns. It is well to note that the bombing period during the day is usually fixed . . . between 0900 and 1100 hours. The standard of bombing has improved remarkably in recent times; even from very high altitudes bombs have been dropped skillfully."

The report went on to discuss countermeasures:

"concentration of fighter defence; allocation and camouflage of AAA guns; not expose planes to enemy photography and reconnaissance; use of decoys; frequently alter locations of AAA guns; flying boats making rescues of enemy pilots must be intercepted."[2]

Bill Martin, B-24 pilot: "But the Japanese were dumb, they really were. They followed procedures . . . ritualistic. At Wewak our favorite trick was to bomb hell out of one strip so they'd all go to land at the other, and then boom! A fresh wave of B-25s would catch them on the deck. At Hollandia we did that several times."[3]

For the Japanese at Rabaul, the air attacks were the beginning of their own imprisonment. The air groups were destroyed in fierce combats and the remnants evacuated in February 1944 to the Marianas. There in June US carrier pilots and fleet AA gunners destroyed 476 Japanese aircraft. By the end of the war few experienced Japanese pilots were alive, even fewer were those who flew at Rabaul, and the man who had flown before Pearl Harbor was a rarity.

For Sisters Catherine, Berenice and the rest of the interned missionaries long months of imprisonment stretched ahead, often under aerial bombardment and acute personal danger from hunting Allied pilots, strafing anything in sight. Sister Catherine: "We had no contact with the natives, so did not know till after the war of their hopes for an early liberation. As for the Japanese, they were kept so busy they had little time for communication with us, and as it was always through our Bishop, we knew little of their feelings at that time. Our main feelings were hope of release and an end of war."[4]

The Chinese community endured the bombing and strafing, employed in building tunnels and shelters and repairing the damage. The men were rotated through a two-week roster: two weeks working for the Japanese and two weeks in the camp at Ratongor. As the war progressed Allied pilots shot at any and all buildings and farm plots. The small figure of 92 Chinese deaths is recorded from all causes for the entire war, and only seven are recorded as through bombing attacks. Many more are believed to have died from one cause or another; as time goes by the survivors pass away this information becomes unavailable and true figures will probably never be known.

Captain Sen, 5/2 Punjab Regiment: "At various times they had their propaganda say that a large company of reinforcements was coming out next month, and every month it was next month. They also said the American Navy had struck and was not going to do any

more fighting for the British, and the British were going to join the Germans. It was a lot of nonsense, their own troops believed it, but they couldn't get us to believe it."[5]

Gordon Thomas: "Many of the Ladies of Pleasure had already departed during the previous month, and December saw the last of them leave amid a flourish of cheers and waving as they sped through the streets, seated on top of their beds and baggage. They were the one remaining splash of colour in a town of dark drab grey and green landscape and uniformed humanity.

"They were doomed, these little Ladies of Ten Thousand Delights, for, after having catered untiringly to the desires of the Services for nearly two years, and collected a sum sufficient to pay off the mortgage on the old Korean homestead, their ships were bombed a day or so out of Rabaul, and only half-a-dozen or so escaped to tell the tale.

"It was a sad ending for those Little Ladies, who had gone through so much, and I always admired their cheerfulness."[6]

In January 1944 Nobuko Tajimura, head nurse, left Rabaul for Japan. In February the evacuation of many other technicians accelerated. Most of the aircrews and groundcrews of units with no flyable planes were sent out, some being captured when their ships were sunk. The ring around Rabaul was tightening.[7]

For Dennis Glen Cooper, intelligence officer of the 475th Fighter Group, the future campaigns in the Pacific held an unusual and challenging job. On arrival at Biak, he was transferred to HQ 5th AF, to be the first rescue intelligence officer in the service. "Our rescue group, which went right through to Tokyo, brought back more than 2,700 men during the time we were working there and it was one of the best-kept secrets in the Air Force. The Japanese never did find out we were operating over their territory."[8]

For some Americans, the journey home was to be anything but easy and plain sailing. After 30 months in the SWPA and 46 low-level attack missions, John Shemelynce was returned to the USA with combat fatigue.

As John saw it, "like a dream. Back in the States with family, girls, cocktail lounges, dancing, sleeping between sheets, paved streets, hot showers and all that which makes the good life."

Moving to Finschafen, he waited for six weeks and finally boarded a ship, unpacked his B-4 bag and went up on deck. In the bag was $900.00 and next to it a pair of the prized RAAF flying boots.

While watching a movie on deck "things started happening" as the ship alongside caught fire. It was said to be carrying ammunition. The steel started to turn cherry-red. John thought, "Here I am, made it through 30 months of the war and now on my way home, I am going to die in this harbor. I took action and immediately jumped off my ship and ran at full speed for the hills that surrounded the harbor. Well, I turned on a burst of speed and made it behind one of those hills and waited and waited but nothing happened. I started back to the ship when I noticed it had started to pull out of the harbor. I immediately turned on another burst of speed to reach the ship. As I came near the ship, it was slowly moving out—about three feet from the dock. I still had a chance, the gangplank wasn't retracted yet. I reached but too late, the gangplank was just out of reach. My ship started to move out of the harbor, no problem, I know the ship will stop after it clears the burning ship, after all, I am not aboard. *Wrong* the ship keeps moving and moving until I could see it disappear over the horizon on a moonlit night. Within one hour from being on ship with money, clothes and ready to sail for the good old USA to nothing but me and a pair of undershorts standing on a dock in New Guinea."

Here was a person with no means of identity, providing a field day for mosquitoes, wondering what to do next. And 16 others were with him. The system came to their rescue, John proving his identity by reciting his army number while a clerk checked it against a copy of his orders. The 17 castaways were quickly put aboard another ship going to the US. The passengers were all controlled military mental cases.

"Then I arrived in San Francisco and was reunited with my B-4 bag all the money and everything except my R.A.A.F. flying boots. My friends had taken care of everything for me. Of course, they did have a few remarks and laughs at my expense, but I was back in the States and laughed with them."[10]

Gordon Thomas: "And then on August 15th 1945 the bonfires started. Office records from every section of the supply unit were brought out and thrown on huge bonfires in the gully. No thought, apparently, of aircraft, for incidentally, there had been no aerial activity for several days. Amongst other rumours we had heard an ultimatum had been issued to Japan, and she had 48 hours in which to consider it, and, rumour had it, if no aerial activity occurred on the 15th then it would mean she had accepted and surrendered.

"This was the 15th and records were being burned. We could not wish for better evidence. All day long huge bonfires were eating up books, papers and careful watchers saw that every paper was destroyed and not a shred of evidence remained."[9]

At the surrender, the Japanese forces in Rabaul did not consider themselves defeated. Isolated, they were prepared to fight. The Allies never came to do battle. A Rabaul Medal was struck by themselves and worn. In 1946 they were shipped to their homeland, and for many Rabaul holds a special place in their memories.

The Americans either finished their wartime service and returned to civilian life or continued with the Air Force. For most, the SWPA became memories, few of them good. The spirit of comradeship and sense of unit achievement were offset by the environment and constant loss of friends.

Colonel Charles E. Lancaster led a small team of USAAF officers to Rabaul to evaluate the bombing campaign. His report aptly concludes:

"At the conclusion of the war, there was nothing left of Rabaul as a town. Jungle had reclaimed approximately two-thirds of the area that constituted the town proper. There was no shipping of any kind in Simpson Harbor. There were six aircraft left on the island and they only flew twice a month and performed no combat with Allied aircraft. The garrison of troops were living like rats in caves and tunnels, and were existing on what they could cultivate in their gardens. Rabaul was a place on a map that represented approximately 90,000 Japanese troops who were absolutely helpless to assist Japan to wage war.

"Air power had destroyed hundreds of thousands of tons of merchant vessels and warships, and isolated thousands of first-line troops. The war had bypassed Japan's most expensively built and heavily manned base of operations in the Southwest Pacific Area. Isolation and stagnation had been forced upon Rabaul simply by the use of airpower, and except for the aircrews that were shot down, this had been accomplished without one invasion soldier setting foot upon this area."

Colonel Lancaster's evaluation of the air attacks consisted of 12 separate points, which have been condensed slightly for this book:

1. Rabaul, main enemy base in the SWPA, was permanently neutralized by airpower alone.
2. Japanese offensive capabilities were greatly reduced by this neutralization.
3. Continuous effective neutralization required daily attacks and reconnaissance.
4. After Allied dominance of the Bismarks, only tactical reconnaissance of Rabaul was necessary.
5. Continuous day-night attacks had a definite effect on Japanese morale and efficiency.
6. Low-level B-25 attacks were considered by the Japanese to be most destructive.
7. Most feared were low-flying P-38s.
8. Most feared bomb was the anti-personnel (Daisycutter).
9. Periodic attacks against airfields did not greatly hinder the Japanese, as others were available and repairs quickly made.
10. Moving into caves and tunnels greatly reduced casualties.

11. Transportation was effectively paralyzed by constant daylight air patrols.
12. Japanese resupply of the garrison was made difficult by the effective Allied isolation of the battle area.[11]

Colonel Lancaster's first point, permanent neutralization by airpower alone, may be strongly disputed by members of the Allied naval surface and submarine fleets and by the ground troops who invaded and held islands and beachheads in the drives to surround Rabaul. Without their operations and the casualties in men, ships and planes inflicted on the Japanese, the defenses of the base would have been much stronger and supplies would have continued to arrive. Once the distant perimeter had been established, air power was used to maintain pressure on the encircled Japanese.

But the Fifth Air Force, flying through weather that often seemed an ally of the Japanese, covering long distances over seas and jungles which showed no mercy to downed crews, showed that Rabaul could be hit, and hit hard, and held the attention of the Japanese while the drive up from the Solomons was launched. When those landings had succeeded and the Japanese were unable to dislodge or destroy the Allied forces, the future of Rabaul became clear. There is no disputing that airpower played a great part in the drive, but it was a part, not the entirety.

Whatever figures are produced at this distance in time, and whatever over-claiming may have taken place on both sides, it is certain that Rabaul was the place where at least 18 Japanese naval air formations were ground down. The USAAF evaluation of the Rabaul attacks includes the following list of such formations which operated from Rabaul. Those listed as 'Withdrawn' were not merely relocated, but left the area of battle as remnants, not to return to the South Pacific.

HQ AAF Intelligence Situation Reports (Sitreps), classified "Most Secret," reflected the problems of the staff in assessing Japanese air strength. Using information from all sources, the Sitreps included totals of Japanese combat aircraft on the various islands. But, as in the Intsums with the lower classification of "Secret," no-one seems to have questioned the never-decreasing number of aircraft accepted as available on the Rabaul fields.

A glance at the list of Sitreps below will show that the Japanese appeared able to replace very heavy combat losses at once, without including losses from any other causes. Recalling the weather conditions, airfield quality and training, the Japanese should have suffered as many flying accidents as the Allies. These losses were not known, or not included.

So, from figures accepted at "Most Secret" level, the Rabaul defenses lost about 600 aircraft in a month, yet the 11 November figure was the same as for 10 October. If losses in transit and due to weather and other causes are "guesstimated," then over 1,000 combat aircraft and crews were consumed in the Rabaul area. Yet these large formations arriving were not observed on radio or by coast-watchers.

The Japanese themselves over-claimed, moreso than the Allies, and their individual claims would have been almost impossible to assess accurately, given that the combats took place in the cloud conditions, often over water and jungle, without camera guns.

IMPERIAL NAVY AIR GROUPS AT RABAUL

Air Group	Aircraft Type	Arrived	Disposition
4th	Medium bomber	14 Feb. 42	Withdrawn 3 Oct. 42
938th	Reconnaissance	Mar. 42	1 plane left, Aug. 45
958th	Reconnaissance	Mar. 42	1 plane left, Aug. 45
1st	Medium bomber	4 Apr. 42	Withdrawn Apr. 42
Tainan	Fighter	12 Apr. 42	Withdrawn 4 Nov. 42
Ginzan	Medium bomber	Apr. 42	Withdrawn May 42
Kisaragu	Medium bomber	10 Aug. 42	Disbanded Dec. 42
705th	Medium bomber	20 Aug. 42	Withdrawn Oct. 43
253rd	Fighter	1 Nov. 42	Withdrawn 10 Jul. 44
204th	Fighter	4 Dec. 42	Withdrawn 4 Mar. 44
151st	Reconnaissance	15 Apr. 43	Withdrawn 10 Jul. 43
251st	Fighter	20 Apr. 43	Withdrawn 1 Sept. 43
702nd	Medium bomber	28 apr. 43	Disbanded 1 Dec. 43
201st	Fighter	Jun. 43	Withdrawn 15 Jan. 44
751st	Medium bomber	15 Aug. 43	Withdrawn 22 Feb. 44
501st	Light bomber	4 Oct. 43	Disbanded 4 Mar. 44
552nd	Light bomber	Dec. 43	Withdrawn 20 Feb. 44
582nd	Light bomber	20 Dec. 43	Withdrawn 23 Feb. 44 (12)

Medium bomber: Mitsubishi G4M Betty
Light bomber: Aichi D3s Val and Nakajima B5N Kate
Reconnaissance: Watanabe E13A Jake and Mitsubishi F1M Pete
Fighter: Mitsubishi A6M Zeke

Sitrep	Date	No. of aircraft	Losses claimed Dest	Prob	Dam	Attack Date	Comment
98	10 Oct	254					
107	15	—	126	0	51	12 Oct	1/2 lost
110	16	329					
111	17	91 (2 fields)					
114	18	232					
115	19	145 (3 fields)					
116		184					
118		222 (19 Oct)	75	29	0	18 Oct	1/3 lost
120	21	248					
126	24	255					
127			15	13	0	23 Oct	1/15 lost
128	25	172					
129			88	25	0	24 Oct	1/3 lost
130		172	58	43	0	25 Oct	1/3 lost
(no totals given for next eight reports)							
139	31 Oct	—	45	13	0	29 Oct	—
143	3 Nov	237 (119 ftrs)	68	23	0	2 Nov	1/3 lost
144	5	192 (115 ftrs)	22	4	0	1 Nov	(USN)
145	5	236 (150 ftrs)					
147	7	214	27	0	0	5 Nov	1/7 lost
148	8	189					
149			36	0	0	7 Nov	1/6 lost
150	10	205					
151	11	252					
		total:	*560*	*150*	*51*		

Veterans of the operations are divided in their attitude to claims of success.

Tom Fetter, 90th Group: "The claims for planes destroyed and damaged were vastly overstated by the Fifth Air Force. I personally had suspected for a long time that claims made were not realistic. In the excitement of an engagement everyone that fired at a fighter that went down made a claim."[13]

Bill Martin, 90th Group: "As far as what the aircrews shot down, oh no, they were never accurate, because as soon as the Zero went by, between us or under us or over us, well, then he dove, headed head down, and unless you saw smoke out of the airplane, and frequently they didn't, the guys are claiming everything in sight, 'I got 'im, I got 'im, I got 'im!' The excitement level in the airplane was tremendous, with machineguns going and people talking . . . no, I don't think really we got as many as we claimed. Except the ground. On the deck, I do believe those claims because we had all sorts of reconnaissance to confirm (the claims)."

Carl Camp, 90th Group: "Yes, I believed the claims. No reason not to. We had seen the results each time we went over and the Japs were not putting forth any counter-claims. But in any case, we believed that if they overclaimed and the damage was not done, well, not to worry; all would come right and lay flat before we were finished."

Bill Moran, 90th Group: "No, I did not believe the claims announced by this command. Seeing is believing, and on many occasions reports were exaggerated by the press as well as by the Bomber Command. As an aerial photographer-photo interpreter I was able to witness, first-hand, many of our 'mistakes.' Basically the reports were correct, but on occasions exaggerated to a slight degree."

Larry Tanberg 38th Group: "As I recall we were not mesmerised one way or another with the count. (I) am sure the fighter groups were more interested in same than we were. All in all, the numbers destroyed were not an item of vital interest to the aircrews then. We were more interested if the overall mission was a success and whether we lost any crews. Our competition was the other B-25 outfits and how they were doing versus us."

Charles King 39th Fighter Squadron: "Yes, I believe the overall numbers of 5 AF fighter pilot claims was accurate. I had high school experience with motion picture projectors and I was the self-appointed custodian of our combat gun camera film. I reviewed it all with each pilot and saw each film numerous times. In time I developed a sense of co-relation between observed results and the confirmed claims. I repeat again it is my opinion that the claims of the 39th were not exaggerated. I was not able to make an observation of the 5th Bomber Command claims to qualify me to comment."

"Corky" Smith 80th Fighter Squadron: "Generally speaking, our claims were fairly accurate. Fighter pilot claims were not respected by higher authority without eyewitness confirmation by another participant or guncamera confirmation. Most of us were honest and the few who were prone to exaggerate were known. Bomber claims were another problem and there were undoubted instances of honest exaggerated claims. A number of bombers might witness the same Zero going down and crashing—instead of one Zero this might be reported as 2-3-4-5 or more separate Zeros. Difficult to know how to weigh bomber crew claims! My personal view was that they were overly high. I saw very few bombers shoot down enemy aircraft."

The most vivid memories off those Rabaul missions for some of the participants illustrates the wide scope of such events. Rather than dramatic military actions, some of the memories which first come to mind are quite personal things.

Marion Kirby: "Freezing feet in the P-38 cockpit at altitude."

"Corky" Smith: "The terrific amount of AA. The huge number of Zeros in the air runs a close second. Many of the Japanese did not fly in formation as we did. Coming into Rabaul was like going into a flying circus with Zeros performing loops, rolls, steep climbs and dives, etcetera."

Tom Fetter, 90th Group: "Personally, as squadron bombardier there was always a feeling of achievement when you made good hits on a target. We bombed by squadron in those days and you had a lot of destruction to hand out when the squadron formation dropped on your release."

Captain Sen, 5/2 Punjab Regiment: "The most frightening thing was the anti-personnel bomb, we used to call them broom-sweepers; daisy-cutters I suppose you call them."

For Charles Ray, bomber gunner, the most awesome thing was the "phosphorus bomb or shell that would explode above us and looked like a large gray octopus with long tentacles reaching out. I never did see them do any damage."

Bill Martin, B-24 pilot: "Those (Japanese) pilots were pretty damn good. I remember one Zero, and that fella was out there at 9 o'clock, went on to 10, and I'll be damned if he didn't turn in right against the six of us."

Rabaul had acquired the reputation as the toughest target in the South West Pacific Area. However, some of the men who flew missions there regard other targets as the toughest.

"Corky" Smith: "I don't think there were tougher assignments than Rabaul. In early '43 Wewak was just as tough and we lost some good people there. Those who missed the early '43 strikes against Wewak will undoubtedly consider Rabaul as the highlight."

Takeo Tanimizu, 253 *Ku*: "In late '44 and '45, when there were very few veterans, now that was tough! For me, flying in Taiwan and home defence with a bunch of green pilots and against superior American fighters, that was tough."

Carl Camp, 90th Bomb Group: "Wewak was tougher than Rabaul by far. We lost more personal friends than at Rabaul."

Harry Young, 43rd Bomb Group: "I have to say Rabaul. After all, it held out longer than the main Japanese Islands did. Rabaul was rough because of the ships which threw out a lot of flak. I remember approaching Rabaul and seeing battleships shooting broadsides at our formation. Then, the area was so big. And they had a lot of airfields with lots of fighters and the area was ringed with anti-aircraft guns."

Bill Welch, 43rd Group: "Rabaul missions were the toughest because you were under fire for a longer period of time."

Bill Martin, 90th Group: "It had to be Rabaul. Nobody had done it in daylight before, and with three airfields you knew they had to have all kinds of airplanes. If the B-25s hadn't got scads of them on the ground they'd probably have made hash of us."

And even after the evident envelopment of Rabaul and the poising of MacArthur's forces to leap westward along northern New Guinea, the individual low-ranking Japanese soldier was fed on propaganda and lies.

Shichizaemon Kasahara was a Japanese soldier of long service in the Rabaul area, and kept a diary throughout his time there. He enlisted in July 1941, trained, went first to Manchukuo, to South China, then to New Britain. Aboard *Kyokusei Maru* in the March 43 convoy, he abandoned it when the ship was hit in the annihilating low-level attacks, was rescued by destroyer *Asagumo*, and returned to Rabaul. Later he was sent to Cape Gloucester (Tsurubu). There he saw destroyers *Ariake* and *Mikazuki* smashed by B-25s. The propaganda fed to the troops was reflected in his diary, as in the entry for 8 September when he wrote "2,000 paratroops and 800 planes assembled at Truk, besides 20,000 men of *Go* Force at an island north of Australia, ready to attack." On 31 October he wrote that he had malaria for a week, and on 7 November noted that "I would be glad if I could go to Rabaul." His last entry is 14 December.[14]

Susumu Hirazawa, of the Kawasaki Unit, also kept a diary:

"30 November: I'm getting disgusted at staying here, for I can't even sleep because of hunger.

8 December: Heard that 1200 new type fighter planes were concentrated at Rabaul and will start bombing the enemy bases.

11 December: I heard that our naval force will carry out an operation in the waters off New Guinea Island and I also heard of the brilliant achievements of 40th and 20th Divisions.

13 December: Heard that 300,000 of the Imperial Japanese Forces under the command of General Yamashita are storming the enemy from Western New Guinea.

16 December: Heard that a big enemy convoy has effected a landing at Merkus Point (Author: Arawe) 43 Consolidated airplanes bombed us today.

24 December: Continuous enemy bombing is almost unbearable." (Last entry)

And a final summing-up from Tom Fetter, 90th Group:

"Rabaul had a mystique of its own. For us it was the big game. We felt like we were finally going to deliver a crushing blow. We found that Rabaul wasn't as tough as we expected and we felt we were really winning at this point."

Notes

1. ATIS Bull 1457
2. ATIS CT 130
3. tape 1983
4. tape, letter 1983
5. Lancaster Report
6. ANU PMB microfilm 36
7. letter, 1984
8. letter, 1983
9. ANU PMB microfilm 36
10. letter, 1983
11. Lancaster Report
12. Lancaster Report
13. all personal quotes from letters 1982-83
14. ATIS Bull 580

Appendix 1

Japanese losses, 12 October 1943, from captured documents and post-war Allied surveys.

E.P. 270

Army aircraft destroyed	2 from 14 *Sentai*, Sally bombers
	2 from 208 *Sentai*, Sallys
	2 unit not listed, Sallys
Army aircraft damaged	8 from 14, 208 and unidentified *Sentais*
Navy aircraft destroyed	9 from 751 *Ku*, Bettys
damaged	3, including one fighter
Army shipping sunk or burned	2
damaged	25
Navy shipping sunk or burned	1
damaged	4, including submarine I-180

Buildings—1 Field Shipping Depot, the Main Field Depot for motor transport and five 'factories' burned

Army Killed in Action (KIA)	47 or 95 (report is unclear)
Wounded	95
Missing	47
Navy KIA	29
Wounded	84

The Military History Section, GHQ, Far Eastern Command, produced a report, which lists the following ships sunk:

Keisho Maru, Tsukinada Maru, Kamoi Maru, Mishima Maru

Damaged were listed as:

Tsukushi Maru, Naruto Maru and destroyers *Mochisuki, Minazuki, Tachikazi* and submarines I-180, I-177 and RO-105.

However, a Washington report lists *Keisho, Tsukinada, Shimi Maru, Mishima Maru, Kiku Maru* and *Daiichi Wakamatsu Maru* as sunk, with damage to destroyers *Minazuki* and *Mochizuki*.

Appendix 2

Japanese losses, 2 November 1943.

Photo-interpretation reports of the mission claimed initially a total of 42,050 tons of shipping sunk or damaged, including damage to a cruiser and a destroyer, a 10,400-ton *Hakuneto Maru*-class hit and burning, an 8,000 ton *Yamabiko Maru*-class hit and burning, a freighter of 4,000 tons hit and burning, another of 7,000 tons damaged, a 1,550-ton *Haruna Maru*-class sunk, a 650-ton *Tokyo Maru*-class freighter transport hit in the stern, a 3,800-tonner damaged, and a 2,000-tonner damaged.

Second phase interpretation showed a *Nachi* class cruiser suffered a direct hit and left harbor; a destroyer bracketed by bombs and left harbor; another ship down by the stern with debris floating nearby; one *Yamabiko class* of 6,800 tons direct hit amidships and burning; one *Tokyo Maru* class of 6,000 tons, bomb exploded under the stern; two freighters totalling 7,000 tons had a direct hit on the stern of one and another hit amidships of the other; one freighter 7,000 tons, damage to the stern; one *Haruna Maru* class 1,500 tons sunk; one destroyer tender 2,000 tons gutted by fire; one naval auxiliary 1,500 tons damaged amidships; one tugboat 500 tons demolished; one flying boat and one floatplane on fire; one destroyer on fire.

ATIS EP 270 & Bull 725:

Captured Japanese documents list 4 Air Army reports for the action: Army KIA 2, WIA 21; houses burned or damaged, 18; munitions burned, "some;" Navy planes missing, 18; damaged, 2; Navy ships sunk, 2; damaged 4. Other documents list the same damage, but with the note "It is probable we suffered more damages than reported," and, "Casualties and other damages are being investigated."

ATIS Bull 1985

Another (captured) list of Japanese ships used by the army sunk or damaged between 1 September and 19 November in the area lists 26 vessels, but unfortunately does not include date and place of the actions. Some of these may well have been hit on 2 November.

USSBS

Recorded damage which survived the destruction of records at the surrender shows the following ships sunk:

Manko Maru	1,503 tons
Shinko Maru	3,119 tons

Cruiser *Myoko* was recorded as suffering slight damage from a near-miss.

However, the report produced by Military History Section, HQ Far East Command, also lists damage to *Hayasaki* and *Arasaki, Shiratsuyu, Haguro* and minesweeper *W36*.

ATIS Bull 1090

Yet another captured document describing shipping crew casualties lists *Yamabiko Maru* as suffering one killed and 23 wounded, under the care of Chief Medical Officer Tokumaru. They were later sent to Japan. *Wakatsuki Maru* also suffered at least 57 casualties, who were sent to Truk and collected there by *Takasago Maru* between 5 and 15 November.[22]

The combination of poor record-keeping by the Japanese, combined with normal wartime destruction and the supervised burning of records makes a precise totaling of the results of 2 November almost impossible.

After the war, the US Strategic Bombing Survey team found they could only credit the attack with sinking three small merchant vessels, a minesweeper and two smaller ships, plus damage to a 10,000-ton tanker. However, the team did note that some of the surviving records remaining at Rabaul had been removed by Australian forces. A search of documents held by the Australian War Memorial, Australian Archives and the Historical Offices of both the RAAF and RAN has not located any further information to that above.

Appendix 3

FIFTH AIR FORCE TABLE OF ORGANIZATION RABAUL RAIDS OF OCTOBER—NOVEMBER 1943

3rd Attack Group
Dobodura

8th BS	B-25s
13th BS	B-25s
90th BS	B-25s
(89th BS	A-20s)

38th Bomb Group
Dobodura

69th BS	B-25s
70th BS	B-25s
71st BS	B-25s
405th BS	B-25s

8th Fighter Group
Port Moresby

80th FS	P-38s
(35th FS	P-40s)
(36th FS	P-40s)

35th Fighter Group
Port Moresby

39th FS	P-38s
(40th FS	P-40s)
(41st FS	P-40s)

43rd Bomb Group
Port Moresby

63rd BS	B-24s
64th BS	B-24s
65th BS	B-24s
403rd BS	B-24s

90th Bomb Group
Port Moresby

319th BS	B-24s
320th BS	B-24s
321st BS	B-24s
400th BS	B-24s

345th Bomb Group
Dobodura

498th BS	B-25s
499th BS	B-25s
500th BS	B-25s
501st BS	B-25s

49th Fighter Group
Port Moresby

9th FS	P-38s
(7th FS	P-40s)
(8th FS	P-40s)

475th Fighter Group
Port Moresby

431st FS	P-38s
432nd FS	P-38s
433rd FS	P-38s

TOTAL AVAILABLE
FOR RABAUL
11 B-25 squadrons
8 B-24 squadrons
6 P-38 squadrons
6 P-40 squadrons lacked range for missions against Rabaul

ROYAL AUSTRALIAN AIR FORCE UNITS INVOLVED

No.	36	Squadron	Beauforts	Kiriwina
No.	38	Squadron	Beauforts	Kiriwina
No.	11	Squadron	Catalinas	Cairns
No.	20	Squadron	Catalinas	Cairns
No.	30	Squadron	Beaufighters	Port Moresby
No.	43	Squadron	Catalinas	Cairns
No.	100	Squadron	Beauforts	Kiriwina

Appendix 4

FIFTH FIGHTER COMMAND CLAIMS OVER RABAUL

Unit	Oct. 12	Oct. 23	Oct. 24	Oct. 25	Oct. 29	Nov. 2	Nov. 5	Nov. 7	Nov. 11	TOTALS
9th FS	—	1	6	—	7	6	2	—	—	22
39th FS	—	1	4	—	3	1	—	—	—	9
80th FS	1	—	12	—	2	8	—	1	—	24
431st FS	—	4	2	—	—	9	—	5	—	20
432nd FS	1	2	6	—	—	5	—	—	—	14
433rd FS	1	4	10	—	6	—	—	—	—	21
475th FG	—	1	—	1	—	—	—	—	—	2
	3	13	40	1	18	29	2	6	0	112

FIFTH FIGHTER COMMAND LOSSES OVER RABAUL

Unit	Oct. 12	Oct. 23	Oct. 24	Oct. 25	Oct. 29	Nov. 2	Nov. 5	Nov. 7	Nov. 11	TOTALS
9th FS	—	—	—	—	3	2	1	1	—	7
39th FS	—	—	1	—	—	—	—	2	—	3
80th FS	—	—	1	—	—	2	—	1	—	4
431st FS	—	1	—	—	—	3	—	—	—	4
432nd FS	—	—	—	—	—	1	—	1	1	3
433rd FS	—	—	—	—	—	1	—	—	—	1
	0	1	2	0	3	9	1	5	1	22

All victory credits as per USAF Historical Study 85. Mission reports differ.
Losses include all causes: enemy action, weather and operational accidents.

No fighters reached Rabaul on the October 18 mission.

Appendix 5

MISSION SUMMARIES

The following tables show the confusing and contradictory nature of 5th Air Force reporting on mission results. The three main sources of information are unit records (R), the official history by Craven and Cate (C) and General Kenney's writings (K). Volumes by historians Steve Birdsall and William Hess were also consulted. The notation (all) indicates that all sources agree on a specific point.

OCTOBER 12

Aircraft	Dispatched	Aborted	Over Target	MIA	Fighter Victories
B-24	87	R: 20	R: 20	R: 2	
		C: 25	C: 62	C: 3	
B-25	R: 115	R: 5	R: 110	1 (all)	
	C: 113	C: 6	C: 107		
	K: 114				
P-38	No data	R: 3		None?	R: 3
		C: 16			K: 26
TOTAL	R: 338			5 (all)	
	C: 339				
	K: 349				

OCTOBER 18

Aircraft	Dispatched	Aborted	Over Target	MIA
B-24	70	70		2 lost in weather?
B-25	R: 54 ?	3 (all)	R: 54	R: 2
				K: 3
P-38	Nothing recorded, not mentioned by others			

OCTOBER 23

Aircraft	Dispatched	Aborted	Over Target	MIA	Fighter Victories
B-24	R: 56	R: 7	R: 49	?	
	C: 57				
	K: 45				
P-38	R: 80			R: 1	R: 12
	C: 100			C: 1	C: 13
	K: 47			K: 2	

Sitrep 107: 49 bombers and 82 fighters claimed 11-5-0 with 2 P-38s lost.
There are also differing and double entries for some squadrons

OCTOBER 24

Aircraft	Dispatched	Aborted	Over Target	MIA	Fighter Victories
B-25	R: 63			R: 2	
	K: 62				
P-38	R: 73	R: 8			R: 39-13-0
	K: 54				K: 35

Some sitreps contain differing numbers for P-38s over the target and for squadron claims. USAF Historical Study 85 credits 31.

OCTOBER 25

Aircraft	Dispatched	Aborted	Over Target	MIA	Fighter Victories
B-24	R: 74	R: 7		R: 1	
				K: 1	
P-38	C: 87	C: 73	C: 8	none	1 (all)
	K: 50		R: 14		

OCTOBER 29

Aircraft	Dispatched	Aborted	Over Target	MIA	Fighter Victories
B-24	R: 52	R: 15		R: 1	
	C: 46				
	K: 37				
P-38	R: 75			R: 3	R: 15-5-0
	K: 57				

Sitrep 139: 41 B-24s and 75 P-38s. 1 P-38 lost, claims for 16-6-0.
Sitrep 140: 52 bombers, 15 aborts. 53 P-38s, 6 aborts. 3 P-38s lost for claims of 16-5-0.

NOVEMBER 2

Aircraft	Dispatched	Aborted	Over Target	MIA	Fighter Victories
B-25	R: 76		R: 76	R: 9	
	K: 75				
P-38	R: 73	R: 5	R: 68	R: 10	K: 41-13-0
	K: 57				C: 42

Sitrep 143: 75 B-25s (25 aborts) and 80 P-38s.
Sitrep 145: 84 B-25s (9 aborts) and 80 P-38s (6 aborts)
Hess: 433rd FS claims 19 victories. Study 85 credits 29.

NOVEMBER 5

Aircraft	Dispatched	Aborted	Over Target	MIA	Fighter Victories
B-24	R: 27 K: 27	none ?	27?	none ?	
P-38	R: 67 K: 64 C: 58			1 (all)	C: 23 R: 2

Sitrep 146: 27 B-24s (no aborts) and 67 P-38s. Claims 2-2-0, losing 1.

NOVEMBER 7

Aircraft	Dispatched	Aborted	Over Target	MIA	Fighter Victories
B-24	R: 27 K: 25	R: 4			
P-38	R: 58 K: 64 C: 64			5 (all)	none

Sitrep 149: 29 B-24s (4 aborts) and 64 P-38s. Bombers claimed 10-3-0.

NOVEMBER 10

Reports mention 8 B-24s dispatched with loss of 1. Squadron reports are unclear.

NOVEMBER 11

Aircraft	Dispatched	Aborted	Over Target	MIA	Fighter Victories
B-24	R: 55	R: 33	R: 12 K: 21 C: 36	R: 1 K: 2	
P-38				R: 1	none

CONTRIBUTORS

Dr. Tetsuo Aso — Surgeon, 60th Anti-Aircraft Battalion

John Brogan — Line chief, 8th Service Group

Ted Dorward — Beaufort pilot, RAAF No. 8 Squadron

Carl Camp — B-24 gunner, 320th BS, 90th BG

Bill Cather — B-25 pilot, 501st BS, 345th BG

Dennis Glen Cooper — Intelligence officer, 475th FG

Tom Fetter — B-24 bombardier, 90th BG

Peter Figgis — Coastwatcher, Australian Army

Carl Hustad — B-17 pilot, 63rd BS, 43rd BG

Makoto Ikuta — Dinah pilot, 10th Sentai

Charles King — CO, 39th FS, 35th FG (P-38s)

Marion Kirby — P-38 pilot, 431st FS, 475th FG

Robert McCandless — Special service officer, 8th FG

Bill Martin — B-24 pilot, 321st BS, 90th BG

Bill Moran — B-24 gunner-photographer, 90th BG

Bill Nance — Sergeant-major, 43rd BG

Sister Catherine O'Sullivan — Missionary nun, Rabaul

Max Osborn — B-24 navigator, 65th BS, 43rd BG

Keichi Owada — Civilian, 8th Naval Munitions Depot

Dennis Petersen — B-24 pilot, 319th BS, 90th BG

Charles Ray — B-24 gunner, 320th BS, 90th BG

Yale Saffro — P-38 crew chief, 80th FS, 8th FG

John Shemelynce — Photographer-gunner, 3rd BG

Takeo Shibata — CO, 201st and 204th Kokkutai (Zekes)

C. M. "Corky" Smith — P-38 pilot, 80th FS, 8th FG

Clint Solomon — B-25 pilot and operations officer, 3rd BG

Cy Stafford — Sergeant, 482nd Service Squadron

John Stanifer — P-38 pilot, 80th FS, 8th FG

Joseph Summers — CO, 482nd Service Squadron

Shiegeo Tanaka — Soldier, 1st Battalion, 81st Regiment

Larry Tanberg — CO, 38th BG (B-25s)

Takeo Tanimizu — Zeke pilot, 253rd Kokkutai

Clinton True — CO, 345th BG (B-25s)

Nobuko Tsujimura — Head nurse, 8th Naval Hospital

Sister Berenice Twohill — Missionary nun, Rabaul

Bill Welch — B-17 pilot, 403rd BS, 43rd BG

Kiyoshi Yagita — Betty pilot, 702nd Kokkutai

Mitsuyasu Yamakawa — Zeke pilot, 253rd Kokkutai

Harry Young — B-24 pilot, 64th BS, 43rd BG

Steve Birdsall — Author and historian

Bill Fogarty — Curator, Australian War Memorial

Kev Ginnane — Photographer

Doris Heath — Japanese linguist, Australia

Lyall Richardson — Australian radio personality and historian

Barry Saxby — Curator, Australian War Memorial

ABOUT THE AUTHOR

Lex McAulay was born in North Queensland, Australia in 1939, where he developed a lifelong interest in aviation. After spending a great deal of his own money buying other peoples' books on flying, he decided to write one himself. Upon seeing the famous photo of the 71st Bomb Squadron B-25 flying through the smoke and splashes over Simpson Harbor, Rabaul, he knew he found his subject. That picture epitomized the courage and determination of the Fifth Air Force, and led to this book.

McAulay has written two other books, both dealing with Vietnam, published in Australia by Hutchinson. He is now researching the attacks on Wewak and Hollandia in August 1943 and March-April 1944. He would welcome information from anyone who participated either as aircrew or ground support.

McAulay and his wife live near Canberra, where most of the military archives are stored. The author may be reached at 160 Copland Drive, Evatt, ACT 2617, Australia.

THE TARGET AND THE DEFENDERS

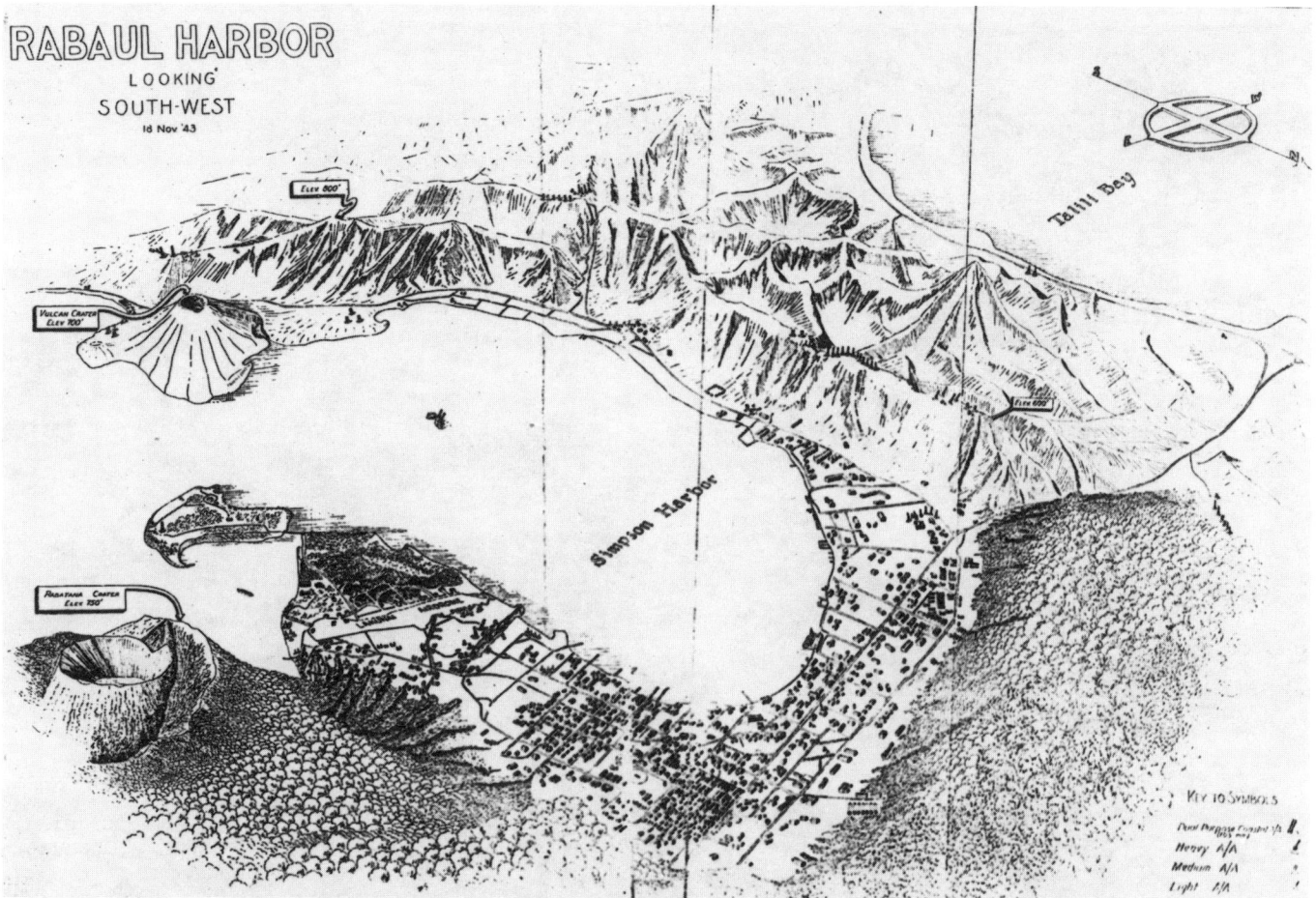

A drawing of Rabaul Harbor compiled by Allied intelligence officers in November 1943. (AWM)

Rabaul in a 1937 photo. Lakunai Aerodrome center. (AWM 106044)

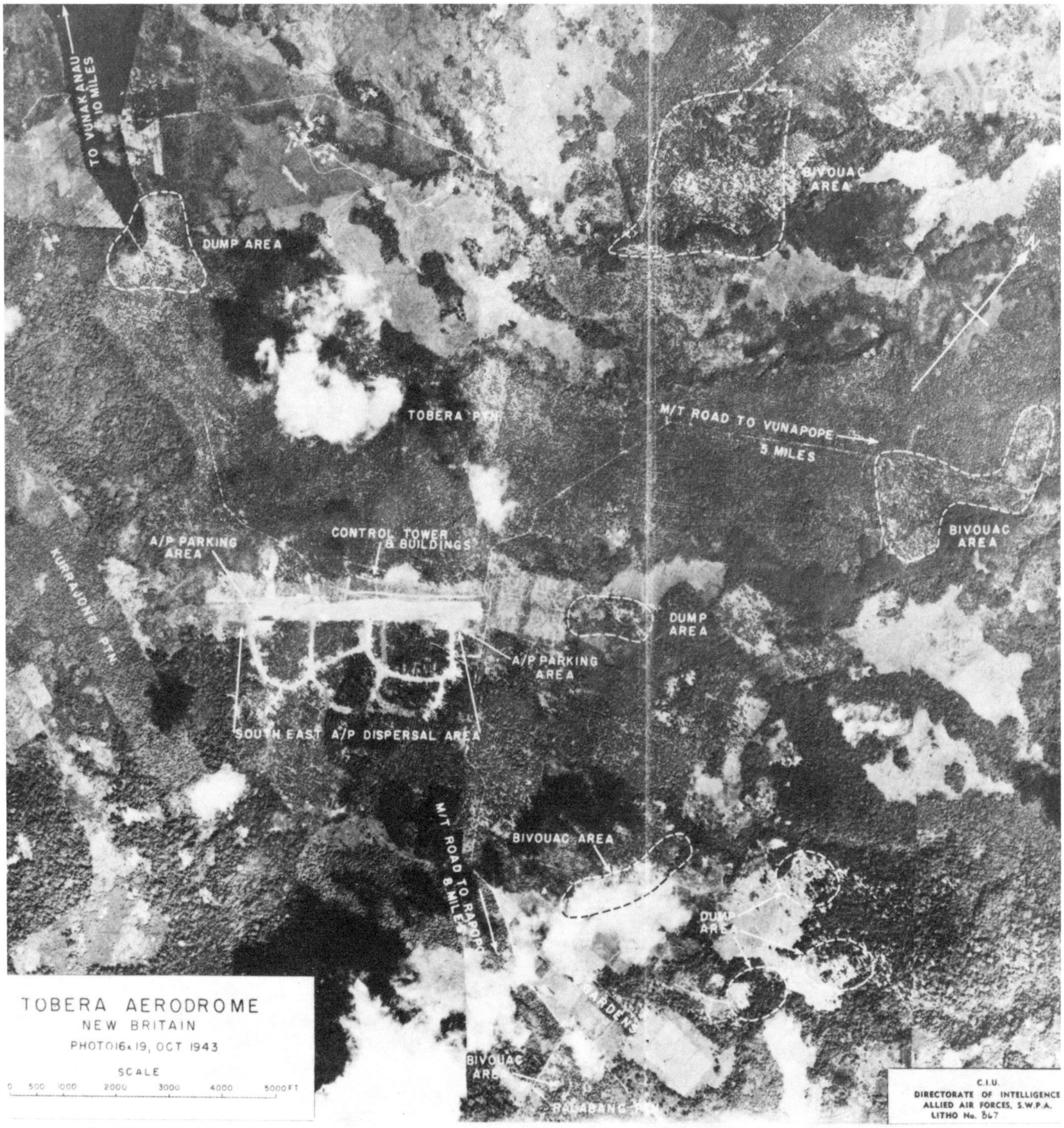

Within the photo:

TO VUNAKANAU
10 MILES

BIVOUAC
AREA

DUMP AREA

TOBERA P'TN

M/T ROAD TO VUNAPOPE
5 MILES

BIVOUAC
AREA

A/P PARKING
AREA

CONTROL TOWER
& BUILDINGS

DUMP
AREA

A/P PARKING
AREA

SOUTH EAST A/P DISPERSAL AREA

BIVOUAC AREA

DUMP
AREA

M/T ROAD TO RAPOPO

GARDENS

BIVOUAC
AREA

RALABANG P'TN

TOBERA AERODROME
NEW BRITAIN
PHOTO 16 & 19, OCT 1943

SCALE
0 500 1000 2000 3000 4000 5000 FT

Photo No. 16A

C.I.U.
DIRECTORATE OF INTELLIGENCE
ALLIED AIR FORCES, S.W.P.A.
LITHO No. 847

CONFIDENTIAL

This October 1943 recon photo shows Tobera Aerodrome and vicinity. (RAAF HO)

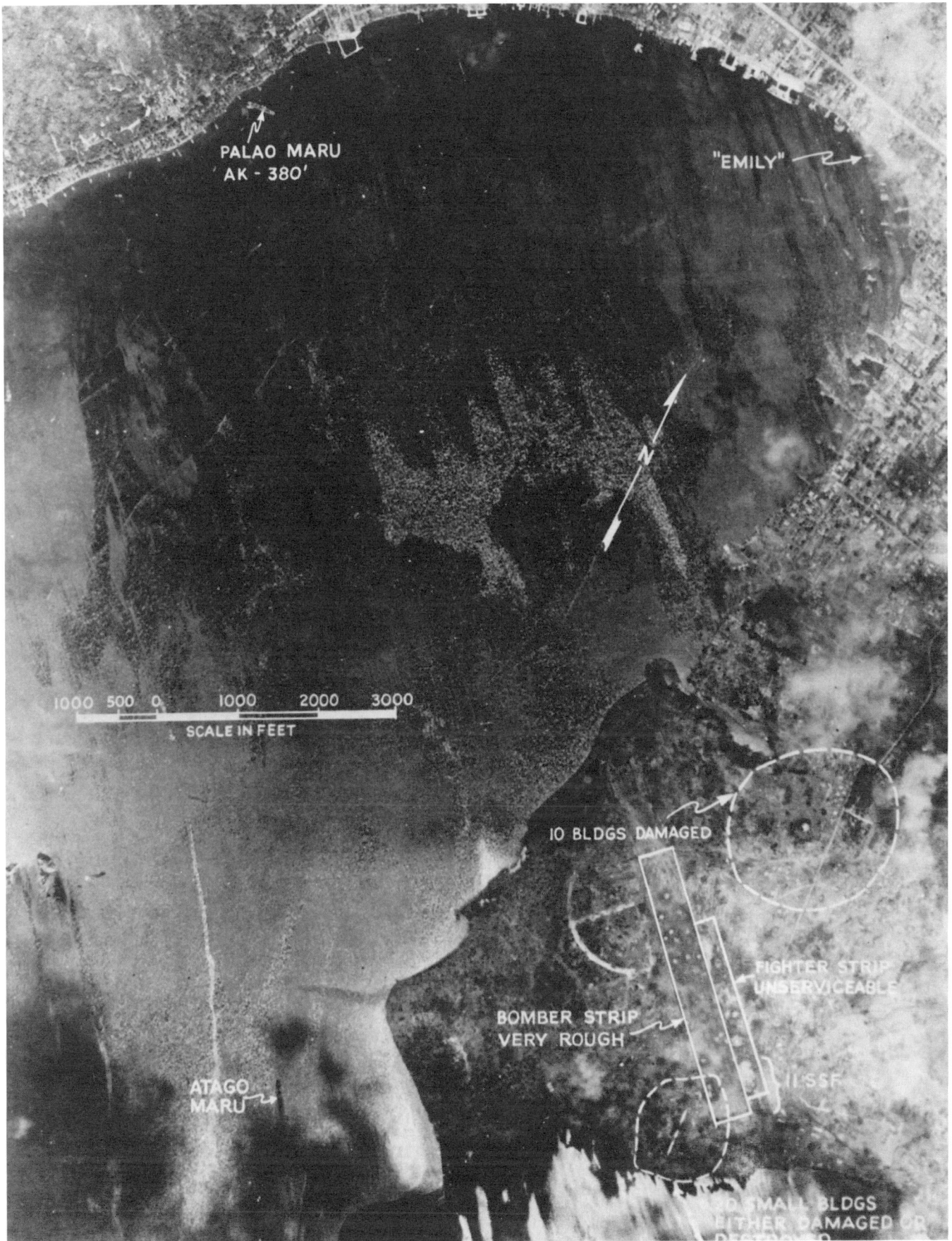

PALAO MARU
'AK - 380'

"EMILY"

N

1000 500 0 1000 2000 3000
SCALE IN FEET

10 BLDGS DAMAGED

BOMBER STRIP
VERY ROUGH

FIGHTER STRIP
UNSERVICEABLE

II SSF

ATAGO
MARU

20 SMALL BLDGS
EITHER DAMAGED OR
DESTROYED

Lakunai following a visit by B-24s. The bomb-pocked runways are clearly visible. (RAAF CPE)

General Imamura, Japanese army commander at Rabaul. (Tetsuo Aso)

Much of Rabaul's air defense was in the hands of Commander Takeo Shibata, leader of 201 and 204 *Kukutai*. (Shibata)

Among the experienced, skillful Zero pilots at Rabaul was Warrant Officer Hiroyoshi Nishizawa. An Imperial Navy pilot since 1939, he flew with 253 *Ku* during September and October 1943. One of Japan's leading aces, Nishizawa was killed in the Philippines in October 1944

Aircraft UI-105 in formation with other 251 *Ku* Zeros

Flying with 204 and 253 *Ku*, Warrant Officer Takeo Tanimizu claimed at least eight victories over Rabaul. At war's end he had destroyed or damaged 30 Allied aircraft

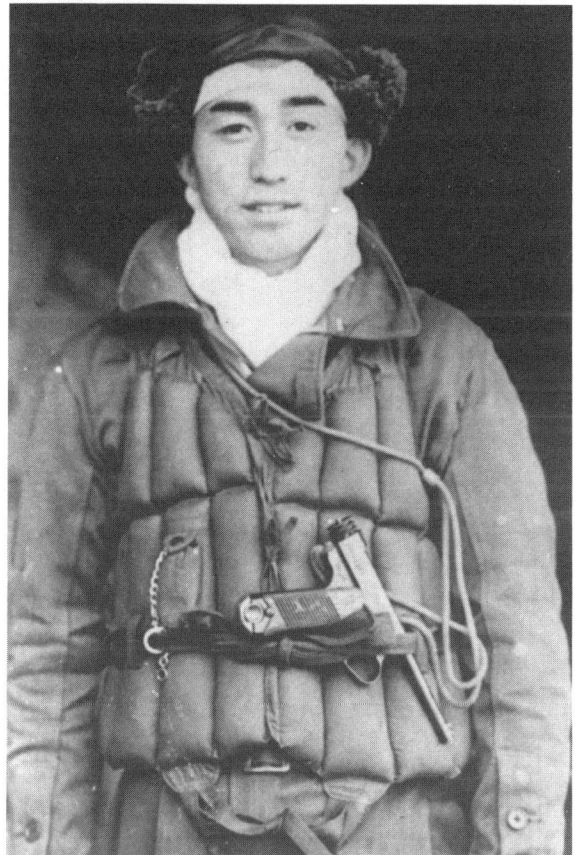

A prewar naval pilot, Petty Officer Sadamu Komachi completed flight training in 1940. He flew from the carrier *Shokaku* before joining 204 and 253 *Ku* at Rabaul and survived some 180 combats from 1941 through 1945

114

One of the Imperial Navy's more experienced fighter pilots, Susumu Ishihara fought in China, Rabaul, Truk and the Marianas. Considered a triple ace by his peers, he joined the postwar Japanese Self-Defense Force but died in a helicopter accident

Mitsuyasu Yamakawa of 253 *Ku* in tropical flying kit, September 1943. (Yamakawa)

Petty Officer Kenji Yanagiya of 204 *Kokutai*. On 18 April 1943 he was one of six pilots escorting Admiral Yamamoto's aircraft when intercepted by P-38s. At war's end Yanagiya was the only surviving Zero pilot of that mission, but he lost his right arm in combat, becoming an instructor

Unwilling witnesses to the air battles over Rabaul were Australian nuns imprisoned by the Japanese. Left rear, Sister Berenice Twohill; right front, Sister Catherine O'Sullivan; left front, Sister Borgia Kelly. (AWM)

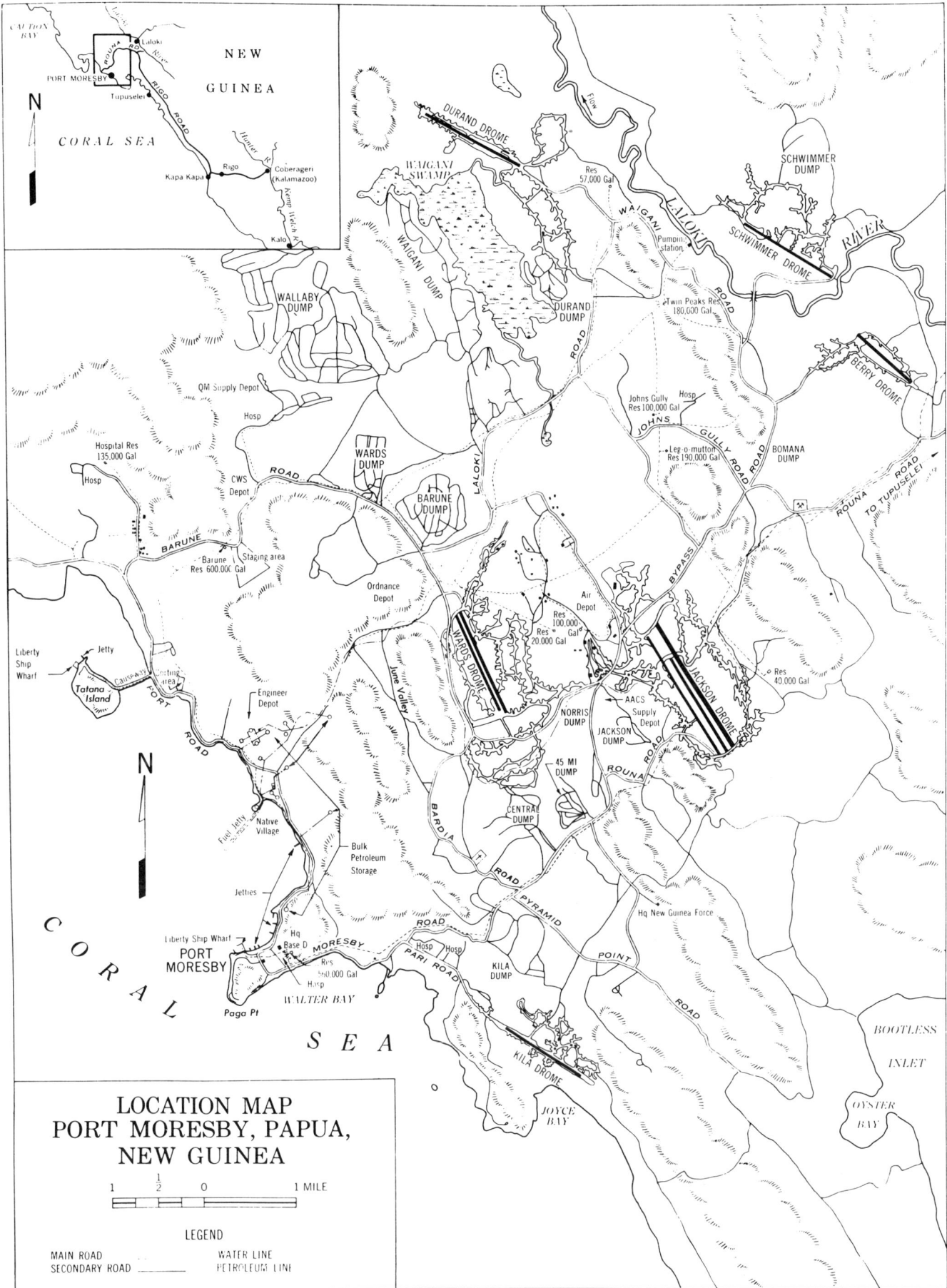

**LOCATION MAP
PORT MORESBY, PAPUA,
NEW GUINEA**

LEGEND

MAIN ROAD .... WATER LINE
SECONDARY ROAD _____ PETROLEUM LINE

The Port Moresby airdrome complex, home of the 5th Air Force B-24 and P-38 groups which attacked Rabaul

THE FIGHTERS

GONA
Cape Killerton
Sanananda Point

Liberty Ship Wharf
BUNA MISSION
Giropa Point
Fuel Jetty
Strip Point
Bulk
Petroleum
Storage
Cape Endaiadere
BUNA

SOPUTA

HARIKO

Petroleum
Pipe Line

Cape Sudest
LST
Landings
Staging Area
Jetties
Hospital

Samboga River

DOBODURA

Hospital

Staging
Area

4Y   4W
HORANDA
DROME   4E
HORANDA
7   ULADA   BORIO
Hospital   10
15

EMBI
LAKES   12

Embi

EMBI   Embi Creek

LOW ROAD
LST Landing
EMBOGO

Hospital

Radio Transmitter
Signal
Depot   Hospital
Bulk Petroleum Storage
Base QM
Depot   Fuel Jetty
HQ Base B

ORO BAY
Liberty Ship Wharves
Cape Sinclair
Engineer
Depot   HARVEY BAY

Girua River
Embogo River
Eroro River

SOLOMON SEA

Inset (Location Map)
NADZABO LAE   FINSCHHAFEN
HUON GULF   SALAMAUA
NASSAU BAY
WAUO   SOLOMON
SEA
BULLDOG
BUNA
ORO BAY
NEW   DOBODURA   KIRIWINA I
GUINEA   PONGANI   GOODENOUGH I
PORT
MORESBY   MILNE BAY
CORAL SEA

LOCATION MAP
ORO BAY - BUNA - DOBODURA AREA
PAPUA, NEW GUINEA

MILES
1   0   1   2   3   4

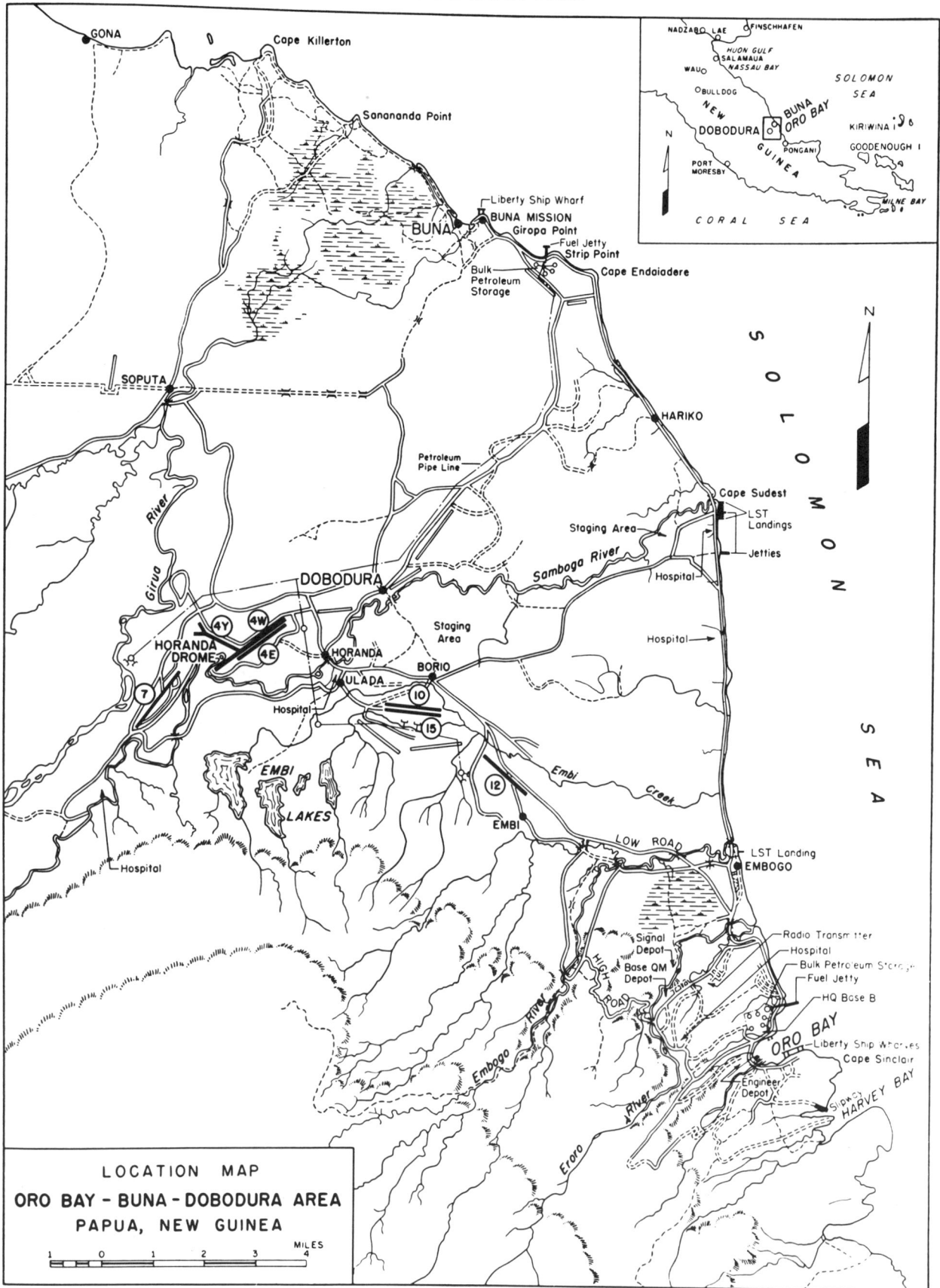

"Dobo"—the Dobodura area—base of the B-25 squadrons engaged in the reduction of Rabaul

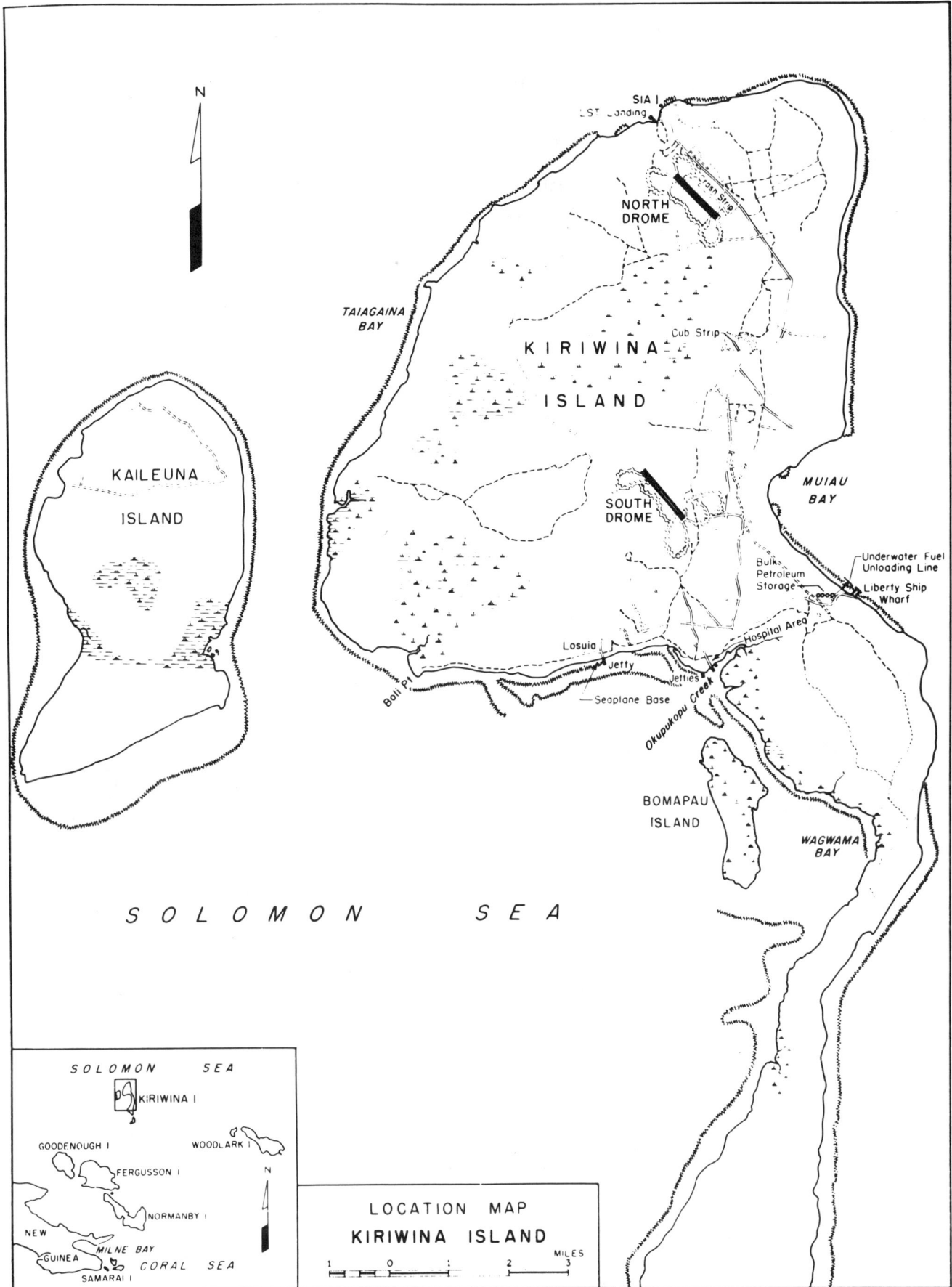

Three RAAF Beaufort squadrons flew from Kiriwina Island, nearer their New Britain targets than longer-ranged B-24s and B-25s It also was a staging base and emergency field for Rabaul-bound B-24s, B-25s and P-38s.

A homey white picket fence and this sign identified HQ of Fifth Fighter Command.

First P-38 squadron in the 5th Air Force was the 39th, which exchanged its P-39s for Lightnings in late 1942

39th FS stalwarts Charlie Sullivan and Ken Sparks indulge in some extra-low flathatting for an Australian photographer. (AWM 14636)

Six "Flying Cobra" aces of the 39th. Front L-R: Charlie Sullivan, Tommy Lynch and Ken Sparks. Rear L-R: Dick Suehr, John "Shady" Lane and Stan Andrews. Lynch was KIA in March 1944 with 22 victories to his credit

120

Charles W. King as a captain, mid-1943. By October he was CO of the 39th FS, leading
missions over Rabaul

Another early P-38 outfit was the 9th FS, 49th Group. Its top scorer was Captain (later
Major) Dick Bong, who made four of his forty kills over Rabaul

Widely regarded as a flier and combat leader, Gerald R. Johnson finished the war as a colonel with 22 victories only to die in an accident in October 1945, two months after his former squadronmate Dick Bong

Colonel George Prentice, first CO of the 475th FG. "Satan's Angels" were the first 5th AF unit formed in the combat area, drawing personnel and aircraft from other groups to make up three P-38 squadrons. (Dennis Glen Cooper)

Captain Danny Roberts, originally of the 8th Group, was tapped as CO of the 433rd FS after "Satan's Angels" were formed. One of the ablest, most popular pilots in 5th Fighter Command, his loss in a midair collision was keenly felt. (Dennis Glen Cooper)

Danny Roberts' personal aircraft, showing his final tally of 14 victories just before his death in November 1943

Many of the 475th Group missions to Rabaul were led by Colonel Charles H. MacDonald, who became group commander. The tall gentleman on the right in this early 1944 photo is Charles Lindbergh, who flew with the 475th

The glamorous Army Air Force. Lieutenant Blythe and 475th FG information officer Dennis Glen Cooper doing laundry at Port Moresby. (Dennis Glen Cooper)

Captain Marion Kirby, 431st FS, whose dominant memory of the Rabaul missions is "freezing feet in the P-38 at altitude." (Dennis Glen Cooper)

The sign says it all. "Headhunters" of the 8th Group's 80th Squadron were one of only six P-38 squadrons available in late 1943. L-R, five aces: Cy Homer, Allen Hill, Art DeGraffenreid, J.T. Robbins and C.M. Smith. By war's end these pilots accounted for 63 aerial victories. (Smith)

Captain C.M. "Corky" Smith, who was impressed by Rabaul's "terrific amount of AA and huge numbers of Zeros in the air." (Smith)

Porky II was the mount of 80th FS ace Edward Cragg, who logged eight kills by August 1943. At war's end he had 15 total.

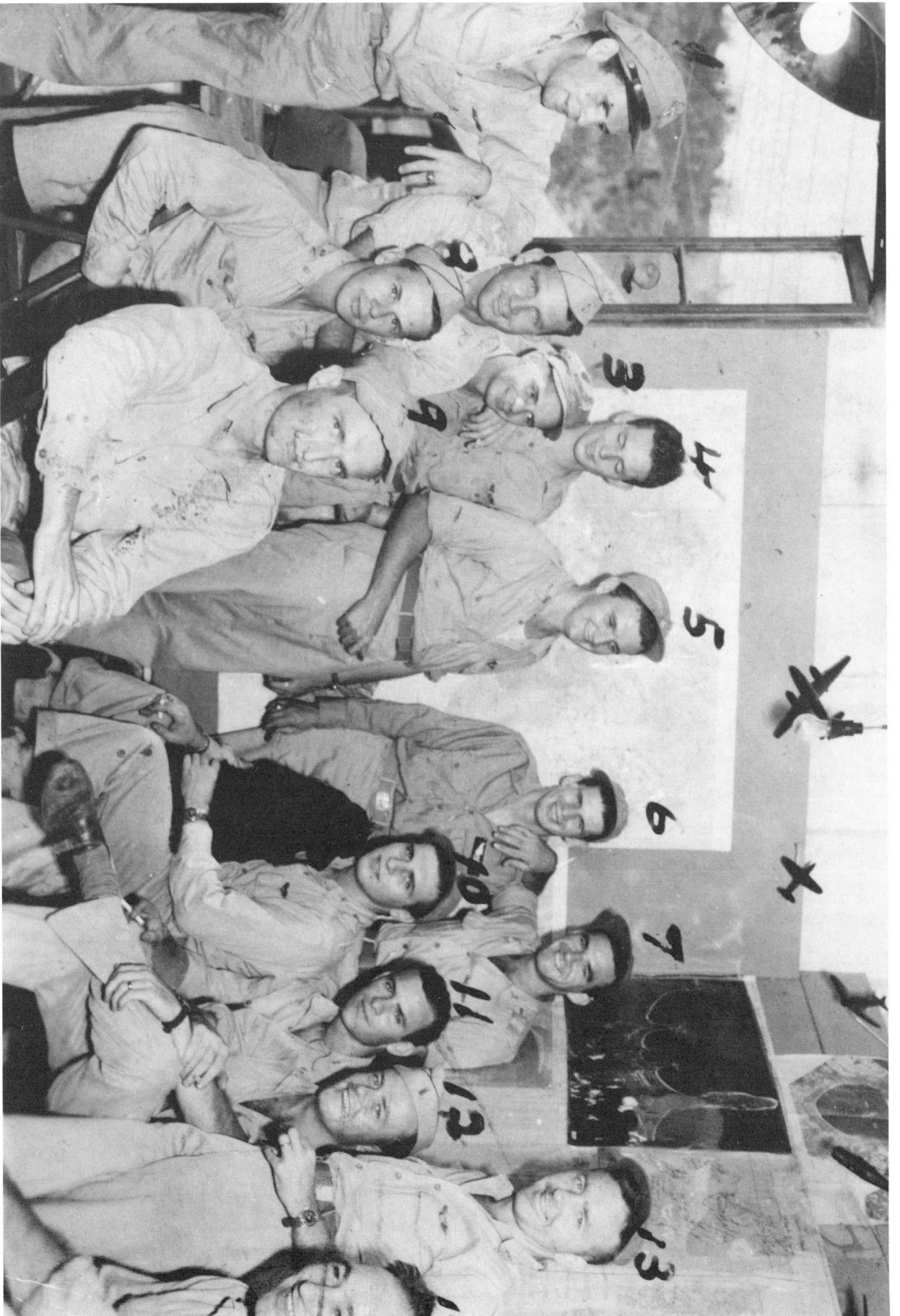

Pilots of the "Headhunters," August 1943. Average age about 24, ten of these men scored confirmed kills and five aces tallied 68. 1. Ed Robertson 2. Freddie Taylor 3. Ken Ladd 4. Bob Siebenthal 5. Ed Cragg 6. Harrison Freeman 7. Don McGhee 8. Raymond Daly 9. John Jones 10. Don Hanover 11. Jay Robbins 12. Corky Smith 13. J.R. "Red" Wilson 14. Swede Hanson

80th FS living quarters, considered elegant by some standards. (Smith)

"Headhunters" officers' club, Port Moresby. The sign above the door says, "Through these portals pass the hottest pilots in the world." (Smith)

THE BOMBERS

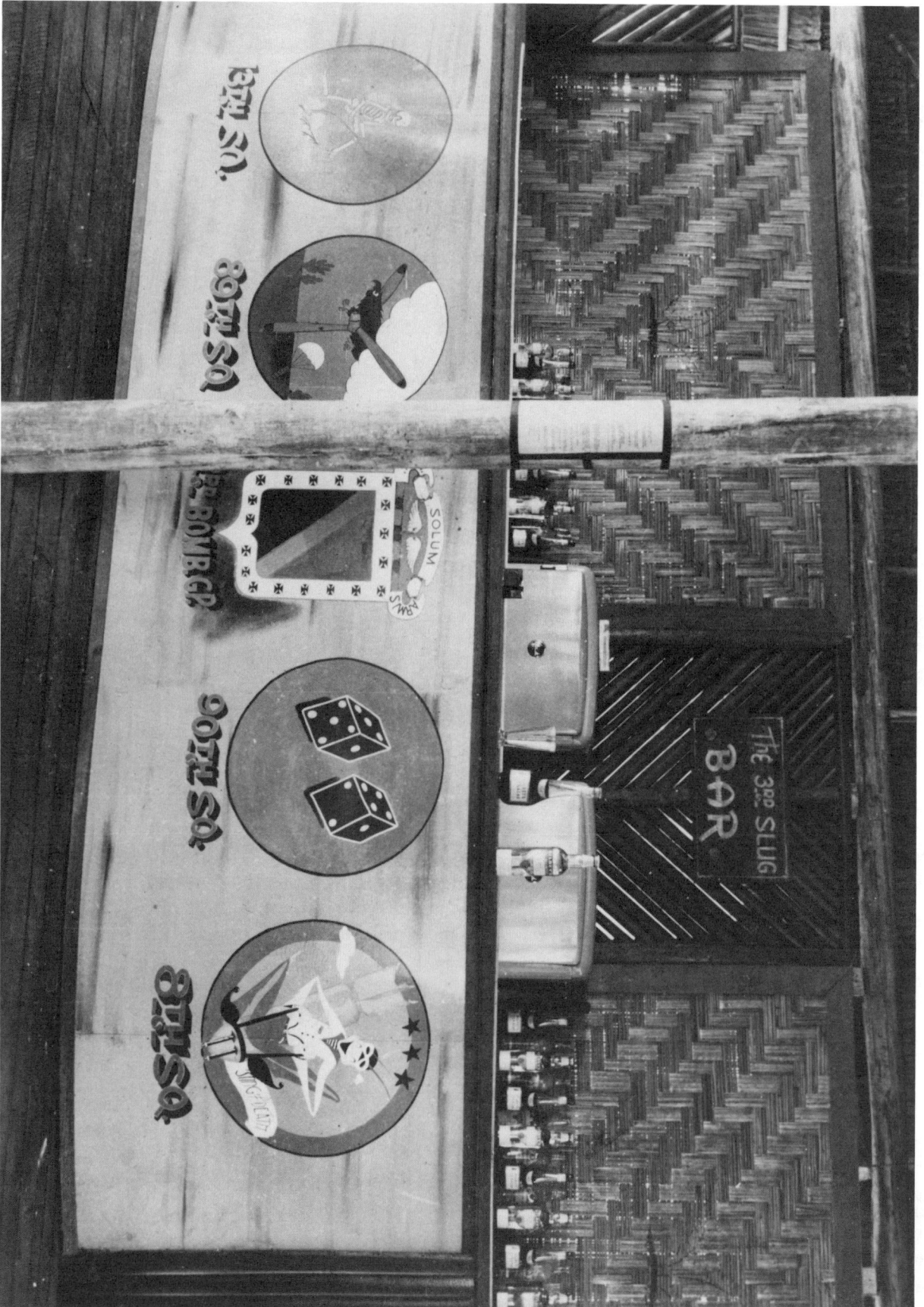

The 3rd Attack Group constructed this bar for its patrons. Visible are insignia of the component 8th, 13th, 89th and 90th Squadrons. (Shemelynce)

John Brogan of 8th Service Group admires typical nose art of the period. *Sad Sack* was a B-25 of the 3rd Attack Group. (Brogan)

John Shemelynce, Third Group photographer. (Shemelynce)

Navigator Max Osborn of the 43rd Bomb Group. (Osborn)

Lucky Lucille flew with the 43rd BG's 65th Squadron. (Osborn)

Major Carl Hustad (front row, left) and his 43rd BG B-17 crew. (Hustad)

Hells Angels belonged to the 400th BS, 90th Group. (Brogan)

Harry Young, left front, piloted *Frisky* with the 64th BS, 43rd Group. (Young)

Another B-24D of the "Jolly Rogers" was *Crosby's Curse,* also assigned to the 400th Squadron. (Brogan)

Two "Air Apaches" of the 499th BS were Edgar "Ted" Sliney (right) and Carl Conant (above). (AWM)

134

A 345th BG Mitchell closely escorted by a pair of 80th FS Lightnings

Master Sergeant Cy Stafford of the 482nd Service Squadron—one of the unheralded men who "kept 'em flying." (Stafford)

The spoils of war. Ted Dorward and fellow Beaufort flier with *Kelvin*, a jeep stolen from the US Army Air Force and freighted to Goodenough Island in a crate marked as a refrigerator. (Dorward)

Beauforts of No. 100 Squadron, RAAF, which flew night torpedo attacks into Rabaul Harbor. (John Harrison)

RAAF aircrew accommodations on Goodenough Island. (Dorward)

THE MISSIONS

Armorers loading para-frags for the 12 October mission. The unit is believed to be the 501st BS, 345th BG (AWM)

Liberators of the 90th BG taxi out in the early morning of 12 October. (AWM)

751 Kokkutai, Vunakanau Aerodrome under attack by 38th and 345th Groups, 12 October. (RAAF CPE)

Taken completely by surprise, 751 *Kokkutai* bombers sit in their revetments as B-25s scatter 1,500 para-frags. (RAAF HO)

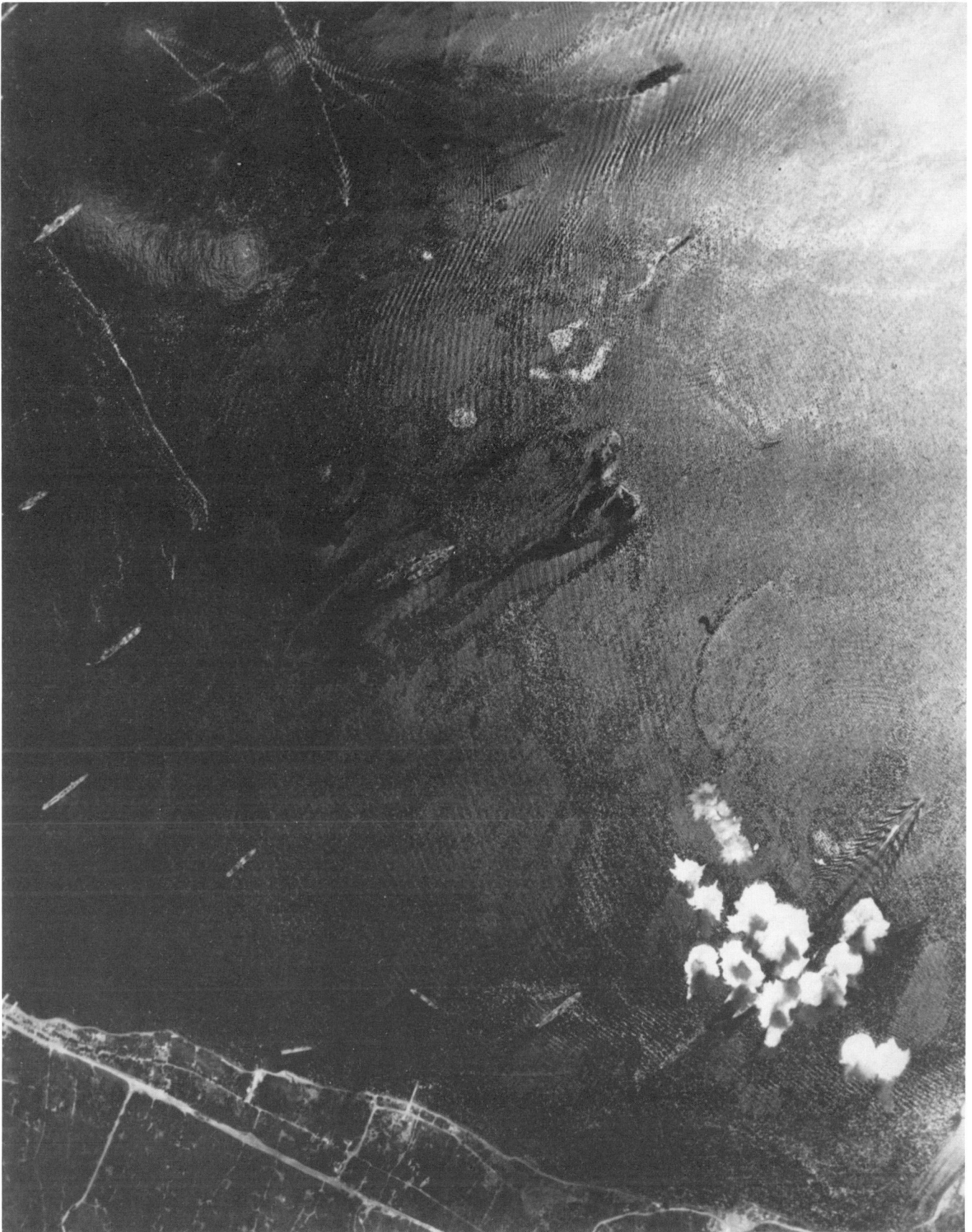

The 90th Group's view of Japanese shipping at anchor in Simpson Harbor, 12 October (Bill Moran)

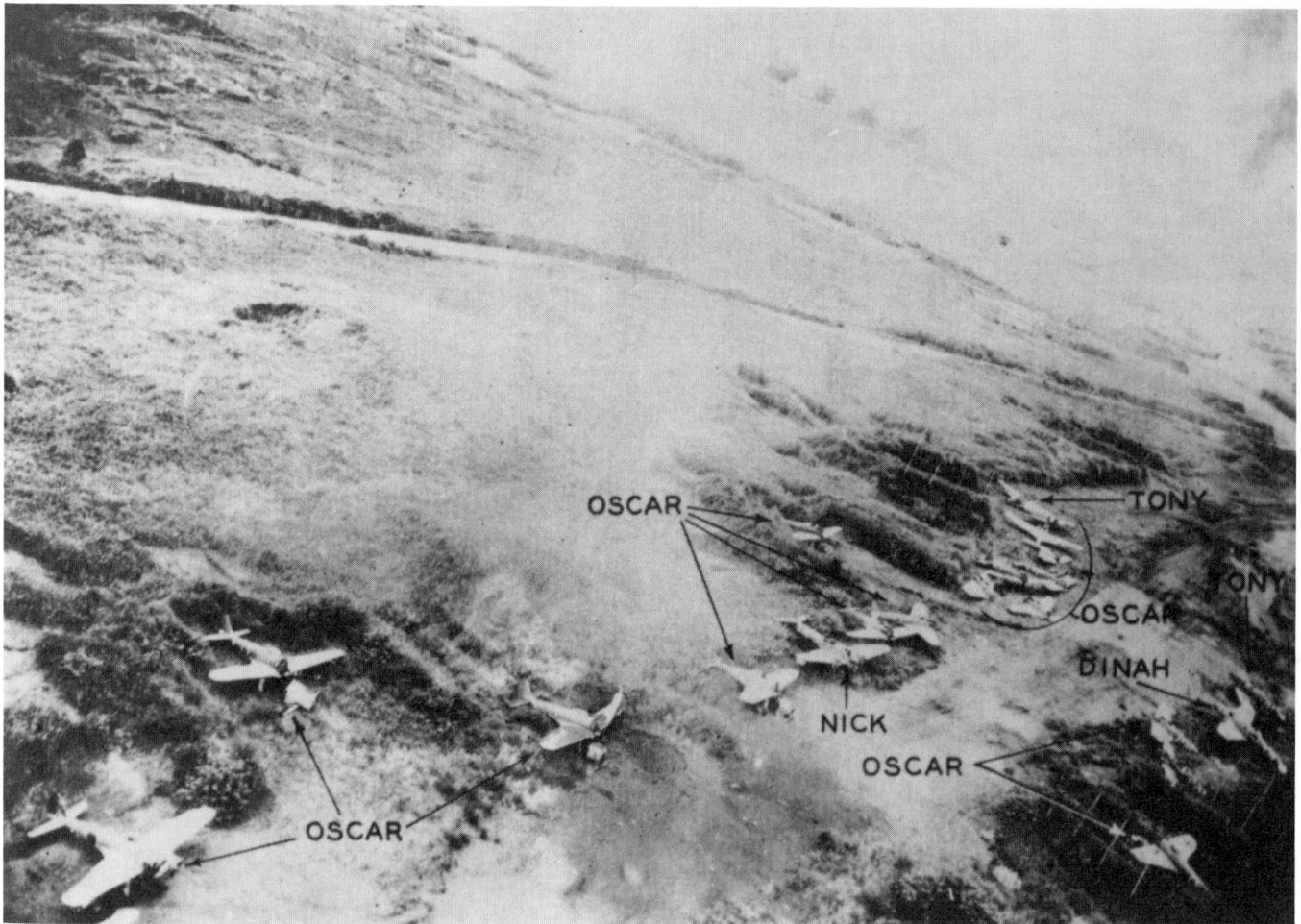

Destroyed and damaged Japanese army aircraft on Vunakanau Aerodrome 24 October.
Looking southeasterly, this photo was taken the day P-38s claimed their biggest victory over
Rabaul

White-tailed B-25s of the 498th BS en route to the 2 November strike (AWM)

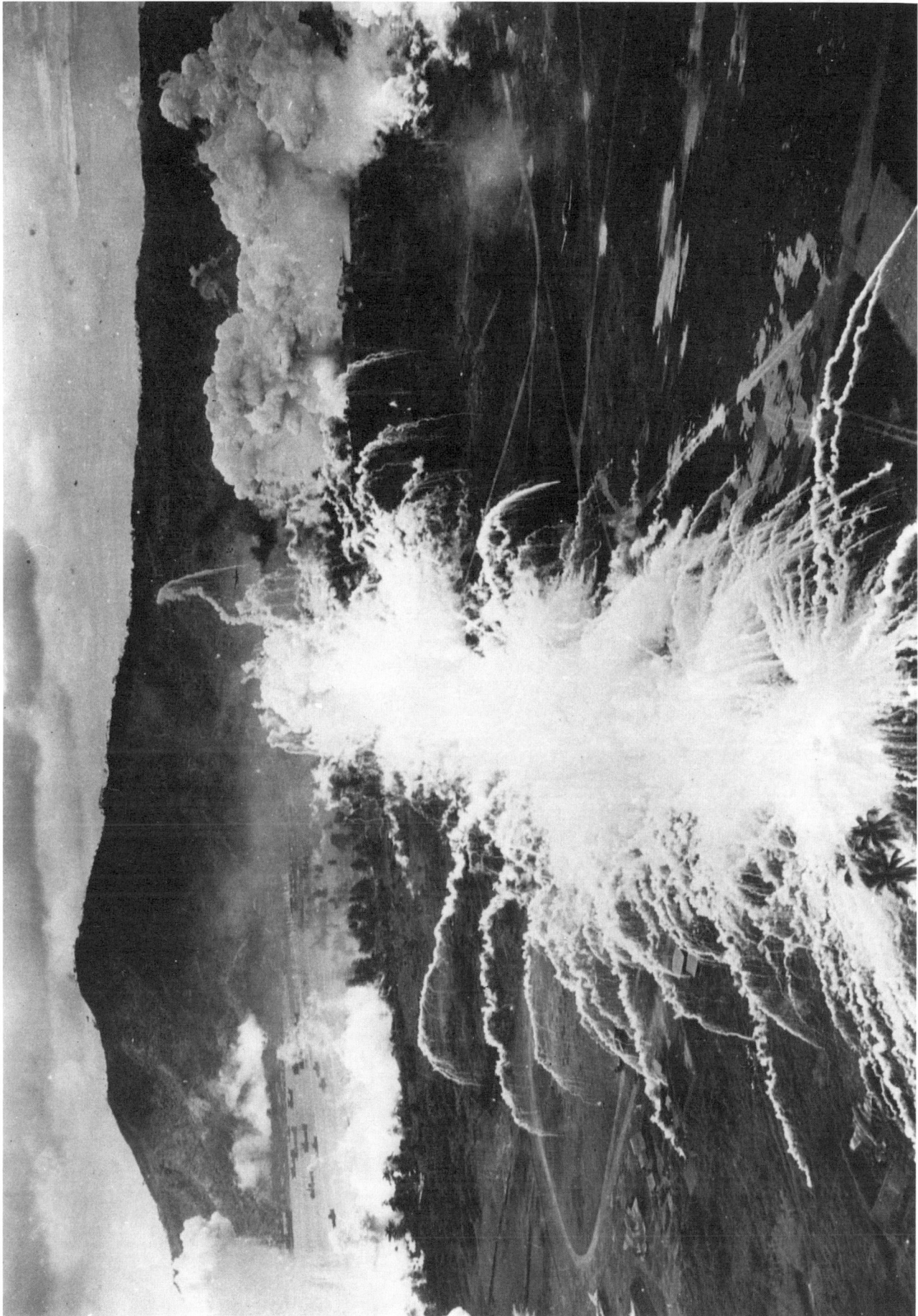

The "Air Apaches" made good use of white phosphorous weapons. Here the 499th BS blankets Lakunai on 2 November, but at least one Zeke is visible, airborne just below the treeline to left. (AWM 100147)

Defense suppression was provided by Mitchells of the 500th BS, dropping phosphorous over AA positions on slopes overlooking the harbor. However, the attackers lost at least 19 aircraft this date. (AWM 100150)

345th Group B-25s ran in over Rabaul Town, noting military supplies stacked in residential areas. (AWM 127603)

The B-25 strike force attacked from the north on 2 November, flying over the volcanoes.
Lakunai fighter field is at the left side of the left-hand mountain. (USAF)

143

Bomb bay open, a 71st BS B-25 flies low over Simpson Harbor as the 38th Group begins its attack. (RAAF CPE)

A spectacular close-up of a Japanese freighter, already burning from a hit amidships, November 2. (RAAF CPE)

A Nachi-class cruiser pushing out to sea, past three merchant ships previously damaged or still under attack (RAAF CPE)

This sequence apparently shows 3rd and 38th Group attacks upon anchored vessels, with obvious results. (AWM and RAAF CPE)

This B-25 pressed its attack on a *Mutsuki*-class destroyer almost to masthead-height, straddling the target
(RAAF CPE)

Amid bomb bursts and heavy strafing, ships attempt to get underway, clearly exposed to attack despite flak bursts
(RAAF CPE)

A lone B-25 gunship pulls off its target, leaving smoke clouds and water geysers behind.
Close examination shows this aircraft had a bombardier nose converted with four .50 cal.
machine guns (RAAF CPE)